VICTIMS
OF CHANGE

CONTRIBUTIONS IN SOCIOLOGY

Series Editor: Don Martindale

Harold Finestone

VICTIMS
OF CHANGE

Juvenile Delinquents in American Society

Contributions in Sociology, Number 20

 GREENWOOD PRESS
WESTPORT, CONNECTICUT • LONDON, ENGLAND

Library of Congress Cataloging in Publication Data

Finestone, Harold.
　　Victims of change.

　　(Contributions in sociology; no. 20)
　　Bibliography: p.
　　Includes index.
　　1. Juvenile delinquency—United States.　I. Title.
HV9104.F525　　　　364.36'0973　　　　76-5327
ISBN 0-8371-8897-0

Library of Congress Catalog Card Number: 76-5327
ISBN: 0-8371-8897-0

First published in 1976

Greenwood Press, a division of Williamhouse-Regency Inc.
51 Riverside Avenue, Westport, Connecticut 06880

Manufactured in the United States of America

Excerpts from Herbert Blumer, *Symbolic Interactionism: Perspective and Method* (Englewood Cliffs, N.J.: Prentice-Hall, Inc., 1969) and Edwin M. Lemert, *Human Deviance, Social Problems and Social Control*, 2nd ed. (Englewood Cliffs, N.J.: Prentice-Hall, Inc., 1972), reprinted by permission of Prentice-Hall, Inc., Englewood Cliffs, New Jersey. Excerpts reprinted by permission of New York University Press from *From the Depths: The Discovery of Poverty in the United States* by Robert H. Bremner, © 1956 by New York University. Excerpts reprinted by permission from Ray Ginger, *Altgeld's America* (New York: Funk & Wagnalls Co., 1958). Excerpts reprinted by permission from Joseph M. Hawes, *Children in Urban Society* (New York: Oxford University Press, 1971). Excerpts reprinted by permission from Richard S. Pickett, *House of Refuge* (Syracuse, N.Y.: Syracuse University Press, 1969). Excerpts reprinted by permission from Lee Rainwater, *Behind Ghetto Walls* (Chicago: Aldine Publishing Company); copyright © 1970 by Lee Rainwater. Excerpts reprinted by permission from William I. Thomas, *The Unadjusted Girl* (Boston: Little, Brown and Company, 1923). Excerpts reprinted by permission from William I. Thomas and Dorothy Swaine Thomas, *The Child in America* (New York: Alfred A. Knopf, Inc., 1928). Acknowledgment is made to Alfred A. Knopf, Inc. for material reprinted from *The Polish Peasant in Europe and America* by William I. Thomas and Florian Znaniecki.

To Don Martindale

contents

acknowledgments

At no time is an individual more of a social being than in the solitary task of writing a book. He becomes aware of the depth of his dependence upon the ideas, books, and articles of others. He is grateful for the labors of his teachers and colleagues. As a sociologist he is likely to be especially appreciative of the gifts of those who provided him with access to the social worlds that he was interested in understanding and who themselves often became friends and exemplary informants about these worlds. He is dependent upon those who offer him encouragement and support to remain at his task.

I have been richly favored in all these respects. The book itself is testimony of my constant intellectual indebtedness to the work of others. I was helped by my teachers but by none as much as by Herbert Blumer, whose belief in the necessity and dignity of criticism if the standards of a discipline are to be maintained were an inspiration. His example encouraged me to attempt a critique of three major sociological theories of juvenile delinquency.

My special interest in the problem of juvenile delinquency was first kindled by the writings and later by the privilege of personal association with the late Clifford R. Shaw. I was moved by the intensity of his feeling for this problem and by the total dedication he brought to its amelioration. The charisma of his spirit and personality has remained as a beacon throughout the years since his passing. The quality of the man was nowhere better reflected than in the caliber of his colleagues, Henry McKay, Solomon Kobrin, and Anthony Sorrentino. McKay matched Shaw in the intensity of his dedication to the subject of his work. He saw romance in his patient, plodding, never-ending task of analyzing the juvenile court statistics on juvenile delinquents. He exposed the myths and misconceptions in which the topic of juvenile delinquency is constantly enmeshed. Kobrin, self-effacing, industrious, and ever knowledgeable and enthusiastic about the latest developments, earned the right to be the colleague and equal of Shaw and

McKay. Sorrentino was a valued colleague who kept the administrative machinery of the Chicago Area Projects from creaking too badly and was a constant haven of friendly warmth.

Shaw had also assembled a group of indigenous community workers who were unparalleled in the skills that they brought to the task of community organization and to their work with juvenile and adult offenders in the inner-city areas of Chicago. Many of them became my friends during the dozen years or so when I worked as a research sociologist at the Institute for Juvenile Research and with the Chicago Area Projects. True men of the world, they were always generous with their insights and knowledge. They included the late Steve Bubacz, Nick Taccio, Joe Giunta, Emil Peluso, Joe Puntil, Joe Losciuto, Ray Raymond, and Jim Hardy. They were and remain a group of rare talents.

For friendly encouragement at strategic moments and for continuing moral support I am indebted to my friends Bob Fulton, Dan Cooperman, Luba Lee, and Connie Goldman.

I am grateful to my colleague John Clark, chairman of the Department of Sociology at the University of Minnesota, for helping to arrange my teaching schedule so that I was able to take a quarter's leave for writing, and to my colleague David Ward who changed his teaching schedule to suit my writing plans.

Finally, I owe a very special debt to my colleague Don Martindale. The idea for this book was initially his. He has since proved to be a cornucopia of encouragement, rich scholarly experience, helpful insights, and painstaking criticism.

introduction

Millions of children and adolescents pass through our system of juvenile justice every year. In 1974 the police arrested 2.5 million individuals under the age of eighteen. Among them were murderers, sophisticated pimps and prostitutes, holdup men, jack rollers, second-story men, thieves, and rebels unable to abide parents and teachers, and who attempted to solve their problems through flight, thievery, violence, alcoholism, and drug addiction. Their number has risen by sixteen times—1,600 precent—during the past twenty years. All too many of them have had previous encounters with the law, sojourning briefly in the juvenile correctional system before engaging in more daring and desperate encounters in the streets, homes, and businesses of the community. These precocious offenders, who come from varied social and economic backgrounds, commit almost 50 percent of the serious crimes recorded. Others are just trying to grow up under extremely trying circumstances. They all wear a common symbolic badge of dishonor: they are all juvenile delinquents, and this tag taints them in their schools, neighborhoods, and, later, the marketplace as they seek jobs and the dignity of adulthood.

Juvenile delinquency is a problem with deep roots in the nineteenth century when social change of great intensity and scope became an endemic aspect of American society. The growth of concern with the problem of juvenile delinquency during the first quarter of the nineteenth century was one indication, among many, of the efforts of reformers from the established middle and upper classes to confront what they viewed as the undesirable consequences of change. The rise of a free market in labor eroded the apprenticeship system and greatly reduced the control that families—of the poor, in particular—could exert over the behavior of their children. Large numbers of uprooted youth found their way to the burgeoning cities of the eastern seaboard like New York, Boston, and Philadelphia. Here the struggle for survival led many into the street trades, begging, and criminal activities.

As they began to appear in the courts, they posed a problem for the existing judicial and penal systems that had implicitly been designed for adults only.

The unattached youngsters who were of native American origin were augmented and eventually overwhelmed in numbers by the stranded sons and daughters of the immigrants. Too frequently the social and economic consequences of immigration worked like a centrifuge separating the young from their familial ties. The large-scale urbanization and industrialization that followed the Civil War intensified the pressures upon the capacity of poverty-stricken families to remain intact. An additional aggravating factor was the introduction of compulsory education, creating a giant new leisure class among the children of the poor without the traditions or institutional resources for using it. Moreover, compulsory education was accompanied by a new type of delinquency, truancy. Accordingly while quantitative data are not available on the actual trends in juvenile delinquents during the nineteenth century, there are many indications that juvenile delinquency was becoming a more serious and difficult problem.

The reformers of the nineteenth century responded to the issue of juvenile delinquency with piecemeal experimentation. In New York City special court hearings for youths accused of crimes were established. In Boston an effort was made to "reach out" to the children of the slums. Boston also initiated a tradition of caring for the disadvantaged in the community rather than in institutions. Undoubtedly the most influential contribution of the nineteenth century to the solution of the problem of juvenile delinquency was the institution; the New York House of Refuge, which opened in 1825, was the prototype. Nevertheless, no fundamental conceptualization of judicial and correctional problems of the young was attempted. This task had to await the so-called discovery of adolescence during the closing decades of the century. The idea that youth represented a distinct stage in the psychological development of an individual's personality resulted from a convergence of influences from evolutionism, individualism, and the growth of interest in the psychology of personality.

Despite the highly persuasive notion of the delinquent as an aberrant adolescent, it proved to be an extremely difficult one to translate into legal procedures that were just and that treated each case as an individual. The philosophy upon which the juvenile court was founded remained extremely vague. As the momentum for reform that had generated the juvenile court slackened, its problems were increasingly turned over to academically trained professionals. Since the work of Cesare Lombroso and the triumph of positivistic criminology, the professionals had been concerned with the offender rather than the offense. What better milieu in which to try out this idea than in the juvenile court? Those who inherited the responsibility for defining the functions of the court in theory and practice included psychiatrists, psychologists, social workers, and sociologists. The sociologists tended to remain outside the system and became the researchers, critics and theorists.

Jane Addams was the first to formulate the view that delinquency expressed a disjunction between the "normal" needs of youth and the situation, predominantly urban, in which they found themselves. This premise set the task for the sociologists of delinquency during the twentieth century. What was the relevant situation for understanding and controlling the delinquent response? What was the nature of the disjunction between the adolescent's needs and the situation? How could the juvenile court and the juvenile correctional system be organized and supplemented to overcome this disjunction? Unlike their psychologically oriented brethren working in the juvenile court, the sociologists avoided posing their problem in terms of the adjustment of the individual, for typically their analysis implied that the situation itself should be changed.

Three major initiatives have been undertaken during the twentieth century to develop sociological theories of juvenile delinquency: those of Clifford R. Shaw and Henry D. McKay, the subcultural theorists, and the labeling theorists. Each has led to some form of institutionalization that implied significant changes in some aspect of the juvenile system of justice. Each has been found wanting both as theory and in its mode of institutionalization. Accordingly the development of the sociology of delinquency during the twentieth century can be viewed as one that resulted from the dynamic interplay between theory and institutionalization. According to the familiar dialectic, the institutionalization of each idea revealed unanticipated consequences and the challenge to the construction of a better theory.

The Work of Shaw and McKay

Shaw and McKay, the major students of delinquency within the framework of the Chicago school, did their work when the consequences of immigration were at floodtide in large cities such as Chicago. Social change during the 1920s was equated with the overlapping processes of urbanization, immigration, and assimilation; moreover, it was these processes of change, as reflected in the community experience of second-generation adolescents, that constituted the situation of delinquency. The particular disjunction between adolescent and situation that was viewed as fostering delinquency was the breakdown of control over the conduct of youth by both the traditional institutions of the immigrant and by those of the host society. Delinquency was simultaneously a product of the social disaffiliation of the second generation and the resolution of such disaffiliation by the construction of an alternative social and moral world. The social isolation generated by the difficulties and barriers to communication with the representatives of conventional institutions and values provided conditions favorable to the flourishing of a nonconventional social heritage. The extralegal traditions of the disaffiliated were sustained by a network of personal relationships based upon local community ties. Such ties helped to generate a highly ramified indigenous society located in the inner-city communities but existing beyond the pale of convention. It consisted of both gangs and personal relationships, which knit together individuals from the various age groups. The Chicago Area Project, which Shaw and his colleagues established, was an attempt to reduce the social and cultural isolation of the second generation of adolescents in the inner-city areas by the deliberate "reaching out" to them on the part of local adults attempting to provide access to conventional institutional affiliations in the ethnic community and in the larger encompassing American society.

The Subcultural Theorists

The premises of social change upon which Shaw and McKay had based their approach to delinquency became less applicable to the residents of the inner-city areas of large cities during the post-World War II period. Urbanization continued apace, but there was a profound change in the migrants, who now increasingly came from the rural hinterlands of America itself rather than Europe. The new arrivals had long been familiar with American society. On the whole, they came to the city because technological changes had displaced them from their traditional rural occupations. Many arrived in a state of demoralization, having long lived in destitution. They joined the lower-class populations of the cities. The problems of survival in the alien milieu were intensified by the social definition of color, which remained in the urban as it had in the rural setting a symbol of inferior social status. Under such circumstances, the disjunction between adolescent and situation in the inner-city areas was postulated as being one of status-linked deprivation of opportunity. The burdens of discrimination and social injustice fell excessively upon the lower-class adolescents. They were constantly confronting intolerable reminders of the inferiority of their position in their family life, in school, in the search for employment, and in their treatment by the judicial and correctional system. In response to these status problems, gang delinquency assumed a more complex and hostile character. For the first time in the twentieth century, sociologists began to be concerned with drug use and violence among juveniles. The typical delinquent as Shaw and McKay had conceived of him had been a thief. Now, this view of the delinquent as largely conforming to a single social type was modified. The central theoretical task became that of developing a conception of gang delinquency, which would take account of this new awareness of the diversity in the illegal activities of adolescents in the inner-city areas and relate it to the status system of the society. Albert K. Cohen paved the way for the formulation of this problem with the concept of delinquent subculture, and his work was followed by that of Richard A. Cloward and Lloyd C. Ohlin and by Walter B. Miller.

The practical implications of the work of the subcultural theorists can be clarified by contrasting them with the presuppositions of the Chicago Area Project. One of the premises of the latter was the inevitability of social mobility among the immigrant groups who at any period occupied the city slums. However, in a situation where low social class status was frequently synonymous with differences of color, such an assumption was no longer tenable. Indeed the fundamental practical implication of the subcultural theorists was the necessity of opening up channels of upward mobility for the adolescents trapped in the urban ghettoes. Such ideas made an important contribution to the formulation of the goals of the war on poverty.

The Labeling Theorists

Beginning in the early 1960s many sociologists interested in delinquency began to reject the premises of the subcultural theorists. Instead of viewing delinquency as a product of the functioning of certain impersonal social environmental forces (such as rigidities and strains in the status system of society), they sought to view delinquency as a particular type of social process. This process was viewed as fundamentally political, in which official control agents attempt to resolve certain social crises and conflicts in which adolescents are involved by defining certain of them as deviants. Since such labeling is one of the consequences of contact with the official agencies of social control, it meant that the professionals were as deeply implicated as any other agent of social control.

Once again certain changes in the society had influenced the working premises of sociologists. The image of American society as a unitary status system or social structure was increasingly replaced by a view of it as pluralistic, highly heterogeneous in its values, and dependent upon an ever-changing set of political processes for whatever social order it possessed. This approach was sensitive to the increasingly pervasive role of intergroup conflict, and delinquency itself became an expression for one mode of resolution of the "generation gap."

For the theorists in this tradition the fundamental axis of interest tends to revolve around the interaction between the official social control agencies and the individuals whom they process. What is particularly striking about this interaction is the astronomical growth in the number of contacts between youth and the official control agencies. This process has placed an unprecedented strain upon the existing judicial and correctional system. It has become increasingly clear that correctional institutions cannot be expected to compensate for the inadequacies of the family, the school, and the other socializing institutions of society. The generation gap, which is involved in many of these problems, cuts across all classes. At the same time the labeling perspective has introduced the idea of accountability—accountability for the control agents, for those they process, and for the communities in which intergenerational conflicts occur. The search for accountability has taken many forms and is now in the experimental stage. Community corrections attempts to render the community accountable for its delinquency problem.

With the emergence of community corrections the problem of juvenile delinquency has come full circle. It first attained the status of a social problem during the early nineteenth century in response to the disruption of the life of hitherto tradition-oriented and relatively small and stable communities. Over the time span of a century and a half, despite an unremitting search for institutional expedients for dealing with youthful law violators, a search spurred by the promise of applying the findings of the social and psychological sciences, the problem has increased in volume and seriousness and has become more and more resistant to understanding and control. There is a current tendency among many practicing and academically oriented professionals to acknowledge too quickly the futility of their efforts and to turn the issue back to the communities. Such a tendency, if carried to an extreme, would indeed be unfortunate because the youth involved represent a substantial share of the future citizens of this country. Social scientists are duty bound to continue their efforts to find ways of dealing effectively with the unchastened children of change.

VICTIMS
OF CHANGE

chapter 1

Delinquency and its control in America: an overview of major theoretical orientations and institutional expedients

Every society identifies classes of disapproved behavior. In the simplest of societies such behaviors are taboo, viewed as magical defilement or sins. As societies grow more complex legal institutions grow up to deal with socially disapproved behaviors, which are redefined as "crimes" subject to sanctions. A major task in every society is to socialize its children into its particular system of approved and disapproved behaviors. In the process—because it is the nature of the young to be initially ignorant, awkward, spontaneous, and censurable—the lines between approved and disapproved behaviors will be repeatedly transgressed. Hence most societies are reluctant to apply the same sanctions to normative and legal violations by their young as they apply to their adults. There have been few societies of either simple or complex type that have applied the same attitudes and sanctions to the normative-legal violations of their approved conduct to juvenile as to adult defenders. Nevertheless, a qualitative transformation occurred in the nature of juvenile offenses, when the transition was made from the type of simple society that Robert Park described as sacred to the new social order, pragmatic and secular, identified with the rise of modern cities.[1]

The change from sacred to secular types of societies in recent time has been accompanied by (in fact, in part, implemented by) the change in human understanding from traditional lore, magic, and religion to science. The explanation of violations of normative-legal codes, whether by juveniles or adults, has been transformed in the process. The theory of juvenile deliquency and the changing forms of institutions designed to cope with it thus are not only intimately inter-related but reflect the transition to contemporary types of secular society and the rise to dominance in them of scientific modes of under-standing.

As a provisional orientation to our subject, it is useful to review quickly the major changes in the mode of explanation and the primary forms of coping institutions addressed to juvenile delin-quency in the United States.

Delinquency as Incipient Pauperism and the House of Refuge: 1820-1898

Through the colonial period and into the first two decades of the nineteenth century American society consisted of relatively small communities of comparatively homogeneous religious (overwhelm-ingly Protestant) and ethnic (60 percent English with the remaining 40 percent of the population largely north European) composition. By 1820, however, such a variety of diverse nationals began to arrive in large numbers that the U.S. Census for the first time began to list im-migrants by nationality. New England was beginning to show the in-fluence of the industrial revolution, and the cities—particularly on the seaboard—were growing rapidly. The first major contingents of non-Protestants appeared and settled in the cities; ethnic and reli-gious tensions often became intense, and juvenile deliquency slipped out of the hands of the family and the church and became a manifest public problem.

These new patterns in intergroup relations were initiated by the in-tense pace of growth experienced by New York City, Boston, and Philadelphia during the opening decades of the nineteenth century. This development coincided with large waves of Irish immigration. The unprecedented stresses to which the traditional social order was now subjected were viewed through the perspective provided by the ideas of the Enlightenment. Originating in Europe during the eigh-teenth century and imbued with humanitarian sentiment, these had strongly influenced the social thought of the new society. There they helped to inspire a large group of earnest, indefatigable social reformers. One important outcome of the latters' efforts to apply the Enlightenment ideas to the social ills of their time was the founding in 1825 of the New York House of Refuge, designed for the correction of criminal and wayward youth.

During this era the delinquent was conceived of as a potential pauper. This conception reflects the response of middle-class reformers during an era when the child was still regarded as a miniature adult and therefore expected to be working. The growth of eastern cities was accompanied by both increased heterogeneity of population and the sharpening of class differences. These cities were still small enough so that members of the community who differed from one another in values and life patterns could not avoid jostling one another in public places. Middle-class reformers began to feel that the security of their way of life was threatened by the pervasive pressure of numerous poor and apparently idle people. The enemy as they defined it was "pauperism," a term that stood for all they most loathed. "Paupers" were people without the motivation to work who were quite content to remain dependent upon the charity and benevolence of others, probably because of an irremediable moral weakness. The point of view from which these reformers approached the problem of poverty was composed of an improbable blending of the moralism of puritanism with the belief in the malleability of human nature and its responsiveness to environmental influences associated with the Enlightenment. The mutual inconsistencies between the two views were resolved by dividing the moral development of the human individual into two stages. Up to a certain point of maturation the clay of humanity could be molded. After that the person's character was permanently set as fundamentally "good" or "evil." The existing environment with all its change and instability was viewed as corrupting and inevitably leading to moral weakness. However, if vulnerable youth could be placed in a carefully controlled environment, that is, in specially designed institutions, they could be inculcated with the appropriate morality. It was believed that once properly trained they could be returned to the community as exemplary citizens. The reformers proposed establishing a separate institution for youth in which potential paupers, whether juvenile offenders or homeless children, might be housed, corrected, and taught to be moral. The fundamental purpose of the institution was captured in its title. It was to be a "refuge," a shelter for youth from the destructive forces of a changing world that left unchecked, would inevitably convert the innocent into malevolent and useless paupers and criminals. So certain were its founders of the righteousness of their mission that they showed little concern with the niceties of the civil rights of the children they institutionalized; admissions included homeless children and convicted juvenile offenders indiscriminately.

Delinquency as a Product of Urbanization and the Juvenile Court: 1899-1945

Throughout the nineteenth century the forces that had thrust juvenile delinquency into public attention grew in strength. A mobile restless population—multiracial, multiethnic—was rushing across an open continent. The cities were growing. The Civil War had rent the country temporarily into warring factions and left new components of demoralization in its wake. The explanatory mechanisms of the Enlightenment (moralism and rationalism) were inappropriate to the new social trends and were being replaced by a more adequate social science. By the turn of the century the field of delinquency was opened to theoretical and institutional reconstruction.

The new developments were best exemplified by Chicago's experience during the closing decades of the nineteenth century. Its emergence as the commercial hub and industrial colossus of the Midwest had rested upon its rapid recruitment of a massive labor force from the peasantry of southern and eastern Europe. Socially and culturally it became a latter-day tower of Babel where the forces of a raw and ruthless industrialism were complicated by profound cultural and class conflicts as wave after wave of newcomers entered the vortex of the city. The glaring contrasts it offered between affluence and poverty, between well-being and suffering, between the complacency of the haves and the restiveness of the have-nots, provided a challenging milieu in which a new generation of reformers, the Progressives, thrived and found support. The magnitude of the problems they faced, such as poverty, health, housing, criminality, and juvenile delinquency, provided a powerful stimulus to the development of the new social perspectives embodied in social work and the social sciences. It was from the point of view of these emerging professions and disciplines that the problem of juvenile delinquency was redefined.

The redefinition of the problem of juvenile delinquency that occurred during the latter part of the nineteenth century is clarified by contrasting the perspectives of the New York City reformers (in the early nineteenth century) and the Chicago reformers (in the late nineteenth century) toward urbanization. In each case urbanization was viewed as an impersonal destructive force, which, in undermining the old sources of morality, left the individual rudderless and without traditional emotional outlets and relationships. The two groups differed, however, in their approaches to these large-scale and apparently frightening phenomena. Although each was apprehensive that the survival of civilization as they knew it was threatened, they differed in the spirit with which they approached its revitalization. The reformers of the early nineteenth century had sought to turn back the clock, to deny urbanization, and to promote reforms that would neutralize its consequences. They sought to stem the tide of change by implementing a moralistic view of man. The reformers of the late nineteenth and early twentieth centuries, in contrast, while recognizing the destructive tendencies inherent in urban civilization, accepted it and determined to humanize it through a broadly conceived program of social engineering based upon empirical inquiry and the principles of the social and psychological sciences.

The new perspective was based in part upon a rejection of the moralism of the earlier era. While it is true that the Progressive reformers never succeeded in fully divesting themselves of moralistic interpretations of social problems, they increasingly replaced it with a new, more dispassionate orientation, that of the individual viewed in relation to his social environment. The influence of Darwin was, of course, crucial, but it was Darwin recast in the light of a growing empirical interest in the psychological makeup of the individual and the functioning of the social environment.

Undoubtedly the most eloquent interpreter of the new intellectual currents, with a special solicitude for their bearing upon the lives of youth, was Jane Addams. One of the most influential of the Progressive reformers, she had succeeded, as did many of the social workers of her era, in discarding the stereotype of lower-class youth as potential paupers. She helped to articulate a new perspective that drew upon the emerging psychological and sociological orientations; indeed, she discussed the problems of youth and delinquency from a social-psychological perspective. She attempted to identify the consequences of urbanization for youth and the conditions under which they attained expression as so-called delinquency. As she sought to view the problem of delinquency from the delinquent's perspective, she became aware of the ambiguity of meaning of delinquent acts. In her sympathetic eyes, delinquency became the expression of certain cravings and wishes of youth that were denied outlet by the urban environment. Delinquent acts represented in part the persistence of activities that had been "normal" or at least tolerated under rural conditions of living; in this sense, ironically, since cities tended to be viewed as at the very heart of change, delinquency in the city represented a kind of psychological lag. In general, then, she interpreted delinquency as the response of youth to the changes and barriers to emotional outlets represented by urban living. The implications of such an analysis for the treatment of delinquents were clear; such treatment had to take account of their psychological makeup in relation to their social environment. For dealing with this problem, with its locus in the community, juvenile correctional institutions were singularly inappropriate.

This interpretation of the problem of delinquency was one of the major influences leading to the establishment of the juvenile court in 1899. Once in operation the juvenile court acted as a catalyst for drawing the psychological and social sciences into the domain of the delinquency problem. The limitations of the court as originally established soon became apparent. Many cases proved to be far beyond the skills and resources of probation officers; a substantial volume of juvenile recidivism persisted despite all efforts at treatment or control. The social and psychological sciences were drawn upon to provide new resources for dealing with youthful violators. Ultimately they were also to furnish a new justification for the court's continued existence: to provide a platform in the community for inquiry and experimentation in dealing with the problems of youth. The clinical skills of psychiatrists, psychologists, and social workers were incorporated into the functioning of the court.

William Healy became the first juvenile court psychologist, and in this capacity he organized the Juvenile Psychopathic Institute in Chicago in 1909. The latter was a diagnostic and treatment center for delinquent children and came to include a full-time staff of psychiatric and social workers. Although not the only clinic in existence during this period to focus upon the problems of juvenile delinquents, it attained preeminence under the leadership of Healy, who brought both clinical skills and a scientific perspective to this new task. On the basis of his clinical work with delinquents Healy went on to establish modern psychiatric casework. His interests also included the evaluation of the juvenile court and the attempt to formulate general theories of juvenile delinquency. Many of Healy's initiatives were pursued by Clifford R. Shaw from a sociological point of view.

Delinquency as Peer Gang Behavior and Work with Street Gangs: 1946-1970

Shaw's comprehensive sociological researches had profound practical implications. His analysis indicated that delinquency was a problem of the inner-city communities. Depiction of such inner-city communities indicated that the juvenile court was so alien to the local community life as to be inevitably limited as a mode of social control. Second, he found that the adolescents who lived in the inner cities had evolved a way of life steeped in unconventional values that differed from those of the larger community. Considerable distances, both social and cultural, separated the delinquents from the court. They tended to live in a separate moral world, composed of its own web of primary group relationships woven from the strands of family, peer group, and neighborhood. Since it was also viewed as a world in disarray, crumbling under the shocks of urbanization and culture change, it was in this enclave that juvenile delinquency was spawned.

Such findings had important implications for the functioning of the court. It would have to find some means to overcome the social and cultural distances that separated it from its youthful clients. It was in part to meet this need that Shaw generated the idea of the "indigenous worker," an agent of social control who could act as a liaison between the distant institution and the child. Moreover, if the delinquent was to be responsive to such a worker their relationship would have to be a personal one. Shaw's harshest criticism of the juvenile court was aimed at the impersonality that prevailed in the relationships between its functionaries and the wayward child. Like his mentor E. W. Burgess he insisted that the delinquent was a person.[2]

The research of Shaw and his colleagues was sufficiently influential to mold the image of the delinquent, which prevailed for several decades after it was first formulated during the 1920s. This is the image of the delinquent as "disaffiliated." Social change was approached as manifesting itself in the breakdown of the control exercised by traditional institutions—the family, the church, and the neighborhood. Furthermore, it could be viewed from the dual perspectives of the inner-city community and the individual. From that of the inner-city, social change was manifested as a decline in the capacity for collective action; from that of the individual, as increasing detachment from traditional group ties. All was in a state of transition; the old ways were being abandoned, often at great social and personal cost, and there was a groping for the new. As one of the burdens created by the social disorganization of the community, the delinquent could be viewed as a casualty of urban life, cut loose from the institutional ties that had sustained youth in a simpler and earlier era.

The problem of juvenile delinquency assumed new forms during the years following World War II. Mass movements of population to the suburbs were accompanied by the immigration of new peoples—southern whites, blacks, Puerto Ricans, and Mexicans, largely from the hinterlands of America itself—into the deteriorating urban cores. Predominating in this movement, and therefore to a large extent defining the quality of this migration, were the blacks. During the Great Depression there had been marked shifts in the orientation from which Americans tended to view their society. A general awareness that there were structural constraints such as social class (and as some claimed, even social caste) endemic to American society grew and intensified. The view of society in terms of social change and social process in the sociology of the 1920s and 1930s, and in that of the Chicago school in particular, gave way to theories emphasizing the structural features of society. As a consequence there was a new attentiveness to the role of social stratification.

In a closely related development, the decline of the melting-pot perspective was accompanied by a growing recognition that America was a society highly differentiated not only by class but also by ethnicity. The social structural point of view, with its sensitivity to social rigidities, was also conducive to an analysis of American society in terms of the inconsistencies between its ideals and its social reality. Perhaps the most striking manifestation of the new orientation was *An American Dilemma*, in which Myrdal sought to demonstrate that a conflict existed between the "American creed" and the actual structure of race relations between whites and blacks.[3]

This structural approach, with its emphasis upon social rank and social differentiation, was congenial to an attempt to view the total society as a unity. Society was conceived of as a social system, that is, an organic unity composed of differentiated yet interdependent parts. The existence of social problems such as juvenile delinquency was interpreted as evidence of the malintegration between some segments of society and the rest of the social system.

In his classic article on urbanism Wirth had noted that the city had increased the contrasts in status among people: "While the city has broken down the rigid caste lines of pre-industrial society, it has sharpened and differentiated income and status groups."[4] One of the consequences of this trend has been that in the cities certain contradictions in the American social system have become most intensified and stressful.

> The American social system . . . is permeated with two conflicting social principles: The first says that all men are equal before God and man. . . . The second, contradictory to the first, more often found in act than in words . . . declares that men are of unequal worth, that a few are superior to the many, that a large residue of lowly ones are inferior to all others.[5]

> The two constitute the realities of American democracy. The democracy of the American Dream is true only because of the social gradation on the ladder where successful men are permitted to realize their ambitions. The social-class system is true only because the precepts of the Dream provide the moral code which enforces the rules of social mobility by insisting that all able men who obey the rules of the game have "the right" to climb.[6]

It was from the perspective provided by such assumptions that juvenile delinquency was interpreted. The structural theorists of delinquency such as Cohen and Cloward and Ohlin selected different aspects of social stratification and inconsistencies in the values of

American society as a basis for their analyses of the type of social malintegration that generated delinquency. Each was equally rigorous in
his insistence upon the group character of delinquency. The burden of
their work was to assert that certain malintegrations in American society inevitably produced delinquent gangs or subcultures.

The policy implications of this position were clear in principle if not
in detail. Some means had to be found to "reach out" to the delinquent gangs to improve their social integration into the existing social
system. The principle of reaching out provided the basis for a critique
of long-established social agencies and ultimately of the quality of services provided by the welfare state itself. The solid crust of bureaucratization that had resulted in the virtual exclusion of many segments of the lower classes from access to social services had to be
broken. The primary agency selected for bridging the distance between gang boys and the rest of the society was the street worker.

This whole era of theory and practice in juvenile delinquency,
which is as yet far from exhausted, can be summarized by its implicit
image of the delinquent as a "frustrated social climber." He was fully
integrated into the society, imbued with its notions of the good and
successful person, and yet lacking the wherewithal to be upwardly
mobile. To move through legitimate pathways appeared to be impossible; to stagnate at the bottom was intolerable to his self-esteem. By
virtue of his social position, he was placed in a bind, testimony not to
the social disorganization of the community but to the powerful hold
of its social organization upon even the least favored of its members.

The Era of Community Corrections, 1971-

The fourth major stage in the attempt to account for and institutionally cope with juvenile delinquency in America is so close to us in
time that it is difficult to attain clarity regarding the social factors that
initiated it. Unlike the previous three stages, the fourth, or contemporary, stage has not been characterized by processes linked to urbanization or by changes in the ethnic composition of the population. Its
distinctive features can perhaps be approached by contrasting it with
the preceding stage. One of the central assumptions of the post-World
War II era was that American society was characterized by consensus.
This assumption was fundamental to Myrdal's *An American Dilem-*

ma; its central hypothesis presupposed a society committed to a common set of values. A similar assumption that American society was characterized by consensus over its central values was also to be found in the work of the leading social theorists of this stage, such as Parsons and Merton.

Beginning in the 1960s this assumption came under increasing attack. The idea that a society is characterized by a consensus over values presupposes that there is a dominant social perspective or orientation shared by all the major segments of the community. What became increasingly salient during the 1960s was not the consensus but the multiplicity of social perspectives that were harbored within the same society.

The dramatic transition from an orientation emphasizing consensus to one emphasizing perspectivism first became explicit during the course of the struggle of blacks for civil rights. The initial goal of the civil-rights movement was the more complete integration of the black population into American society through the strategy of desegregation. This goal and this strategy both presupposed the idea of consensus, the belief that the disadvantaged position of the blacks could be attributed to their isolation from the mainstream of American values and could be ameliorated by their incorporation into this mainstream. However, the resistance the civil-rights movement encountered had two consequences. First, it demonstrated the limitations of purely legal means for bringing about social change and suggested that there was no alternative but to resort to political means to attain group goals. Moreover, the use of political means in this context required the deployment of resources in order to confront openly the authority of the existing government at federal, state, and local levels. Second, the resistances that blacks encountered in bringing about change were conducive to enhanced mutual identification on their part accompanied by a growth in their social solidarity. These developments in turn were propitious to the cultivation of orientations and perspectives that were uniquely and distinctively black. The politicization of the black struggle for recognition and equality in American society provided a model for many hitherto submerged and voiceless groups. The feminist movement, the gay rights movement, and the movement for prisoners' rights all entered the public arena in order to alleviate the discrimination to which they were vulnerable in the existing social system.

As these groups awakened to their political potential, American society suddenly appeared to become fragmented into antagonistic segments, and the American social order was becoming increasingly problematic. Each dissident group, as it became politicized, redefined its identity and its place in society. Rather than viewing American government as an instrument through which the pluralism of American society was channeled and accommodated, it was increasingly viewed as the special organ of the interests of powerful groups and the defender of the status quo. Pitting themselves against this leviathan, each of these groups viewed itself as relatively powerless and beyond the pale of conventional politics. Consequently new strategies and tactics of civil disobedience were devised in order to dramatize their causes and to gain political concessions. Each movement nursed a profound sense of the injustice of its lot under the existing social system.

The new image of the delinquent typifies these new trends. It is that of the delinquent as "aggrieved citizen." What is striking about this new image is that unlike the images associated with previous stages, this one represents an effort to view his world from the perspective of the delinquent himself. The image of the delinquent as "potential pauper," as "disaffiliated," and as "frustrated social climber" in contrast are all designations from the perspective of the reformer or the sociologist.

We have attempted to single out what we have called perspectivism as the central characteristic of the contemporary era. Undoubtedly it is intimately related to various other tendencies occurring during the same period. For example, some might argue that the outstanding feature of the contemporary era is the decline in the legitimacy of the government and of other traditional social institutions, such as the family and the church. It is accordingly an era in which the meanings of a great range of traditional behavior have come under question. Others might argue that the tearing away of the protective layer provided by the belief in consensus has exposed the skeletal structure of society with its dependence upon power relationships and conflict processes. We have chosen to place the emphasis upon the concept of perspectivism because of its analytical value for our present purpose. It enables us to move from the general social context of social change to the more specific topic of the sociology of delinquency during this era.

There is no doubt that developments in the sociology of deviance, particularly its emphasis upon an interactionist approach, provide an unusually accurate reflection of the changing intellectual climate of the contemporary era. The interactionist approach views deviance as a phenomenon that emerges out of the reciprocal interplay between two perspectives—that of the control agents and that of the potential and actual deviants. Without the participation of official agencies of control to make the legal rules and enforce them, certain acts and the individuals who perform them would never come to be defined as deviant. Without other individuals who live according to perspectives that conflict with those of the agencies of control there would be no deviance. Deviance becomes an emergent, generated by the interaction and confrontation between the representatives of legal authority and the representatives of alternative perspectives. As Lemert suggests, deviant phenomena presuppose the differentiation of society. [7] So viewed, the fundamental issue for the sociology of deviance becomes that of how certain differentiated segments of the society become defined as deviant and with what consequences for themselves and the rest of society.

Perspectivism provided a platform for a thorough criticism of the existing judicial and correctional system. The latter was increasingly identified as an institutionalized expression of certain powerful interests who bent these institutions to promote their own welfare rather than that of the clients. Inevitably such an attitude led to a profound skepticism of the whole existing correctional system. It was viewed as authoritarian, arbitrary, and capricious, imbued with notions of the rehabilitative ideal. Interactionist analysis of the juvenile justice system encouraged the allegation that it treated the delinquent as an object—something to be processed by impersonal, bureaucratic procedures. The whole idea of stigma, which has become so prominent during this period, can be regarded as a process through which a human being is transformed from an individual with some control over his own behavior and destiny to one who has been virtually forced to forfeit such control. The counterpart to the idea of human rights in the race relations struggle became the idea of accountability in the sphere of corrections. In this context, accountability applied to all of the parties involved—the offender, the control agents, and the community itself. Because accountability thrives best within a democratic context, there was a general movement toward the construction of a whole set of alternative nonauthoritarian peer-oriented institutions in which this prized quality could be cultivated. The outcome, in short, was the movement toward community corrections.

After some two hundred years of American history the problem of delinquency has come full circle. It arose when social forces broke it out of the sphere of the primary groups, the core of the sacred society. The dream of theorists and reformers in the 1970s is to take the problem out of the hands of the institutions of the secular society and place it in the hands of a new sacred society.

NOTES

1. Robert E. Park, "The City as a Social Laboratory," in Ralph H. Turner (ed.), *On Social Control and Collective Behavior* (Chicago: University of Chicago Press, 1967), p. 5.

2. E. W. Burgess, "The Study of the Delinquent as a Person," *American Journal of Sociology* 28 (May 1923); 657-680.

3. Gunnar Myrdal, *An American Dilemma* (New York: Harper, 1944), p. xlvii.

4. Louis Wirth, "Urbanism as a Way of Life," in Albert J. Reiss, Jr., ed., *Louis Wirth on Cities and Social Life* (Chicago: University of Chicago Press, 1964), p. 80.

5. W. Lloyd Warner, *Democracy in Jonesville: A Study of Quality and Inequality* (New York: Harper, 1949), p. xiii.

6. Ibid., p. 297.

7. Edwin M. Lemert, *Social Pathology* (New York: McGraw-Hill, 1951), pp. 21-23.

chapter 2

Gentlemen reformers, charity workers, and the house of refuge: juvenile delinquency in the nineteenth century

In New York City at the opening of the nineteenth century, and in Chicago at its closing, many reformers preoccupied themselves with the problems of immigrant and lower-class youth. Indeed, youth and how it could be socialized (and if necessary resocialized) was one of the major concerns of middle-class people throughout the nineteenth century. The growing momentum of urbanization and industrialization was constantly upsetting conventional assumptions about the place of youth in the community. Earlier, in an economy in which agriculture was primary, the control of children and young people had been delegated to the family quite successfully. In the urban environment, however, the family was no longer able to perform this function effectively. During the course of the nineteenth century many varied efforts were made to come to terms with this fundamental transformation. Questions such as the following were raised: Was the family to be distrusted, ignored, and bypassed? Or was it to be placed upon a pedestal and idealized in hopes that its former effectiveness might thus be restored? Or were its limitations and capabilities to be confronted and supplemented by other public resources in order to provide for the welfare of youth? Each of these possible approaches and others vied for priority. Moreover, because juvenile delinquency so deeply dramatized the plight of the urban family, it provided the forum in which these issues were most openly confronted.

The Emergence of the Gentlemen Reformers

During the early decades of the nineteenth century Americans, particularly those living in large eastern cities like New York City, Boston, and Philadelphia, became aware that they were living in a changing world. The tempo of social life picked up as mobility across the land and up the social scale increased. The population grew and the number of enterprises multiplied. Between 1790 and 1830 the population of New York State increased five times. The number of factories grew rapidly on convenient river locations.[1] Americans had no precedent for making sense of this kind of world. The norm until then had been the small, relatively self-contained rural community. Many of the assumptions they had hitherto made about society were now being contradicted by what was happening around them. They had lived in an orderly world where everyone knew his place and where there was a place for everyone. Now there were strangers everywhere, some of whom were ambitious and began to compete for the wealth, status, and power that growing urban communities offered. Others appeared to be idle, drunken, and disrespectful individuals who challenged all the accepted verities of the social order and morality.

The segment of the population most sensitive to these trends was the old Protestant middle class. Successful merchants and professionals, they were men with a strong sense of public responsibility who had inherited a tradition of exercising authority over their communities, as leading functionaries in church and government. Now, because of the rapid growth, control of public policy through such direct and personal means was no longer so feasible. In reaction they grouped together and formed voluntary associations and attempted to exercise their control collectively. The world as they viewed it then gave cause for both utopian hopes and simultaneous feelings of distress.

The evidences of growth in business, commerce, and industry in New York City led to visions of its future in which the possibilities of development appeared to be unlimited. DeWitt Clinton (governor of New York, 1817-1823, 1824-1826) in 1825 expressed it as follows:

The city, he declared, "will, in course of time become the granary of the world, the emporium of commerce, the seat of manufactures, the focus of great moneyed operations, and the concentrating point of vast, disposable, and accumulating capitals, which will stimulate, enliven, extend, and reward the exertions of human labour and ingenuity, in all their processes and exhibitions. And, before the revolution of a century, the whole island of Manhattan, covered with habitations and replenished with a dense population, will constitute one vast city."[2]

Perceived simultaneously but in sharp contrast to this highly optimistic estimate of the future were some of the sordid realities of the present:

People on the eastern coast of the United States could look upon the cities of Boston, New York, and Philadelphia and view the breaking down of long-established colonial controls and the emergence of disruptive forces. Something had gone wrong. Young ruffians ran in gangs through the streets, and watchmen found hungry urchins asleep under doorsteps. Beggars and cutpurses jostled the wealthy on busy thoroughfares. It had been less than fifty years since the supposedly perfect nation had been devised, but the noble plans of the forefathers already seemed in jeopardy. Even while the blood of life still coursed through the veins of Thomas Jefferson and John Adams, the perfect experiment seemed on its way to destruction.[3]

The rapid growth of New York City had been accompanied by the sudden emergence of a segment of the population, largely composed of destitute immigrants, that the reformers thought threatened their own interests and their values. They feared these people as possible sources of violence and anarchy. They were all too aware of the havoc the street mobs caused during the French Revolution and saw these outcast people as possible sources of similar civil disturbances. There were, indeed, some human obstacles that appeared to be strewing the road to utopia, and the old middle classes were determined to remove them. The idea of reform had already taken solid root among them. During the eighteenth century Americans had shared in the growth of the humanitarian sentiment that during the eighteenth century had characterized both Britain and Europe: "Humanitarian activities of many kinds were undertaken in the early republic, presaging the great reforming crusades of the mid-nineteenth century, and the centres of these experiments were the large commercial cities of New York, Philadelphia and Boston, which possessed the necessary conditions of a conscientious middle-class, an adequate supply of funds, and social evils in need of attention."[4]

The zeal for reform had already manifested itself in efforts to improve the system of justice. The new republic had inherited a system characterized by an emphasis upon capital and corporal punishment. Under the influence of Beccaria, who had proposed that crime could be dealt with by moderating punishments and increasing the certainty that the sanctions of the criminal law would be applied to violators, several of the eastern states had revised their criminal codes and constructed prisons for criminal offenders. This innovation had rather quickly led to disillusionment as it became evident that the rate of crime was not declining. Observers noted that the contacts permitted among prisoners in such institutions tended to defeat the goal of reformation. A new generation of reformers was soon to demand prisons based upon the principle of solitary confinement.[5]

New York City, in particular, provided the milieu for a very active group of reformers. These were all members of established families, or individuals who had achieved success as merchants and professionals. They included an unusually large number of Quakers, considering they formed a relatively small proportion of the population of the city. They were cosmopolitan men who kept informed of reform movements in other communities and abroad through correspondence and travel. They were also avid believers in the ideas of the Enlightenment. The secular ideas of progress and the perfectibility of man harmonized well with the newer theological view of man. The rigidities of older Puritan views of individual salvation as inexorably predetermined were softened by ideas favoring the possibilities of self-redemption and self-regeneration. Locke's doctrine that children's minds were formed entirely during the course of their experience, the notion of the tabula rasa, proved to be especially influential. These reformers held a world view of man as an incongruous amalgam of moral principle and environmental determinism. It was a mixture that provided an ideological framework congenial to a series of intense reform efforts during the early decades of the nineteenth century. I have found it convenient to refer to this group of reformers as the "gentlemen reformers." For the most part they were men who remained at their occupations and who interested themselves in reform as their avocation. They were amateur rather than professional reformers, but they were highly dedicated and diligent.

The Problem of Pauperism

The gentlemen reformers were responding to more than the stimuli provided by a favorable ideology when they undertook their program of reform. Much of New York City's rapid growth was attributable to immigration from abroad; the largest in numbers and the most conspicuously visible were the Irish. They were impoverished, and the males turned to whatever employment was available. This led to their engagement as laborers on many construction projects both in New York and farther inland. The stress of making the transition from one society to another under conditions of virtual destitution was in many cases destructive of family solidarity. Illness took a heavy toll. Many abandoned their families. The major victims of such developments were the children. Many became homeless and had to survive on their own, through finding employment, or through begging and stealing. They were the unreached. At a time when, stimulated by Locke and the ideas of the Enlightenment, the gentlemen reformers were placing heavy emphasis upon the virtues of formal instruction and the laborious inculcation of morality and were ingeniously creating a network of schools, they found it impossible to bring schooling to these "street arabs."

The gentlemen reformers worried that the homeless children were destined to become paupers or criminals. In particular the idea of pauperism most disturbed their equanimity; it was the very antithesis of their own most cherished sober, middle-class values. Industry, thrift, punctuality, and sobriety constituted the very foundations of their lives. Paupers were those who manifested the very opposite. What was particularly disturbing to them were evidences of lack of industry and drunkenness.

Because the Irish were relatively numerous among the newcomers to the city and because of their difference in religion, their favorable attitude toward drinking, and the poverty of large numbers, the reformers began to perceive pauperism and crime in terms of the Irish stereotypes:

The image which the largely Anglo-American leaders of New York City seemed to hold concerning Irish parents was that of slatterns and drunken hell-raisers. The authorities and the dominant ethnic group, somewhat dismayed at the thought of increased Irish influence, probably had little desire to see "Paddy Murphy" in any other light. To have argued that the Irishman was equal in ability to "Native Americans" would have been to point out that he had been somehow treated unfairly. Few chose this avenue of explanation. A far easier path lay in the direction of stereotyping the Irish family itself, since if it could be proven deficient, factors such as immigration and intemperance could be blamed for rising crime rates and increased pauperism.[6]

The gentlemen reformers were at their most innovative in their selection of the problem of delinquent youth for special concern. In response to their concern with the problem of poverty, they had initially organized as the Society for the Prevention of Pauperism. In 1823 they disbanded this organization and reconstituted themselves as the Society for the Reformation of Juvenile Delinquents. As the new name indicates, they selected the problem of delinquency as the major point of intervention for their whole attack on the problem of poverty. They might well have selected a different target for reform, and, indeed, they did make halfhearted and unsuccessful attempts to close up what in their view were the purveyors of temptation and vice, the taverns and the theaters. They did not even try to provide employment opportunities and other services to the poor. These alternatives would have been completely unacceptable; the implication that there was some public responsibility for the provision of employment was strongly contrary to their laissez-faire economic doctrines. The furnishing of services to the poor would have been regarded as almsgiving.

The reformers found in delinquent youth a virtually new problem. The colonial era had had a place for poverty and traditional ways of dealing with it. The adult pauper might have been remanded to a family, placed in an almshouse, or, if a transient, forced to move to another community, but in any case he had a place in the scheme of things. There had, however, been no category for the homeless child. Poor children and orphans had been dealt with through apprenticeship, a contract binding the child to work for a craftsman or merchant but also requiring his incorporation into the family as a family member. However, as Mennel has indicated, there had been a gradual deterioration of apprenticeship as an effective source of social control throughout the eighteenth century. As it became subject to economic exploitation there was an increasing tendency for apprentices to desert their masters.

> Craftsmen and merchants began to see them [their apprentices] as workers valuable for their labor and little else. These masters had neither the time nor the inclination to regard apprentices as members of the family—a development not entirely unwelcome to the children but one which left them at the mercy of public authorities when they committed crimes.
>
> The tendency to view children as economic units affected both public policy and organized benevolence. As society's primary design became the promotion of individual and national wealth, philanthropy became miserly and minimized the scope of institutional care in order to spur poor children to work.[7]

Moreover, during the eighteenth century the increasing distrust among social classes led the established classes to doubt that poor families were able to raise their own children properly. This response had not been limited to America but had already taken root in England.[8] "During the eighteenth century, juvenile delinquency slowly ceased to mean a form of misbehavior common to all children and became instead a euphemism for the crimes and conditions of poor children."[9]

The growth of the labor market, the high valuation placed upon child labor, and the increasing social distance between the classes were all conducive to awareness on the part of the middle classes of the problems of social control posed by the children of the poor. The same trend appeared in England. Leading prison reformers on both sides of the Atlantic, such as Elizabeth Fry, John Howard, and Benjamin Rush, agreed on the need to create special institutions for the incarceration of young criminal offenders.

> Although these reformers were known primarily for their exposition of the degrading conditions in most prisons of the time, they became, in the course of their work, enthusiastic about the

benefits of specially organized incarceration, particularly for young persons convicted of crimes. John Howard, for example, was "delighted" in 1778 following his visit to a correctional establishment for juvenile offenders in Rome. [10]

A part of this enthusiasm for the creation of juvenile institutions was a reaction to the failure of existing penal institutions to deter criminality or to prevent recidivism. The hope was always there that measures that had failed with adults might prove to be effective with children. There was another apprehension, which had to do with the use of adult judicial and correctional institutions to deal with the young. At the beginning of the nineteenth century youth were treated by the law as miniature adults, which meant that they were tried as adults and sentenced as adults. Inevitably this meant that sizable numbers of children began to be incarcerated in prisons. The gentlemen reformers were already aware that urbanization was associated with a growing proportion of young convicts. [11] One highly influential report presented to the Society for the Prevention of Pauperism in 1822 dealt with the issues as follows:

> It is with pain we state that, in five or six years past, and until the last few months, the number of youth under fourteen years of age, charged with offenses against the law, has doubled; and that the same boys are again and again brought up for examination, some of whom are committed, and some tried; and that imprisonment by its frequency renders them hardened and fearless. [12]

Another observation was also quite disturbing to the reformers. They learned that judges, struck with the harshness of their limited alternatives for disposing of youthful offenders, shied away from applying the law and treated them with leniency. The fact that the very severity of the existing system led to many deviant youths escaping all social control provoked the reformers.

The influential ideas of the Enlightenment also propelled the reformers in the direction of creating a special correctional institution for juveniles. As Rothman has pointed out, during the decades after 1820 Americans in the Jacksonian era began to erect a whole galaxy of institutions—"penitentiaries for the criminal, asylums for the insane, almshouses for the poor, orphan asylums for homeless children, and reformatories for delinquents. . . ." [13] To be sure, the gentlemen reformers did not restrict themselves to the creation of only houses of refuge. Among their institutional innovations were the African Free School Society and the New York High School.

The reformers were convinced that the existing volume of deviance, whether in the form of poverty, crime, or mental illness, threatened the very fabric of society. They attributed delinquency to the destructive impact of a hectic, disorderly social life, joined to freely available sources of vice and profligacy. The inadequacies of community life were aided and abetted by the disorganization of the family. Because deviance was viewed as a product of a bad environment, reformers believed deviants could be helped by exposing them to a good environment. Complementing this view of the environment was a view of human nature as being highly pliant at birth and as remaining tractable until a certain age, when the mold in which the individual was formed hardened permanently. It was a world view congenial to reform, but reform that would tend to be directed to the young. Finally, the doctrine of progress in a rapidly developing society inevitably heightened future consciousness and magnified the role of youth as the guarantors of the future.

The House of Refuge

The creation of the New York House of Refuge in 1825 was preceded by several years of intense inquiry and discussion among the gentlemen reformers. They had surveyed and collated information from other American communities and from such countries as England, France, and Switzerland, which culminated in the issuance in 1822 of a *Report on the Penitentiary System in the United States*. This report advocated "the erection of new prisons for juvenile offenders." [14] One of the most active reformers, John Griscom, Quaker, chemist, and principal of New York High School, in 1818-1819 had visited various specialized juvenile institutions in Europe. Some of the impressions he received from his visit are highly revealing of the orientation with which he and his colleagues approached their tasks. The most influential experience of all proved to be his visit to a school for the children of convicts and other delinquent children in which the children were trained to do industrial work. It had been established by the London Philanthropic Society in 1788 and was designed to

> establish a fund, not to be sunk in gratuities without any return, not to be a perpetual current from the purses of the rich to the miseries of the poor . . . the object in short to unite a spirit of charity with the principles of trade, and to erect a temple of philanthropy on the foundations of virtuous industry. [15]

Griscom had responded quite differently to Johann Pestalozzi, the Swiss educator "who emphasized individual development and self-realization as the core of the educative experience." [16] Griscom dismissed Pestalozzi's approach with its emphasis upon the personal relationship between the educator and his students as well meaning but impractical. He favored a regimen that emphasized impersonality, routine, and uniformity.

Given the social background of the reformers and their world view, it was inevitable that a distinctive institutional pattern was implemented in the House of Refuge. Its daily activities were organized around work, education, and morality. In using the contract system to introduce the children to the world of industry, the emphasis upon work was valued more for the habits of regularity and self-discipline that it exacted rather than for its potential for teaching special skills. The educational methods utilized were influenced by the Lancasterian method. "Under the system of Englishman Joseph Lancaster, one master could teach a number of children who would, in turn, teach younger children, and so on, down the line." [17] Heale has described the methods the reformers introduced in order to promote morality:

> Reformation was encouraged by a complex system of rewards and punishments, whereby the children were divided into four classes "according to their moral conduct," and could be promoted to a higher class or demoted to a lower for good or bad behaviour. Membership of the highest class carried with it certain privileges, such as that allowing "occasionally . . . on Saturday at dinner, a pudding or pie, fruit, etc. in addition to the usual fare," and punishments ranged from privation of play and exercise, through gruel without salt for all meals, to fetters and handcuffs *"only in extreme cases."*

The reformers had great confidence in these techniques. . . . They seemed to take it for granted that the systems of rewards and punishments adopted in the Lancasterian schools or in the House of Refuge would produce a virtuous and well-trained mind. . . . As well as trying to force a code of behaviour on the poor, the reformers also sought to teach their charges by example. In the free schools and the House of Refuge they seemed to be trying to create small models of their ideal society, in which those in the lower classes would raise themselves to the higher by industry, self-help and good behaviour; the inmates of these institutions were presumably expected to draw the appropriate moral for their conduct in the outside world. . . . There was relatively little reliance on moral preaching. . . .[18]

The Motives of the Reformers

We come to understand the gentlemen reformers much better when we realize how they conceived of themselves:

Clifford Griffen has characterized early nineteenth-century philanthropists as conservative reformers—men who regarded themselves as the only legitimate heirs to the ideas and traditions of colonial theocrats and of the Federalist founding fathers. Defining themselves as God's Elect, they felt duty bound to develop charitable organizations in the secular sphere in His name. Benevolent activity was part of their moral stewardship—their trusteeship to relieve the suffering of the needy and to correct the behavior of the deviant.[19]

As true believers in the system of capitalism, they brought its values to the design of their new institution: "Their general purpose was to save children from lives of crime by inculcating them with middle-class values—neatness, diligence, punctuality, and thrift."[20] One of the reasons that John Griscom had rejected the educator Pestalozzi's system with its basis in personal human interaction was the assumption that it would be too expensive. "To Griscom, and to later Americans, despite their well-meaning concern, the problem of delinquency has meant a search for the most efficient, often impersonal, and least costly means of disposing of unwanted youth."[21]

The sense of rectitude and the conviction of superiority with which these reformers approached lower-class youth expressed both religious conviction and the values of their social class. "Unconcerned with their own prejudices, refuge managers concentrated on developing institutional routines."[22] Certain consequences for the delinquency issue followed from such a paternalistic and ethnocentric orientation. Their mode of dealing with the problem, guaranteeing as it did continuing social distance between themselves and the delinquents, was conducive to the development and persistence of stereotypical views of the delinquent. It was also consistent with such views that they should experience few qualms about depriving the juveniles of the protections of due process. "Of the first sixteen children admitted to the House of Refuge, nine had not committed a punishable offense."[23] Inmates included destitute and orphaned children as well as those found guilty of felonies in state and local courts.

Furthermore, the reformers implemented their hostility and distrust of the lower classes by endeavoring to sever permanently all ties between these children and their families. The managers of the House of Refuge retained for themselves the power and the right to determine the conditions of reentry of released inmates to the community. They could apprentice or indenture them to whomever they chose, and they could withhold all information concerning the children's whereabouts from the latters' family.

The kinds of modifications in viewpoint that might have ensued upon greater intimacy with the problem is suggested by the career of Joseph Tuckerman, who in 1826 was appointed by the Unitarian Association of Massachusetts to carry his "ministry at large" among the poor of Boston. He became America's first "street" or "detached" worker. Since he could not "reach" the poor through a conventional ministry, he decided to follow and serve them in their own milieu. What is of special interest here is that increasing familiarity with the problems of the poor led him to modify his emphasis upon the necessity for them to undergo individual spiritual regeneration. He became interested in the varied problems that confronted the poor in the urban community.

As a result of his investigations of the poor in their homes and his growing awareness of their everyday problems, Tuckerman became interested in a great many practical programs that involved wages, housing, education, and the delinquency of children. Although he never abandoned completely an individualistic explanation of poverty, he argued that the community had collective responsibilities to the poor and that to some extent at least these obligations could be met only through legislation. [24]

Tuckerman appears to be the first representative of a tradition intimately associated with Boston and Massachusetts of seeking to develop noninstitutional means of dealing with delinquency.

Institutionalization of the House of Refuge

The opening of the House of Refuge in New York in 1825 established a precedent which was quickly followed by the gentlemen reformers of Boston and Philadelphia. The Boston House of Reformation opened in 1826, and a refuge was opened in Philadelphia in 1828. However, after 1850 the impetus toward the reform of juvenile misbehavior through the creation of institutions declined. "By the early 1850's the evolution of juvenile custodial institutions—whether they were houses of refuge or reform schools on the family plan—had reached a point of stagnation." [25] There were several reasons for this development. As the New York House of Refuge, for example, came to depend increasingly upon the state for support, the gentlemen reformers became less and less influential in its management and the formulation of its policies. According to Rothman in *The Discovery of the Asylum,* the House of Refuge had been part of a larger movement to reform deviants in segregated institutions and by so doing to provide a model for the improvement of society. The lack of realism of this goal was inevitably reflected in the decline of enthusiasm for the House of Refuge. This attenuation in idealistic hopes was not accompanied by its dismantling; however, in mid-century it was forced into a struggle for survival. It did not fare well in the competition for public resources, whose value was reduced even further by extensive inflation. It adjusted to such rigors by extending its dependence upon the contract system. With the establishment of more and more workshops by outside entrepreneurs with the sole aim of profit, the other aims of education and training in morality became subordinate.

At mid-century American society was changing in manifold ways, all with some bearing upon the institutionalized form assumed by the New York House of Refuge. When they first confronted the unfamiliar aspects of an urbanizing and changing society, Americans of the Jacksonian era had tended to believe that deviant behavior threatened the very foundations of society. As the century wore on, urbanization and its consequences became somewhat more familiar and less threatening—general concern with problems such as sectionalism and race relations assumed priority over deviance.[26] The increasing importance of industry in the country's economy also took its toll, making appropriate apprenticeships more difficult to find for released inmates. "Indenture to farmers and craftsmen declined steadily after 1850, and the number of outright discharges increased commensurately."[27]

Ironically the very changes that threatened the House of Refuge in its originally conceived form contributed to its survival and institutionalization during the latter half of the nineteenth century. Of all the institutions for deviants built during the preceding decades it remained highest in general repute. A new generation of penal reformers was highly critical of penitentiaries for adult offenders and turned with renewed interest to institutional innovations for youthful offenders. It was a hope that received tangible expression as the House of Refuge idea phased over into that of the reformatory as the nineteenth century progressed. This favorable judgment of the House of Refuge related to the functions that accrued to it within the evolving correctional system. In the view of its founders it was to be a place of first resort, a place where the moral inadequacies of the deviant implanted by a destructive environment could be transformed into moral virtues. In its institutionalized form it became a place of last resort. Using an institution for this purpose gradually became increasingly acceptable for the care of lower-class deviants in a rapidly growing society, characterized by increasing complexity in its ethnic and religious divisions and by increasing social distance between the lower and the more comfortable classes.

The New York House of Refuge became a holding operation for the youthful wastage of a rapidly growing metropolis. Custody replaced reformation as the primary goal. "The House of Refuge over its first quarter-century of existence, had become a miniature Auburn State Prison...."[28] The services that it provided were regarded as so indispensable that it moved twice, each time to a greatly expanded plant.

In 1854 when it was moved for the third and final time it "had become by far the world's largest repository of delinquent children."[29] This reliance upon the House of Refuge was not noticeably affected by the consciousness that many of its inmates later reappeared as convicts in the state's penitentiaries and prisons. The superintendent of the New York City Penitentiary once remarked, "It is as regular a succession as the classes in a college . . . from the house of refuge to the penitentiary, and from the penitentiary to the State Prison."[30]

Despite its gradual metamorphosis into a prison for juveniles the House of Refuge retained some redeeming features from the point of view of the reformers of the mid-century. It was able to avoid some of the difficulties encountered by other institutions—such as the penitentiaries and mental asylums—by retaining some control over its admissions. Whereas the others became repositories for the most intractable and hopeless individuals—the recidivists among the criminal offenders and the senile among the mentally ill—the managers of the Houses of Refuge continued to function within certain limits. They kept the age of admission down to sixteen and retained control over the length of stay of inmates. "In the 1850's the typical detention period at the New York refuge was sixteen months. . . ."[31] The turnover, consequently, was relatively rapid, and a stream of inmates was constantly being returned to the community. Those who were not amenable to the discipline and routine of the institution were shipped out on whaling expeditions, or sometimes they were permitted to escape unobtrusively. These houses, therefore, were able to retain some of the aura of optimism and hope that are so easily associated with youth. In the less punitively laden atmosphere, some of the illiterate inmates were able to learn to read and do arithmetic.[32]

During the first decades of their operation, the Houses of Refuge admitted a disproportionate number of Irish youth:

in 1830, a substantial minority in the New York refuge was American-born; by 1850, only one-third of the residents of the Philadelphia refuge came from American families, while forty-two percent had parents born in Ireland; in Masachusetts in 1850, forty percent of the inmates were Catholics, most of whom were Irish, and this in a state where the foreign-born composed nineteen percent of the population.[33]

Such data are worth noting because they suggest how prototypical the House of Refuge was of all subsequent institutions created for the correction of juveniles. It acted as a kind of backup institution for those cases in which the basic social institutions—the family, the church, and the school—were unable to exert their control. Such conditions have been most common among the newcomers to the cities. Each wave of new arrivals has provided the grist of its youth for the mills of the reformatories and prisons. Each successive group contributed its quota to the House of Refuge: "Instead of the Irish, Italians, then Puerto Rican, and Southern Negroes became defined as dangerous. . . ."[34]

Charity Workers and the Critique of the Reformatory

The second half of the nineteenth century witnessed a gradual erosion of public confidence in the Houses of Refuge and related institutions. Such criticism was primarily a product of the emergence of new points of view toward the problem of juvenile delinquency. Beginning with Charles Loring Brace in the 1850's, critics had begun to propose noninstitutional alternatives for the treatment of juvenile misbehavior. These criticisms gathered momentum for the next fifty years but remained largely ineffectual until the Progressive era at the start of the twentieth century. It is interesting to speculate why, despite the mounting of attacks against it, institutionalization continued to be predominant. It is not that new initiatives were lacking. Separate trials for youth were established in New York State, and probation was introduced in Massachusetts. What appeared to be required was some conception of the form that a noninstitutional agency for dealing with the problems of juveniles might take. It was not until the end of the century that the idea of the juvenile court was developed.

In order to understand the nature of the criticisms which they made and the alternatives which they offered, it is helpful to note some of the characteristics of the critics. They were recruited largely from a new breed of practically oriented philanthropists, the charity workers, who as the nineteenth century wore on began to think of themselves more and more as social workers. What was remarkable about them was the pragmatic manner in which they began to modify their views as they worked with poor people. The moralism with which they tended to start their work became increasingly tempered by a growing awareness of environmental factors and of the complexity of the processes that lead to poverty. Beginning their careers as charity workers, as staunch conservatives and representatives of the upper classes, many became liberal reformers under the impact of their personal experience with the issues of poverty. Unlike the gentlemen reformers of an earlier era, for whom reform had been an avocation, this new group made social reform their vocation. They became professional reformers devoting their careers to one or more aspects of the problems of the poor. It was from among the ranks of these charity workers who became social workers that the most influential of the critics of institutionalization were drawn.

Charles Loring Brace was the first to make his mark. He was one of the first individuals to observe at close hand, carefully and systematically, the growth of slums on Manhattan Island in New York City. These slums had not been so pervasive or so visible during the earlier decades of the century. Brace was forced to take a stance toward the all-embracing nature of urbanization. Like the gentlemen reformers before him, his experience with the problem of poverty very quickly resulted in his decision to devote his career to working with the young. "Once his decision was made, Brace devoted thirty-eight years of life to his self-chosen task of saving children in New York."[35] The medium through which he carried on his work was the Children's Aid Society. Two ideas appear to have been basic to his point of view: the importance of individual enterprise and the family. During the earlier part of his career he had initiated his highly controversial plan to place homeless city waifs with farm families in the West. However, as time went on he became more reconciled to the necessity of training children for life in the urban environment, and he resourcefully devised a variety of schools, lodging houses, and institutions to assist them. Because he idealized their enterprise and self-reliance, he had a particular fondness for newsboys and organized special lodging houses for them. In conformity with his philosophy they were charged nominal sums for rent. His emphasis upon the family was captured in his phrase, "The family is God's reformatory." In his attitude toward the importance of the family, he represented a drastic reversal of the distrustful attitudes of the gentlemen reformers.

It was from such a platform that he became the first notable critic of the institutionalization of juvenile delinquents. What disturbed

him most was the conviction that institutions such as the House of
Refuge, by virtue of their size, severe discipline, and inflexible routine,
eliminated individuality and personal responsibility, converting the
inmates into machinelike creatures who were unfit to do well outside
the institution. [36] This criticism did not have much effect at the time.
It was voiced during the decade of the 1850s when the House of
Refuge was actually undergoing a renewal in popularity.

A more extended critique was offered several decades later in 1891
by Homer Folks, a social worker and reformer whose career was devoted to making social provision for children and families outside of
institutional settings. [37] Although it reflects a considerable growth in
sophistication and subtlety over that of Brace, the intimate kinship
between the two is unmistakable. Folks listed the five major failures of
the correctional institution as follows:

> 1. The temptation it offers to parents and guardians to throw
> off their most sacred responsibilities. . . .
> 2. The contaminating influence of association. . . .
> 3. The enduring stigma . . . of having been committed. . . .
> 4. . . . renders impossible the study and treatment of each
> child as an individual.
> 5. The great dissimilarity between life in an institution and
> life outside. [38]

It is doubtful whether a critique of institutions as penetrating as
this one could have been formulated by anyone without considerable
insight into the influence exerted by personal relationships and associations upon the behavior of the individual. Implicitly assumed in
these various points is an environmentalism as thoroughgoing as the
gentlemen reformers ever entertained, yet it differed from theirs almost totally in substance. The gentlemen reformers thought man responded mechanically to the rewards and punishments afforded him
by his setting. In contrast, Folk viewed the environment as primarily
social, as composed of parents, peer groups, and the individual's view
of himself. It is a view that finds a place for such symbolic processes as
stigmatization. Any such view of the environment would inevitably
have to attribute considerable significance to the family as the individual's first social environment. It is to be noted, too, that the moralism of the gentlemen reformers had not disappeared. Folks's moral
concern, however, was not with the child but with the child's parents.

None of the points Folks advanced dwelt upon the protection of society. His criticisms were formulated solely in terms of the interest of the child. He believed that institutionalization not only violates the child's integrity but also threatens his sense of individuality. The import of these points is clear. Some mode of working with the child in his own environment, which does not remove him from the responsibilities that his parents should exercise over him, was to be preferred. In his attempt to apply his ideas, in 1890 Folks committed his agency, the Children's Aid Society of Pennsylvania, to accept responsibility for the supervision of delinquent children who had been convicted by the criminal courts and who normally would have been institutionalized. The experiment was not undertaken without misgiving: "We have sometimes left our wards in their home with fear and trembling, and returned half expecting the next mail to announce their evildoing and disappearance," Homer Folks recalled. "But we have been happily surprised as weeks passed by and all the reports were hopeful."[39]

Overview of Nineteenth-century Developments

When the problem of juvenile delinquency forced itself on the attention of Americans in the early decades of the nineteenth century, the challenge it presented was taken up by gentlemen reformers, upper- and upper-middle-class white Anglo-Saxon Protestants who generally subscribed to eighteenth-century rationalistic interpretations of man and society. Delinquency, from this perspective, was an individualistic problem best treated at the level of the individual. In the attempt to get the individual early before he came under the influence of the adult criminal and to provide an environment that would guide him toward a rational and responsible adulthood, the House of Refuge was invented. It quickly was institutionalized and hardened into the reformatory or reform school.

Throughout the century the problem of juvenile delinquency grew progressively more serious, leading to the rise of a new type of professional specializing in the problems of the poor, the impoverished, and the delinquent. Such charity workers, who were on their way to the development into a wide spectrum of professional social workers, increasingly subscribed to a social environmentalist theory of social problems, and they brought the theory and practice of the reformatory under critical review. They began to experiment with a variety of informal arrangements designed to keep the delinquent out of the reformatory.

The theory and practice of juvenile delinquency in America was on the threshold of major changes.

NOTES

1. David J. Rothman, *The Discovery of the Asylum: Social Order and Disorder in the New Republic* (Boston: Little, Brown, 1971), p. 57.

2. Charles N. Glaab and A. Theodore Brown, *A History of Urban America* (New York: Macmillan, 1967), pp. 72-73.

3. Robert S. Pickett, *House of Refuge: Origins of Juvenile Reform in New York State, 1815-1857* (Syracuse: Syracuse University Press, 1969), pp. xviii-xix.

4. Michael Heale, "Humanitarianism in the Early Republic: The Moral Reformers of New York, 1776-1825," *Journal of American Studies* 2 (1968): 161.

5. Ibid., 163.

6. Pickett, *House of Refuge*, pp. 16-17.

7. Robert M. Mennel, *Thorns and Thistles* (Hanover, New Hampshire: The University Press of New England, 1973), pp. xxii-xxiii.

8. Ibid., p. xxvi.

9. Ibid.

10. Ibid., p. xxiv.

11. Pickett, *House of Refuge*, p. 39.

12. Cited by Joseph M. Hawes, *Children in Urban Society: Juvenile Delinquency in Nineteenth-century America* (New York: Oxford University Press, 1971), p. 29.

13. Rothman, *The Discovery of the Asylum*, p. xiii.

14. Mennel, *Thorns and Thistles*, p. 11.

15. Cited by Mennel, *Thorns and Thistles*, p. xxvi.

16. Ibid., p. 25.

17. Pickett, *House of Refuge*, p. 35.

18. Heale, "The Moral Reformers," pp. 173-174.

19. Mennel, *Thorns and Thistles*, p. 5. Citation from Clifford S. Griffen, "Religious Benevolence as Social Control, 1815-1860," in David B. Davis, ed., *Ante-Bellum Reform* (New York: Harper & Row, 1967), pp. 81-96.

20. Mennel, *Thorns and Thistles*, p. 18.

21. Pickett, *House of Refuge*, p. 187.

22. Mennel, *Thorns and Thistles*, p. 18.

23. Ibid., p. 13.

24. Glaab and Brown, *Urban America*, p. 92.

25. Hawes, *Children in Urban Society*, p. 86.

26. Rothman, *The Discovery of the Asylum*, p. 252.

27. Mennel, *Thorns and Thistles*, p. 62.

28. Pickett, *House of Refuge*, p. 161.

29. Ibid., p. 176.

30. Cited by ibid., p. 160.

31. Rothman, *The Discovery of the Asylum*, p. 263.

32. Ibid., p. 264.

33. Ibid., p. 262.

34. Pickett, *House of Refuge*, p. 17.

35. R. Richard Wohl, "The 'Country Boy' Myth and Its Place in American Urban Culture: The Nineteenth-Century Contribution," *Perspectives in American History* 3 (1969): 112.

36. Rothman, *The Discovery of the Asylum*, p. 259.

37. Mennel, *Thorns and Thistles*, p. 112.

38. Ibid., p. 111.

39. Cited by ibid., p. 112.

chapter 3

Chicago in the 1890s: a milieu congenial to social reform

Chicago at the turn of the century had a milieu uniquely favorable to movements of social reform. Like New York City at the beginning of the nineteenth century, Chicago at the century's end was undergoing very rapid population growth and economic development. The major aspects of this growth are well presented in the following citations:

> No city in the history of the world had grown more rapidly than Chicago grew then. In 1840, it had fewer than five thousand residents. For the next fifty years, its population more than doubled in every decade but one—the decade of the Great Fire of 1871. By 1890, more than a million people lived in Chicago. From 1880 to 1910, the population rose by a half-million every ten years.[1]

> Industry grew even more rapidly than population. In the decade from 1880 to 1890, the number of factories almost trebled. The capital invested in them increased more than 300 percent. The number of workers more than doubled, the total wages paid to them more than trebled. Cost of materials and value of product

each rose more than 100 percent. In 1890 Chicago beat its old record for construction; it put up 11,640 new structures, costing 448 million. [2]

In 1889, more than 70 per cent of the inhabitants of Chicago were literally foreign-born. About 30 per cent were classed as "American," but even of this 30 per cent many were second-generation Europeans. But, the business, the money, the prosperity, the power, were chiefly in the hands of the 30 per cent. Only one of the great meat-packers, Nelson Morris, had come from Europe; the rest, Armours, Swifts, Libby's, were all native. The merchant princes were all native, the bankers, the real-estate dealers, the big manufacturers—the Bartletts, Cranes, Fairbanks, Fields, Keiths, Kimballs, Kirks, Hutchinsons, Leiters, Lyons, McCormicks, McNallys, Medills, Ogdens, Pullmans, Wards, Wentworths, even the Mandels and the Rosenwalds (not yet considerable figures) and their prosperous and powerful associates, were all native. It was they who had "made" Chicago, and they believed it to be their own. [3]

Paralleling New York City's earlier experience, rapid population growth in Chicago was accompanied by the emergence of sharp class and cultural cleavages. The manpower required by Chicago's industrial expansion was largely provided by the new immigrants from eastern and central Europe rather than the old immigrants from the British Isles and northwest Europe. Largely of peasant background the newcomers were quite alien to an urban and factory civilization. They differed from the more established residents in language and religion; they were from authoritarian, political regimes; and they had had little experience with democracy.

If the Chicago and the New York City of the two eras both embodied urbanization and industrialization in their most intense form, the differences between them were equally consequential. Unlike the Jacksonian Americans who had been apprehensive that geographic and social mobility threatened the basis of social order, the Chicagoans embraced rapid social change as their fundamental premise. Theirs was a community whose driving enterprise had by 1860 won ten trunk railroads; by 1880 it was connected with its tributary regions by 15,000 miles of railroad. It surpassed its continental rival, St. Louis, and between 1860 and 1890 grew from the eighth to the second among American cities.[4]

In Chicago the abundance of the American economy was fully evident. According to Bremner, it was this awareness that generated the belief that poverty could be eliminated: "This conviction of abundance was the wellspring of the humanitarian movements of the Progressive era."[5] This hectic pace of growth had profound repercussions for the social structure of the burgeoning metropolis. The virtually limitless financial success of the favored few was accompanied by a heightening of class cleavages. Such divisions generated considerable violence as in the Haymarket bombing of 1886 and the Pullman strike of 1894. The ability of the Protestant elites to manage the city as they chose was challenged from below. Chicago now exhibited a unique combination of circumstances that was conducive to social reform: it was characterized by profound social cleavages, considerable unrest in the lower classes, and intransigence in the upper classes.

In order to grasp more fully, however, the conditions that led to the creation of the juvenile court, it is necessary to take some account of the ideological factors that were conducive to reform. In the next chapter it will be argued that Chicago at century's end was propitious to the development of a distinctive outlook or ethos, which became articulate in the work of a distinguished group of humanists, such as Theodore Dreiser, Louis Sullivan, Clarence Darrow, Jane Addams, and John Dewey. This ethos was to exert considerable influence upon the manner in which the Chicago school of sociology formulated its problems, and, through this school, the innovative work by Clifford R. Shaw in the sociology of delinquency.

This ethos, which helped to mold the distinctive form of the juvenile court, was a response to the moral issues suggested by social change. The humanists were concerned with understanding Chicago as a new kind of social reality and ultimately with making institutional innovations that would introduce humanitarian values into its functioning as a community. The rapidity of change Chicago experienced produced some new insights into the nature of man. Development at this pace and scale occurred only because other values and considerations were subordinated to the goals of material achievement and financial success. Success became the catchword.[6] Earlier in America, success had been viewed as an attribute of the individual. However, the transformation of Chicago from prairie town to metropolis had been accomplished not by individuals working on their own but rather under the impetus of individuals with ideas for enterprises and the gift for leadership and large-scale organizations.

> ... Chicago by 1890 was a city of organization, where the efforts of an individual man counted for little. It was a city of monopolies, which closed off the former precious opportunities for ordinary men. A man could not gather together a few dollars and set out to compete with the McCormick reaper works, which employed more men than the city had held people fifty years earlier. It was still possible for men to start from modest origins and rise to the top, but most of them did so in peculiar occupations: Clarence Darrow in law, Theodore Dreiser in literature, John Dewey in teaching, Altgeld in politics. [7]

Social change tends to render the relationship between man and his environment problematic, but most problematic become his relationships between himself and his fellow men. George Pullman built a model community for his employees and watched helplessly while they rebelled against it. What did he owe to them? Marshall Field acquiesced in the execution of the Haymarket anarchists despite the complete absence of evidence against them. What did he owe to them? The Chicago experience rendered problematic in a thoroughly practical way the relationship between the individual and the group. As secularized, the problems of morality became social psychological. It is not surprising that one of the leading theoretical products of the Chicago school of sociology was the social psychology of George Herbert Mead.

It was such ideological and moral issues that influenced the Chicago reformers. In dealing with poverty, one of the problems was deciding whether reform would start with the individual or the group. Charity workers, who were beginning to call themselves social workers, saw the individual as the target for change. Settlement house workers saw social conditions as the target.

The differences in approach were crucial. To begin with, charity workers emphasized the individual causes of poverty, while settlement workers stressed the social and economic conditions that made people poor. Charity organizations sought primarily to help paupers and the unemployed; settlement workers, on the other hand, believed that they could work best with the working class above the poverty line. It was not so much the "poverty of clothes," as the "poverty of opportunity" that concerned settlements. There were other contrasts. Unlike charity societies that were built on the assumption that the upper class had a responsibility to help the needy, the settlement movement was based, Jane Addams expressed it, "on the theory that the dependence of classes on each other is reciprocal." Thus, the philosophy of the charity organization movement led to philanthropy, and the philosophy of the settlement movement, to reform.[8]

The difference between the two approaches, however, tended to be one of relative emphasis and priority only; both were characterized by an environmental approach.[9] The social workers dealt with the individual through environmental manipulation. The settlement house workers defined the neighborhood as the target of change but also viewed their task as that of contributing to the personality development of individuals. Both sought to empathize with the poor.

In addition to specific information, agents of the organized charities contributed a technique of social research. The "case method" which they perfected was an attempt to treat each family or individual as a unique problem. This meant the rejection of preconceived notions about "the poor," "the depraved classes," or "the oppressed," and the substitution of efforts to discover pertinent and significant data about particular family histories.[10]

Through friendly contact with the poor, settlement workers acquired, not just a knowledge, but an understanding of the daily life and trials of the urban masses. The best of them identified their own interests with the welfare of their neighbors. Where others thought of the people of the slums as miserable wretches deserving either pity or correction, settlement residents knew them as fellow human beings—and insisted that they were as much entitled to respect as any other members of the community. Numerous young men and women who lived and worked in the settlements during the 1890's carried this attitude with them into later careers in social work, business, government service, or the arts. It was the most important single contribution of the settlement movement; and it was destined to exert a great influence on the course of both social work and social reform in the twentieth century. [11]

Chicago witnessed the development of highly distinguished practitioners of both perspectives. One need only mention Edith and Grace Abbott, Sophonisba Breckinridge, and Julia Lathrop among the social workers and Jane Addams and Graham Taylor among the settlement house workers. Although it was the settlement house workers who became deeply involved in reform, the social workers also contributed. Indeed, both shared the same reform interests: the child and his family. The two perspectives were not isolated by sectarian feeling, and the practitioners were bound together by the most intimate ties of colleagueship. Collectively they comprised a fellowship of which Jane Addams was the most famous member. Most of them were of upper-middle-class origin, members of families whose heads had attained success during the settlement of Illinois and the growth of Chicago.

Our argument is that it was a coalition of reformers representing both the individualistic and the group perspectives toward the problems of youth who devised and implemented the idea of the juvenile court; for what is distinctive about the court is its premise that the treatment of delinquent youth should take account of the individual in his family and community setting.

The Creation of the Juvenile Court

The establishment of the juvenile court in Illinois in 1899 was one of three contemporaneous developments that institutionalized the changing status of youth in American society. Together with the introduction of compulsory education laws and child labor laws, the juvenile court act gave substance to the "discovery of adolescence." [12] The gentlemen reformers had, of course, recognized the problem posed by the homeless children and youthful beggars and street thieves of their day and had responded to it with the creation of the House of Refuge.

However, this institution was hardly different from institutions for adult deviants (prisons, mental hospitals, and almshouses) established during the same period. [13] The problems of all deviants, children and adults alike, were regarded as attributable to moral deficiencies in their child rearing, which had rendered them vulnerable to the temptations of their environment. If children differed, it was only by a matter of degree. They received the special attention of reformers because their very youth allegedly rendered them more pliable to the influences of a changed environment. There was nothing distinctive about the regimen established for them at the refuge.

The social placement of youth into the special status of adolescence was a long-term consequence of the impact of urbanization and industrialization upon the structure of family relationships. One of the first indications of widespread concern with the problem of youth was the growing number of books on child rearing written by American authors, which began to appear after 1825. The central theme of all these books was the decline in parental authority and the methods through which this authority could be reestablished. [14] Toward the end of the century the city came to be viewed as the prime corrupter of the young. [15] Children became subject to closer examination and study, and their depiction in literature became more probing and realistic. It was in the city that a certain amount of cleavage between parents and children became inevitable. People moved there seeking an improvement in their fortunes and found, inexorably, that life there required a profound modification of their most intimate personal relationships. In the urban milieu they were no longer able to exert the traditional familial authority over their children, who had begun to march to the sound of a different drummer, to the irresistible beat of the peer group. "It is pertinent to recall ... the deep concern of many nineteenth-century Americans about the growth of peer-group contacts." [16] Both intergenerational cleavages and the intensity of the peer group phenomenon were most marked among the immigrants and lower classes. It was among the least advantaged segments of urban society that the disruption of the social bonds linking the generations attained their most dramatic form. The institutional changes in education, work, and the law, which gave social reality to the category of adolescence, were primarily reflective (as they were consciously intended to be by the reformers who proposed them) of the social problems posed by lower-class youth.

With regard to the children of the foreign born who are still children and who appear in the juvenile courts. . . . These children
are the children of the poorer classes of the community whether
foreign or native born. The juvenile courts do not exist for the
children of the well-to-do. Since there is a large proportion of
immigrants among the people who are poor, it is expected that
the children of immigrants will be more largely found in the
courts established for the children of the poor.[17]

Indeed, as Bremner has indicated, "Much of the history of philanthropy and social reform can be written in terms of efforts to rescue
the children of the poor from the bad consequences of their poverty."[18]

We have witnessed in our own generation how the movement to de-
segregate the schooling of black and white children led to the cumulative uncovering of the interlocked problems of ghetto life, to what
Clark called "the tangle of community and personal pathology."[19]
Something analogous was involved as the Chicago reformers sought
to make the juvenile court into an effective instrument for the advancement of youth welfare. It was not particularly beneficial to
modify the child's legal status if elsewhere his status remained that of
an adult. The effective functioning of the court required compatible
changes in the child's other institutionally defined statuses. This recognition led the reformers into allied campaigns for compulsory
schooling and the abolition of child labor. The new status of adolescence became a product of a whole network of reforms.[20]

The founders of the juvenile court, envisaging it as the cornerstone
of a comprehensive child care system, delegated to it the care of neglected and dependent children as well as the delinquent; however, its
most radical departure concerned the treatment of the delinquent. It
was designed to treat the youthful offender as a child primarily and
only incidentally as a law violator. In order to accomplish this aim it
sought to transform the court experience into a judicial setting that
functioned through the medium of personal relationships. The trial
was an informal hearing in which the judge explored the child's problem with the child, his family members, his friends, and the probation
officer. The model underlying the court was a familial one. It was to
seek to emulate the manner in which benevolent parents would deal

with their own children. This objective is made clear in the Illinois Juvenile Court Act which became law in 1899:

> This act shall be liberally construed to the end that its purpose may be carried out, to wit: That the care, custody and discipline of a child shall approximate as nearly as may be that which should be given by its parents, and in all cases where it can properly be done the child placed in an improved family home and become a member of the family by legal adoption or otherwise. [21]

Since the formation of the juvenile court represented the culmination and response to almost fifty years of criticism of the institutionalized handling of juvenile delinquents, it was primarily concerned with treatment in the community. Accordingly its central contribution to the evolving system of correctional services was the task assigned to the probation officer, who became the agent of the court in the community. As his role evolved, its ideal statement represented a nice summation of some of the key values of the Chicago reformers: careful inquiry into the circumstances of the individual case, assessment of the situation, and friendly supervision. A set of environmental assumptions guided his work. By intervening and seeking to manipulate the situational influences to which the child was responsive, he sought to prevent the latter's progression to more serious criminality.

The juvenile court was deeply influenced by a conception of the family as a beleaguered institution in the city. The court was planned as a resource to find hidden strengths in families where these existed, to interpret the child's needs to the family, to support the exercise of parental responsibility, and, ultimately, if all such efforts failed, to remove the child from his family for temporary or permanent placement elsewhere.

The Institutionalization of the Juvenile Court

As it began to function, the Chicago juvenile court very quickly manifested itself as something quite different from the hopes of its founders. It had been envisaged as an omnibus agency for dealing with the varied problems of children. Consistent with this aim, it had been given jurisdiction over neglected and dependent as well as delinquent children. It was to deal with as many of these problems as possible through the use of community resources rather than through institutionalization. The role of probation officer had been conceived with this purpose primarily in mind. However, as probation proved to be inadequate to the task of dealing with such problems effectively, there was increasing resort to the traditional response, the institutional placement of children.

> Cook County juvenile court's early records ... show that institutional commitment was a basic tenet of the child-saving philosophy. One-third of all juveniles charged with delinquency were sent to the John Worthy School, the state reformatory, or transferred to the criminal courts. Almost two-thirds of the "delinquent" girls were committed to state and local institutions. [22]

The reformers also failed to improve juvenile institutions. "If the child savers were alive today, they would find that little has changed in the institutions for delinquents." [23] They did not even succeed in completely segregating juvenile offenders from incarceration in police stations or jails or from trial in the criminal courts. The familial model was soon jettisoned for the traditional penal model in the case of "unresponsive boys."

> The bleakness and impersonality of the institutions were matched by the uncompromising professionalism of juvenile court officials. "Troublemakers" were characterized as ungrateful and malicious, requiring swift measures of retaliation. Henry Thurston, Chief Probation Officer of the Cook County juvenile court from 1906 to 1908, warned that the "persistent repeater will bring inevitable disorganization into the district work of a probation officer and arouse resentment in the hearts of many of the best friends of the probation idea. All right-minded people are willing to have boys and girls have chances to do the right thing, but after they persistently throw chances away, the same people have a right to insist that these young people be really controlled, even if it takes a criminal court process to do it." Thurston and his chief assistant, John Witter, suggested that some "unresponsive boys" could be made to "respond" to treatment if threatened with a criminal prosecution. [24]

The old punitive attitudes toward offenders lingered just below the surface. "Juvenile courts . . . provided new bottles for old wine . . . ways of supervising delinquent children, which, while not formally incarcerating them, provided penal sanctions for persistent wrongdoers."[25] The reformers themselves, however, were not at first discouraged. Pragmatically they tended to envision the juvenile court as only one step, albeit a highly important one, toward providing better services for the neglected, dependent, and delinquent children of the poor. The growing realization that the court provided no panacea for the problem of the adolescent provoked a variety of responses. For some, the court's emerging difficulties implied the need for greater cooperation on the part of the community in order to remove the conditions that initiated the problems of youth.[26] Some social workers, like Julia Lathrop and Homer Folks, contended that progress lay in "understanding and combatting poverty, crime, and disease—the larger social problems of which delinquency was only one part."[27] Jane Addams had a different response; she proposed that the work of judge and probation officer be supplemented by newly developing clinical skills. "Jane Addams recalled that 'at last it was apparent that many of these children were psychopathic cases and they and other border-line cases needed more skilled care than the most devoted probation officer could give them.'"[28] A third response was to view the court as a center of inquiry. "The court served as a laboratory for the professional study of juvenile delinquency."[29] On the whole the court's lack of success with difficult children and persistent offenders led to varying degrees of disillusionment among its founders. Increasing familiarity with the range of cases dealt with by the court and the growth of insight into the complexity of factors involved in such cases led to reduced expectations as to what the court could realistically accomplish.[30] The functioning of the juvenile court was soon enveloped in public apathy.[31]

With the hindsight of history it is easy to identify some of the constraints that appear to have eluded the founders. A constant theme running throughout the nineteenth century is the fear experienced by many middle-class individuals of the threat that lower-class youth posed to the security of their society. Charles Loring Brace had called these youth the "perishing and dangerous classes." This fear was sufficiently compelling to move him to devote his life to helping the street children of New York City. The House of Refuge owed its origin in large part to the same kind of fear. Understandably, it was a feeling that surfaced most intensely during times of rapid urbanization. Under such circumstances what the middle-classes wanted above all was control over the children of the poor. This is precisely what the juvenile court offered them. This is not to impugn the genuine idealism of the reformers. However, as this idealism waned, the court became institutionalized as a legally sanctioned comprehensive instrument of paternalistic and impersonal social control.

The "discovery" of the "youth problem" was an inevitable accompaniment of urbanization and industrialization. As a problem it had already engaged the attention of English philantropists and reformers several decades before the incorporation of the Society for the Reformation of Juvenile Delinquents in 1823. Its emergence appeared to be linked to familial disruption among the poor and to an increasing differentiation of the population by class and cultural differences. The problem manifested itself in the emergence of a whole segment of lower-class youth who were alienated from the conventional social institutions—the family, the church, the school, and the world of work. The middle classes came to view this group with uneasiness and apprehension as a standing threat to the stability of their society. The New York City reformers tended to construct an ethnic stereotype of the alienated youth as Irishmen. From the perspective of such a stereotype the youth problem was self-explanatory since it was accounted for by the moral deficiencies of the Irish. Among the Chicago reformers the ethnic stereotypes of alienated youth were not so salient. This is partially because in Chicago the diversity of cultural backgrounds of the immigrants to the city was not as conducive to the stereotyping of any particular ethnic group. The Chicago reformers also had a far more sophisticated grasp of the complexity of the problem.

It is to the understanding, control, and welfare of this alienated segment of the urban community that much of the philanthropic and reform effort of American society has been devoted since the early nineteenth century. In differing eras varying conceptions of the problem were held and various measures for its amelioration proposed. For the gentlemen reformers, juvenile nonconformity was attributed to the moral deficiency resulting from the ineffectiveness of family discipline. Such conformity could be induced only through a period of institutionalization devoted to the resocialization of the aberrant individual.

The gentlemen reformers viewed the problem of deviant youth as being single and indivisible. Poverty, moral inadequacy, homelessness, and juvenile crime were all viewed as varying aspects of the same issue. It was because they viewed the problem in this omnibus fashion, with criminality as one of its manifestations, that the issue of the civil rights of youthful offenders never arose. Moreover, because of their own unshakable sense of moral righteousness and public responsibility, they never for a moment questioned the identity between their own values and the welfare of society.

The Chicago reformers held a radically different conception of the youth problem. Their perspective was one that challenged the moralistic interpretation of juvenile delinquency. They linked delinquent acts to a multiplicity of environmental factors such as poverty, culture conflict, and lower-class origin. Simultaneously, the individuality and personality of the juvenile was fully acknowledged. The new conception was succinctly stated as follows:

> According to Homer Folks, the probation officer should view the offense of the delinquent "as the joint product of his individuality and his environment and [the officer] seeks to influence both factors so that they will work together for good." These reformers stressed the multiplicity and interrelationship of delinquency's causes. [32]

In this view the family attained a new importance. The gentlemen reformers had viewed the family as the source of training in the moral values and the child as a passive recipient, the tabula rasa. Once the job of training was accomplished, the family's influence was completed and the individual's morality permanently set. The dual emphasis of the Chicago reformers upon individuality and environment introduced a functional view of the relationship between the individual and his environment. Two new considerations were brought to the fore. The concern with the individuality of the youth suggested that he was actively—not passively—related to his environment. The use of "environment" implied that it was as relevant to his current behavior as it was to his past socialization. The continuing involvement of his environment in the child's behavior was clearly identified. Moreover, it was assumed that the most important part of the child's environment was his family.

Both the House of Refuge and the juvenile court became something other than had been envisioned by their founders. In each case the problems for which they had been established proved to be more difficult to solve than they had anticipated, and neither was effective with persistent juvenile offenders. For an account of the rate of recidivism among House of Refuge inmates only anecdotes are available. For data on the recidivism of cases adjudicated by the Chicago juvenile court there are the following findings from a follow-up study by William Healy. Although published in 1926 there appears to be little doubt that it can be regarded as representative of the functioning of the court since its inception.

> Tracing the lives of several hundred youthful repeated offenders studied long ago by us and treated by ordinary so-called correctional methods reveals much repetition of offense. This is represented by the astonishing figures of 61% failure for males . . . and 46% failure for girls. . . . Thus in over one-half the cases in this particular series juvenile delinquency has continued into careers of vice and crime. [33]

In each case this ineffectiveness, to the extent that it was unanticipated, is to be related to the limitations of the reformers' perspectives. The gentlemen reformers were betrayed by a simplistic environmentalism into believing that a mere change of environment could accomplish the reeducation they espoused. The problem of juvenile court reformers was more subtle. Their view of child misbehavior as a product of interaction between the individual and his environment was extremely ambiguous. They were the pragmatists and open-minded eclectics par excellence. The development of a clear point of view required that the vagueness of individuality and environment be clarified by the articulation of a theoretical point of view. This was the task transmitted to the twentieth century together with the practical challenge of finding measures to cope with the persistent juvenile offender.

By the end of the century the response to the problem of juvenile delinquency had reached a turning point. Several waves of reform had been tried. Persistent recidivism, the hard core of the problem, remained intractable. During the twentieth century the key workers in this field became the academics and the theorists. The concepts of the individual and the environment were to prove as difficult to define theoretically as they had been to work with practically.

NOTES

1. Ray Ginger, *Altgeld's America* (New York: Funk & Wagnalls Co., 1958), p. 5.

2. Ibid., p. 95.

3. James Weber Linn, *Jane Addams* (New York: D. Appleton-Century Co., 1935), p. 100.

4. Charles N. Glaab and A. Theodore Brown, *A History of Urban America* (New York: Macmillan, 1967), p. 110.

5. Robert Bremner, *From the Depths: The Discovery of Poverty in the United States* (New York: New York University Press, 1956), p. 129.

6. See Ginger, *Altgeld's America*, pp. 9-10.

7. Ibid., pp. 7-8.

8. Allen F. Davis, *Spearheads for Reform: The Social Settlements and the Progressive Movement, 1890-1914* (New York: Oxford University Press, 1967), p. 18.

9. See Roy Lubove, *The Professional Altruist: The Emergence of Social Work as Career, 1880-1930* (Cambridge: Harvard University Press, 1965), p. 82.

10. Bremner, *From the Depths*, p. 55.

11. Ibid., p. 66.

12. David Bakan, "Adolescence in America: From Idea to Social Fact," *Daedalus* 100 (Fall 1971): 979-995.

13. David J. Rothman, *The Discovery of the Asylum: Social Order and Disorder in the New Republic* (Boston: Little, Brown, 1971).

14. John and Virginia Demos, "Adolescence in Historical Perspective," *Journal of Marriage and the Family* 31 (November 1969): 633.

15. Ibid.: 635.

16. Ibid.: 637.

17. Edith Abbott, *Report on Crime and Criminal Justice in Relation to the Foreign Born for National Commission on Law Observance and Enforcement* (Washington, D.C.: United States Government Printing Office, 1931), p. 14.

18. Bremner, *From the Depths*, p. 212.

19. Kenneth B. Clark, *Dark Ghetto* (New York: Harper & Row, 1965), p. 106.

20. Ginger, *Altgeld's America*, p. 226.

21. Cited by Joseph M. Hawes, *Children in Urban Society: Juvenile Delinquency in Nineteenth-century America* (New York: Oxford University Press, 1971), p. 170.

22. Anthony M. Platt, *The Child Savers* (Chicago: University of Chicago Press, 1969), p. 152.

23. Ibid.

24. Ibid., p. 151.

25. Robert M. Mennel, *Thorns and Thistles* (Hanover, New Hampshire: The University Press of New England, 1973), p. 144.

26. Ibid., p. 152.

27. Ibid., p. 151.

28. Hawes, *Children in Urban Society*, pp. 249-250.

29. Mennel, *Thorns and Thistles*, p. 157.

30. Sophonisba P. Breckenridge and Edith Abbott, *The Delinquent Child and the Home* (New York: Russell Sage Foundation, 1912).

31. Francis A. Allen, "The Juvenile Court and the Limits of Juvenile Justice," *The Borderland of Criminal Justice* (Chicago: University of Chicago Press, 1964), p. 43.

32. Mennel, *Thorns and Thistles*, p. 151.

33. William Healy and Augusta F. Bronner, *Delinquents and Criminals: Their Making and Unmaking* (New York: The Macmillan Co., 1926), p. 201.

chapter 4

Toward a science and a profession of delinquency control

The entry of men like William Healy, a psychiatrist, and Clifford R. Shaw, a sociologist, into the delinquency field during the opening decades of the twentieth century brought to it professional and scientific perspectives that had been lacking. The introduction of the scientific point of view encouraged a systematic search for the causes of delinquency. The cumulative growth of a body of empirical data, provided the basis for a new critical spirit. Thus, Healy, from the very beginning of his association with the juvenile court, was concerned with evaluating its effectiveness through carefully gathered data. Shaw's sociological findings furnished rich materials for a thorough critique of the existing juvenile correctional system and suggested new directions for its future development. There now ensued a concerted effort to replace moralistic by objective approaches, to make values explicit, and to seek rational principles upon which to base policies of social control. Henceforth, in principle, practice was to be guided by theory derived from empirical data. In addition, proponents of a scientific approach became eloquent advocates of a nonpunitive approach to the treatment of juvenile delinquents. Each in his own way came to represent an empathic, humanistic approach to the delinquent.

William Healy[1]

A pioneer such as Healy is not likely to be concerned about the inconsistencies and ambiguities manifested in his work. Nevertheless, there are ironies in his career that illuminate some of the issues involved in approaching juvenile delinquency from a scientific point of view. For example, he approached his task as clinic director as researcher as well as clinician. As researcher he was committed to the search for empirically grounded generalizations about delinquent behavior. As clinician he was committed to the task of understanding and seeking to assist individual juvenile offenders. The tension between the two activities proved to be a highly fruitful one for him, even though he ultimately subordinated his theoretical ambitions to the demands of his work as a clinician.

> Selection of our cases has not been made by their possession of a given quality; all along we have been simply searchers for *any* driving forces. Review of our case studies will plainly show this. Nor has our aim been the development of any philosophical system or scientific theory concerning delinquency or delinquents. In view of the immense complexity of human nature in relation to complex environmental conditions it is little to us even if no set theory of crime can ever be successfully maintained. Such statements as, "Crime is a disease," appear dubiously cheap in the light of our experience. Altogether our task has been not so much gathering material for generalizations, as ascertainment of the methods and the facts which will help towards the making of practical diagnoses and prognoses.[2]

Despite this commitment to the individual case, Healy did attempt to test existing theories of criminality, such as Lombroso's theory of criminal stigmata.[3] Healy patiently photographed hundreds of heads, measured hundreds of craniums, and tracked down other alleged "stigmata of degeneracy."[4] His findings disabused him of any belief he might have had in the possible validity of Lombroso's theory. After systematically seeking to test existing theories he came to the following conclusion:

Collecting data from case after case soon showed us that the whole concept of the causation of delinquency could not possibly be so simple as previous writers had made it out to be. The causative factors, as I termed them, were always multiple. Even the same types of factors played their parts in varying degree in different cases and were interwoven, often in intricate fashion.[5]

Interestingly and perhaps predictably, Healy was unable to rest content for long with a multiple causal approach. Profoundly influenced by psychoanalysis he advanced the theory that the individual delinquent was the product of mental conflicts that had their origin in unsatisfactory family relationships. It did not prove to be a very convincing theory in terms of its limited ability to encompass even the evidence of his own cases, but the very attempt to formulate a theory was in itself revealing of the varying pulls to which Healy was subject.

The second conflict to which Healy was exposed concerned the target population for his services. When the psychopathic clinic was established in 1909 it was clearly intended to be a resource for the juvenile court. Its clientele as such was comprised predominantly of lower-class children. This arrangement did not last long. Healy's pioneering work in the clinic led to the establishment of psychiatric child guidance clinics in several cities throughout the country under the auspices of the Commonwealth Fund Program for the Prevention of Delinquency. As these clinics evolved, their concern moved away from the juvenile court:

At first the work . . . was concerned mainly with the study and treatment of children already under supervision of the juvenile courts. By properly directed methods of treatment it was believed that the social rehabilitation of such children and the consequent reduction of delinquency in the community could be definitely advanced. In practice, however, it soon became evident that work with children who present behavior problems would be more effective if the problem were recognized and dealt with before the behavior had become so serious as to necessitate some form of court action.[6]

Healy, whose reputation after all, had been made by his first major publication, *The Individual Delinquent* (1915), showed that he was quite aware of this trend.

> In recent years the definite shift away from attempting to deal extensively with the problems of delinquency is due principally to the fact that the clinic cannot have control enough over the individual or over his social situation. Aside from the individuals who became delinquent mainly because of inner conflicts and frustrations, it is plainly discernible that in the complex of factors which make for delinquency there are many social elements, deprivations and pressures that cannot possibly be bettered by clinical effort alone.
>
> The conception that the guidance clinic may be of great aid in a program for the prevention of delinquency remains thoroughly valid, but indispensable for any such program is well-conceived, cooperative, social effort. . . . Whatever is undertaken, I am convinced that any project for the prevention of delinquency will be confronted with the necessity for modification of the spirit or ideology of community life. . . . As it stands at present in most large communities, it is impossible for child guidance clinics, through their work with individual cases, to be playing any very important part in the prevention of delinquent and criminal careers.[7]

There is no evidence that Healy himself deserted the cause of the delinquent child. When he moved from Chicago to Boston in 1919 he continued his work with the juvenile court there. However, he did not oppose the transformation of the psychiatric child guidance clinic from an auxiliary to the juvenile court to a specialized service for middle-class families.

The third conflict that Healy's work reflects is by all odds the most subtle. His training in psychiatry and the influence of psychoanalysis had led him to focus upon the relationship between the individual's intrapsychic conflicts and delinquency. To the extent that he was able to specify the sources of such mental conflicts he found them in the individual's familial relationships. In contrast, his extensive personal and practical familiarity with juvenile offenders, and particularly the recidivists, the most serious juvenile offenders, led him to an increasing awareness of the role of community influences upon delinquency.

Because Healy never developed a clear conception of what he meant by the term "community," his references to it are elusive and ambiguous. Since the awareness of the community was merely grafted on to his psychological preoccupations, he never developed a clear conception of what he meant by the term. Nevertheless, he grasped intuitively that the psychological factors he emphasized in his work did not function independently of community influences:

> Inherent in our data is the implication that there are many intangible, imponderable elements in community life that influence the ideas and mental attitudes of young people in ways that are productive of delinquency and crime. The general standards and community atmosphere in regard to law breaking must play an immensely important part.[8]

Despite such seminal insights into the role of the community, Healy never extended his working conception of the social environment much beyond the scope of the family.

From the Chicago reformers Healy inherited the problem of juvenile recidivists. "The most evident facts concerning crime are first, its usual beginnings in early youth and, second, the frequency of recidivism."[9] "By juvenile repeated offenders we mean young people who have continued in delinquency after very definite efforts on the part of some one in authority to check their misconduct."[10] He undertook to make follow-up studies of this group of offenders both in Chicago and Boston. As illustrative of this work we may take a series of 920 cases that he studied in Chicago between 1909 and 1914 and then followed up in 1921-1923.

> ... Outcome was to be counted as Success when the individual was living in the community without known detriment to the community and had engaged in no criminality. . . .
>
> Conversely, Failure denoted actual delinquency. All individuals having adult court records and adjudged guilty, as well as those committed to adult correctional institutions, were regarded as failures.[11]

In the concluding section of the previous chapter we have already quoted the findings of this study—a figure of 61 percent failure in work with male juvenile recidivists and 49 percent failure with females. Healy encountered considerable difficulty in interpreting these findings.

> Surveying our data on age of first court appearance, nativity of parents, religious affiliation, whether or not families are normally constituted, family economic status, physical and mental conditions of the offender, character of the offenses—in none of these to any large extent do we find significant differentiation between the Success and Failure groups.
>
> ... We cannot fail to discern that Success did occur under any and all categories of conditions. Many mentally abnormal, properly cared for, do not develop criminalistic ideas and if already started in delinquent ways their misconduct tendencies may be checked. We are surprised to find no great contrasts between the outcomes of those who have and have not engaged in harmful habits. .... To whatever group of facts we turn, some measure of Success is found; even among the groups with the most extreme figures of Failure there are enough who do not become criminals to warrant the conclusion that no conditions, whether of mind or body or life situations, preclude the possibility of checking the development of a criminal career. [12]

Such findings bring some rigor to statements that can be made about juvenile recidivism but not much illumination of the conditions under which it occurs. Healy responded to such findings with a call for more research. He also candidly admitted the limitations of existing scientific knowledge and was resigned to the necessity for correctional institutions.

> According to the best scientific knowledge of the present time (we do not at all know what this will be fifteen or twenty years from now) certain individuals are practically incurable in the sense of their being made non-offenders in society. After most careful studies for classification, so that there can be little or no attempt at excusing poor therapeutic endeavor, such individuals should be held apart. It is an intelligent and clear-sighted

provision that has led to the establishment of colonies or institutions where such individuals may be segregated for indefinite periods. [13]

Clifford R. Shaw

It is at this point in Healy's career that it becomes appropriate to introduce Shaw's work. [14] To what extent he was directly influenced by Healy cannot be ascertained; nevertheless, despite the different disciplines in which each was trained, there is much continuity in the problems that engaged both men.

Shaw was a practicing clinician and a research sociologist. The life history technique of research, which he did so much to advance, provided a felicitous medium through which he could synthesize and express both interests. Later when he ceased publishing life histories, his clinical interests found expression in the practical work with delinquents of the Chicago Area Projects.

What is of special interest in Shaw's development is the manner in which the problems he inherited from Healy dovetailed with the point of view he assimilated as a member of the Chicago school of sociology. Healy had been interested in general theories of delinquent behavior as well as the process through which specific individuals became delinquent. This standpoint was highly congruent with the dual emphasis of the Chicago school upon the study of the individual through case studies and of general community factors through human ecology. Shaw also inherited from Healy the key problem of recidivism among juvenile offenders. Indeed, in his first life history, *The Jack-Roller* (1930), he indicated that this was one from among a large sample of juvenile recidivists being studied. "The case is one of a series of two hundred similar studies of repeated male offenders under seventeen years of age, all of whom were on parole from correctional institutions when the studies were made." [15] Healy's insight into the role of the community in the experience of the delinquent was strongly reinforced for Shaw by the Chicago school's concern with the same concept.

Shaw was working within a distinctive historical context. The conceptual tools with which he worked were derived from his training in the Chicago school of sociology. Shaw was also responsive to the work of a number of Chicago's great humanists and reformers, such as Jane Addams who at the turn of the century formulated what may be called the *Chicago ethos.*

The Chicago Ethos

The Chicago ethos was an orientation or point of view toward man and society that was distinctive to the city. This ethos was largely the creation of a group of humanists who resided in Chicago and who in their work responded to the varied stimulation that it provided. Numbered among them were Louis Sullivan the architect, Theodore Dreiser the novelist, Clarence Darrow the lawyer, John Dewey the philosopher, Thorstein Veblen the social critic, and Jane Addams the founder of Hull House. They sought not merely understanding of the unruly leviathan at their doorstep. Their purposes were both moral and technical: the development of ideals and standards appropriate to the new setting and the pragmatic exploration of new forms of association that would contribute to the humanizing of the community life. Each in his own way contributed to the construction of a new image of man in relation to society. Their influence, individually and collectively, far transcended the limits of Chicago because the conditions to which they were responding, far from being unique to Chicago, were typical of urbanism and industrialism in general. These conditions were:

1. The rapidity of the economic and population growth of Chicago.

2. The heterogeneity of its population, including considerable class, social, and cultural cleavages.

3. The complex, confused moral quality of its life. Crass materialism was intricately involved with spiritual aspiration, quantity with quality, inhuman brutality with human sensitivity, and provincial egoism with cosmopolitan altruism. Humanity and inhumanity formed part of the same seamless web. It was such a spectacle of grandeur, on the one hand, and of life as "nasty, brutish, and short," on the other, as at once to delight and challenge, if not overwhelm, the most devoted student of human nature.

What image of man was appropriate to this massive, rough-hewn spectacle? How were the relations between man and society to be conceived? How were the processes of growth and communal living to be given direction and humanized? The city was rampant with exploitation, suffering, and poverty. How were these to be transformed into conditions consistent with human dignity and offering opportunity to all to better themselves? According to Ginger in his discussion of the Chicago humanists, the key terms that emerged to embody their perspective were "process," "interactions," and "context." [16]

"Process" suggests change occurring through many small increments, and although such change manifests a kind of order and moves toward ends, both the order and the ends are subject to influence by chance and by other factors beyond man's control. "Interactions" refers to man as inherently, inescapably, and permanently a social being and as forever engaging with other human beings. "Context" refers to the environment, with particular emphasis upon the social environment. It is clear that each of these terms is permeated with the conception of change as the stuff of social life and that what order exists presupposes change as continuous.

In order to grasp some of the views that were distinctive of the Chicago humanists it will be useful to contrast them with the views of man and human nature that had prevailed earlier among the gentlemen reformers. The earlier view had posited a duality of body and mind:

> The body was the seat of those base impulses which to the orthodox meant original sin. But the mind was made up of capacities classified under the faculties of understanding, feeling, and will. Through the will man could rule his baser impulses and translate his innate moral ideas into action. Properly disciplined by early formal training, reason and will could enable individuals to eliminate traditional shortcomings in themselves and in society. [17]

This view was highly individualistic and rationalistic. It assumed that the distinction between good and evil was absolute, universal, clear, and unambiguous. Virtue was viewed as resulting from the striving of the isolated individual.

In Ginger's discussion Abraham Lincoln came to stand for a variation on this outlook. It had been Lincoln's belief that there was no inherent contradiction between the effort of the individual to further his own material interests and at the same time to advance the common good. As exemplified in his own life, individual ambition and social compassion could be found working strongly within the same individual. Stated differently, for Lincoln there was no inconsistency between individualism in economics and democracy in politics. It was the purpose of a democratic society to promote the conditions that would favor the cultivation of these qualities by all citizens. "By this vision, the worthy goal is to improve your status and to do so by your own efforts—and yet to remain a human being who has deep regard for the material and intimate needs of other human beings."[18]

Ginger goes on to point out that these ideals might have been appropriate to a rural society but that they became grossly distorted when applied to an urban setting. In the city the distinction between action that furthered the individual's own interests and that which contributed to the common good became very difficult to make. In the Chicago ethos the center of moral concern shifted from the contest between mind and body to the nature of the relationship between the individual and his society. The individual had needs of his own, which received expression in ways that distinguished him from other individuals and which required that he be viewed as possessing a degree of autonomy relative to the groups of which he was a member. He was thus to be regarded as somewhat detached from his group memberships. At the same time his needs could be met only by entering into relationships with others and by participating in group activity. Morality became a matter of learning how to balance the satisfaction of his needs against the satisfaction of the needs of others and the requirements of the group. This is accomplished by seeking to put himself in the place of others in order to take account of their needs. Inherent in human existence is an unceasing conflict between the interests of the individual and those of the group. At one moral extreme is the individual who would subordinate other individuals completely to the satisfaction of his own needs; at the other moral extreme is the individual who would subordinate himself totally to the satisfaction of the needs of others. A humane, civilized society requires reconciliation between both extremes. Morality must be built upon the dual pillars of honest self-knowledge and sensitivity to the needs of others. It is possible for the action of the individual to serve his own interests and also to benefit the group but only under the condition that he empathize with others in the planning of his action.

This viewpoint had particular applicability to the modern urban industrial society of which Chicago was a prominent example. The rapidity of growth that had occurred had been accomplished by subordinating all other considerations to the attainment of material success. Society was riven by group and cultural cleavages. The elites attempted to maintain their position by monopolizing the instruments of power, such as the police and the government. The use of power, too, needed to be humanized by empathizing with the role of other groups. This meant that capitalist entrepreneurs should temper the use of their economic and political power by taking account of the perspectives and needs of the groups that they sought to control. This growth in the scope of social consciousness was a condition for the emancipation of the working classes.

Using Lincoln as her model, Jane Addams depicted what this point of view required of the leader:

> The man who insists upon consent, who moves with the people, is bound to consult the feasible right as well as the absolute right. He is often obliged to attain only Mr. Lincoln's "best possible," and often have the sickening sense of compromising with his best convictions. He has to move along with those whom he rules toward a goal that neither he nor they see very clearly until they come to it. He has to discover what people really want, and then "provide the channels in which the growing moral force of their lives shall flow." What he does attain, however, is not the result of his individual striving, as a solitary mountain climber beyond the sight of the valley multitude, but it is underpinned and upheld by the sentiments and aspirations of many others. Progress has been slower perpendicularly, but incomparably greater because lateral.[19]

The Chicago Ethos and the Problem of Youth

Two of the Chicago humanists, Jane Addams and John Dewey, devoted themselves to the problems of children. One of the most influential publications of their era is Jane Addams's *The Spirit of Youth and the City Streets*.[20] It appeared in 1909, ten years after the founding of the juvenile court, and much of it is devoted to a discussion of the problem of juvenile delinquency. It is one of the classic contributions to the "discovery of adolescence" and is also an incisive critique of urban civilization from the perspective of the working-class adolescent.

By the "spirit of youth" Jane Addams refers to a loosely defined set of needs and capacities, such as the play impulse, the sex drive, the wish for adventure, and the capacity for idealism. Adolescence is viewed as the period during which individuals assert their inner dispositions and seek to make connection with the social world around them. This development is accompanied by the accession of powerful new feelings, which can attain expression only through becoming attached to rich systems of public symbols. The force of such feelings leads youth to transcend the limitations of their own personal relationships and to seek to regenerate the larger world through their idealism.

Addams viewed contemporary urban civilization as preventing these potentialities from developing into values that would simultaneously allow adolescents to fulfill their lives as individuals and contribute to the renewal of the life of the community. She deplored the excessive sensory stimulation provided by the city because in encouraging the release of mere appetite, it provided little incentive for more demanding yet ultimately more rewarding modes of personality development. She was deeply concerned that life in the city did not provide adequate institutional means through which working-class youth could make the transition to adulthood. The only occupations accessible to them were monotonous jobs in factories as machine tenders, which did not provide them with a sense of participation and thus eliminated all possibility of self-expression through their work. As one consequence, industry was characterized by shoddy, tasteless products, since their form and content were removed from the human personal contribution that the individual worker might have made. Under such stultifying conditions of employment many youths became exhausted after a few years of work, or moved from job to job, or just quit the labor force and took to hanging around the streets. The existing city was viewed as a citadel of materialism, its enterprises managed by men whose overriding objective was financial success and who remained exploitative and insensitive toward its working-class youth. The main theme of the book, accordingly, is a detailed treatment of the severe disjunction between the forms of city life and the varied needs of adolescents. Addams discussed the damage wreaked by this disjunction on both the individual personalities of youth and the quality of life in the urban community. The community as a whole suffered because by closing off channels to the broader social participation of adolescents it intensified the separation and distrust between the generations. The adolescents suffered because they were deprived of constructive outlets for their idealism and were without the means to attain adulthood with dignity.

The great civilizations of the past had allowed the expression of the play impulse by making provision for public recreation; they provided games, drama, pageantry, and public ritual. Modern cities have tended to ignore such needs or have met them through commercialization. Addams was impressed with the powerful force represented by the sex interest and commiserated with youth because in the city it was difficult for them to learn how to channel this interest. The social organization of traditional societies had both controlled and provided occasions for the expression of these interests; in the city such arrangements had atrophied. In the absence of such organization many youths were tempted into casual and exploitative heterosexual relationships, which inhibited the growth of the love sentiment into tenderness and to a generalized idealism. Conditions of life in the city were regarded as also being particularly constraining to the expression of the love of adventure.

Although Jane Addams's appreciation of the function performed by traditional social organization in the maturation of youth undoubtedly expressed some nostalgia for an older and simpler society, it is also true that she recognized that in the city there could be no return to the traditional authoritarian modes of controlling youth:

> Unless we mean to go back to these Old World customs which are already hopelessly broken, there would seem to be but one path open to us in America. That path implies freedom for the young people made safe through their own self-control.[21]

Addams proposed the emancipation of young people from various oppressive aspects of their life in the city. As a leading social reformer she envisaged youth as a human resource for tempering the materialism of contemporary urban society. To accomplish this end she espoused reforms of the key institutions of society—family, economy, and school—reforms that would allow children to experience adolescence as a period of personal growth toward a potential contribution to the community. She sought to implement this view of adolescence by appealing to the better instincts of adults, arguing that it was they who were stifling youth and that it was they who would benefit by the application to the community of the keen sense of justice of the young. She pleaded for the release of youth from both the dead hand of the past and the oppressive circumstances of the present in order to harness their innate idealism and generosity toward the regeneration of community life.

The Spirit of Youth is a tour de force of empathy with working-class adolescents. The whole basis of Addams's criticism of city life is provided by her attempt to view the world as adolescents viewed it. One of the insights resulting from her work was a new relativity in the assessment of motives. A wish for adventure, for example, was inherent in the child's experience and would inevitably seek some kind of expression. Whether it took a socially sanctioned or a delinquent form was dependent upon the child's situation, the opportunities available to him, and the responses of others. Many kinds of activities that might have been viewed as pranks in the country were responded to as delinquency within the greater constraints imposed by the city setting. The situation, as well as the individual's disposition, had to be taken into account. Such assessment was not a simple matter; it required that the person making the judgment seek to place himself in the child's position to gain a better understanding of the situation.

This method of assessing the motives of others by putting oneself in their place had important implications for the control of youthful offenders. If their behavior were a product in part of the situations in which they found themselves, the punitive modes of control were not only useless, they were also bound to be ineffective. Implied in this point of view is that efforts at delinquency control and prevention should concern themselves as much with the situations in which behavior occurs as it should with the individual himself.

There was considerable similarity between many of Shaw's attitudes toward delinquency and those of Jane Addams. Both suspended moral judgment while they sought to understand specific types of behavior. Both sought to look at the world from the perspective of the delinquent. This implied a search for the meaning of his behavior as

arising out of the interaction between the individual's dispositions
and his social situation. Both Addams and Shaw were social reformers who worked in the community seeking to modify situations that
were conducive to delinquent behavior. In the work of Jane Addams,
Shaw found precedents for his humanistic interest in the delinquent
and in the community approach to delinquency.

W. I. Thomas and R. E. Park

The influence of the Chicago ethos continued to be evident in some
of the central themes of the Chicago school of sociology; it was particularly salient in the work of two of its leaders, W. I. Thomas and R.
E. Park. Both in *The Polish Peasant* (1918) and in the conclusion to
The Unadjusted Girl (1923), Thomas formulated a set of problems to
which he believed sociologists should address themselves. They revealed, among other things, his profound concern for the freedom of
the individual and his wish to find scientific means of modifying the
attitudes associated with the materialism of the city.

Among the general problems involved in the study of attitudes and values—the history of personality development and
the measurement of social influences—are the following:

1. *The problem of abnormality—crime, vagabondage, pros-
titution, alcoholism, etc.* How far is abnormality the unavoidable manifestation of inborn tendencies of the individual, and
how far is it a matter of deficient social organization—the failure of institutional influences? . . .
2. *The problem of individualization.* How far is individualism compatible with social cohesion? What forms of individualism may be considered socially useful or socially harmful? . . .
4. *The problem of the sexes.* In the relation between the sexes
how can a maximum of reciprocal response be secured with a
minimum of interference with personal interests? . . .
5. *The economic problem.* How shall we be able to develop
attitudes which will subordinate economic success to other
values? How shall we restore stimulation to labor? . . . [22]

Since Thomas had been impressed with Park's work and had been instrumental in recruiting him for the sociology department of the University of Chicago, it is not surprising that there was considerable similarity between the two men in their value positions. As it had been for Thomas, a concern for freedom was central to Park's approach to the study of society. Turner notes the impact of this value commitment as follows:

"Foremost among the guiding values for his approach to applied sociology is the counterpart to his theoretical emphasis upon social control: a concern with reconciling or balancing the requirements of human collaboration against the goal of individual freedom."[23]

If both Thomas and Park shared central values with the Chicago reformers, they differed from them considerably in the spirit of their enterprise. They strove for a nonmoralistic approach to the city. Moreover, they viewed it not concretely as did Jane Addams but theoretically and abstractly as a form of social association. The core of their interest in the city was as a locus of social processes, and particularly those processes associated with social change. Consistent with their concern with the individual as well as society, they viewed social change as it is reflected in both the makeup of the individual and in the forms of association. Indeed, their profound interest in social change theoretically directed their attention to the individual and his experience. Park made this relationship clear in the following:

> The customs of the group impose themselves upon the individual, and his habits are consciously and unconsciously formed in conformity with them. On the other hand, the habits of individuals support group custom. Changes in habits undermine customs, and eventually destroy its influence and authority. . . . Changes in the content of custom are brought about by changes in the experience of individuals—changes in attitude and in habit.[24]

With social change there is a shift in the nature of the bond between the individual and the group. The traditional equilibrium no longer prevails in which group custom molds the habits of the individual and the habits of the individual serve to reinforce and assure the continuity of group custom. It is the kind of society and individual posed by this new state of affairs that they both devoted themselves to studying.

Their interest in the individual under conditions of his relative emancipation from the traditional hold of the group had its counterpart in their interest in the group-related issues of social order and social control. Both cultivated an "interactionist" point of view, which strove to encompass both individual and group within a single conceptual framework. In formulating this point of view they were seeking to differentiate their position from earlier conceptions of the individual and society. They opposed a moralistic approach to the individual, on the one hand, and various environmental determinisms of group behavior, on the other.

> The moralist complains of the materialization of men and expects a change of the social organization to be brought about by moral or religious preaching; the economic determinist considers the whole social organization as conditioned fundamentally and necessarily by economic factors and expects an improvement exclusively from a possible historically necessary modification of the economic organization itself. From the viewpoint of behavior the problem is much more serious and objective than the moralist conceives it, but much less limited and determined than it appears to the economic determinist. [25]

Both Thomas and Park viewed the traditional forms of association based upon the kinship group and supportive local community as declining in importance and in the process of being replaced by membership in a larger community. In this larger community social control was based primarily upon the law. Both viewed delinquency as an aspect of this transition in modes of social control. It reflected the inadequacies of both the traditional and the new modes of control. Youth were no longer responsive to the personal controls associated with the traditional primary group. The old forms of social control based upon "ordering and forbidding" were no longer effective. Youth were equally unresponsive to the impersonal control represented by the law. Both men hoped that empirical sociology would contribute new conceptions of social control adapted to youth, which would be more effective under the conditions of urban living.

Thomas and Park appear to have been the major intellectual influences upon Shaw's work. From Thomas, ultimately, Shaw derived his conception of the individual delinquent and from Park his conception of the community as the setting for delinquency in its group aspects.

One of Thomas's major theoretical and methodological concerns was to study the individual as he underwent the transition from traditional to modern society. In Thomas's view all human behavior was situationally oriented and proceeded from a "definition of the situation," a rule, prescription, or scheme, which preceded and guided the individual's behavior. The individual experienced his definitions as acts of decision. In traditional society dominated by the primary group, the group definitions of the situation could be imposed upon the individual. However, the individual did not have to be content with such definitions, for he could bring his own point of view to bear and was quite capable of imagining alternative schemes of behavior. In the urban setting, the traditional definitions associated with the primary group lost their coercive power, leaving much greater scope for the individual's behavior to be guided by his own definitions of the situation. Thomas called this process "individualization," and he was particularly concerned with its moral implications. These could vary greatly, depending upon their relations to the norms of society. The meaning of individualized behavior thus became exceedingly problematic.

Because the experience of the individual was such a crucial aspect of a changing society, Thomas was quite concerned with developing special techniques for its study. It was for this purpose that he introduced the use of human documents, such as the life history, to illuminate the individual's definition of situations, the possible conflict between his definitions and the prevailing norms, his response to the decay of the primary group definitions, the manner in which crucial definitions of the situation had molded his personal development. Shaw's pioneering work with the life history of delinquents closely adhered to the standards that Thomas had enunciated.

Shaw turned to Park for his conception of the relationship between social change, community processes, and juvenile delinquency, for Park's central concern was social control. In seeking a conceptual framework within which to interpret juvenile delinquency it was inevitable then that he should view it against the background of changing modes of social control. Like Thomas, Park started with the impingement of a larger world upon the smaller more personal world. It was this broadening of the sphere of required participation that was connected with the emergence of the problem of juvenile delinquency. It was difficult for the young person to identify with the goals of the larger community since they were impersonal and transcended his own personal interests. New forms of social control, such as the law, had been devised in order to regulate his behavior in this larger setting.

> It is in the community, rather than in the family, that our moral codes first get explicit and formal definition and assume the external and coercive character of municipal law. . . .
>
> It is in this community with its various organizations and its rational, rather than traditional, schemes of control, and not elsewhere, that we have delinquency. Delinquency is, in fact, in some sense the measure of the failure of our community organizations to function. [26]

In Park's view, with the breakdown of the social controls based upon intimate, personal relationships there had been two waves of efforts to establish controls upon a more rational basis. In the first wave the churches, schools, and courts had attempted to provide avenues for the participation of youth in the larger community; however, they were rather distant from the individual, and youth tended to experience participation in them as somewhat oppressive.

Since the closing decades of the nineteenth century, a whole new wave of social agencies had come into being in order to promote the conformity of youth to the standards of the larger community:

> The older social agencies, the church, the school, and the courts, have not always been able to meet the problems which new conditions of life have created. The school, the church, and the courts have come down to us with their aims and methods defined under the influence of an older tradition. New agencies have been necessary to meet the new conditions. Among these new agencies are the juvenile courts, juvenile protective associations, parent-teachers' associations, Boy Scouts, Young Men's Christian Associations, settlements, boys' clubs of various sorts, and I presume, playgrounds and playground associations. These agencies have taken over to some extent the work which neither the home, the neighborhood, nor the other older communal institutions were able to carry on adequately.
>
> These new institutions, perhaps because they are not to the same extent hampered by our earlier traditions, are frankly experimental and are trying to work out a rational technique for

dealing with social problems, based not on sentiment and tradition, but on science. [27]

In his attempt to visualize how science might provide principles for
the operation of these new agencies, Park made an eloquent plea for
the need to recognize the individuality and the need for freedom of the
delinquent:

> Any effort to re-educate and reform the delinquent individual
> will consist very largely in finding for him an environment, a
> group in which he can live, and live not merely in the physical or
> biological sense of the word, but live in the social and in the so-
> ciological sense. That means finding a place where he can have
> not only free expression of his energies and native impulses, but
> a place where he can find a vocation and be free to formulate a
> plan of life which will enable him to realize in some adequate
> way all the fundamental wishes that, in some form or other, ev-
> ery individual seeks to realize, and must realize, in order to have
> a wholesome and reasonably happy existence. [28]

Park referred to Thrasher's findings on the important role played
by gangs, particularly in the slum communities: "If I ventured to state
my opinion in regard to the matter, I should say that these gangs have
exercised a considerably greater influence in forming the character of
the boys who compose them than has the church, the school, or any
other communal agency outside of the families and the homes in
which the members of the gangs are reared." [29] Park noted that in the
city effective social control still continued to be exercised by primary
groups, but now by groups, such as the gang, which arise in new forms
and in response to the new conditions, of urban living. He suggested
that effective control of youth in the larger community might be accomplished by finding ways of associating the new primary groups
(such as the gang) with the more formal institutions of social control.

In his subsequent work Park continued to pit the two ideas of the
impersonality of the expanding urban community against the personal primary group relationships, which evolved as enclaves within
the metropolis. The development of human ecology admirably served
his purposes for emphasizing the dramatic counterpoint between
these two themes. Ecological processes provided the scaffolding for

the structure of the expanding and differentiating metropolis as a unity based upon symbiotic rather than conscious human relationships. Against the backdrop of these massive impersonal processes, individuals went about the business of carving out smaller, more manageable worlds based upon personal relationships. As a conceptual scheme, ecology not only provided a useful grid for the mapping of the various social worlds; it also, by implication, pointed up the problem of social control, for it suggested that individuals were more responsive to the controls of their smaller worlds than to those of the larger impersonal community. The problem of social control was to find rational principles through which impersonal and personal realms could be integrated in ways that maintained the freedom of the individual.

The pragmatic temper of the Chicago reformers was reflected in their response to the difficulties encountered by the juvenile court after it was established in 1899. When it became apparent that it was unable to prevent a substantial volume of juvenile recidivism, the reformers turned to the clinical skills and evenually to the research skills represented by the psychological and social sciences. This step resulted in a transformation in the social character of the problem of juvenile delinquency. Henceforth, it was to fall within the special domain of the professionals and the academicians. They were to become the critics of the existing system, the source of new ideas for delinquency control derived from their parent disciplines and their own empirical research, and leaders in the quest to understand rather than condemn the juvenile offender. They were to be chastened by the experience of learning that their own potential for effecting change was quite limited and that even their most carefully considered ideas were subject to institutionalization, to consequences just as undesirable as the existing arrangements.

Clifford R. Shaw's life work is so instructive because it not only reflected but gave direction to the new conception of delinquency as a problem for the professional. Historically he stood at the point of convergence of several movements of thought and action that were realistically seeking to find ways of realizing human values, such as individual freedom, in a modern urban civilization. Chicago at the turn of the century provided a crucible in which early nineteenth-century ideas of rationalism, individualism, laissez-faire, and democracy were melted and reformed into new ideas of the relation between man and society.

A typically Chicago ethos emerged, which rejected the moralistic and rational approach to the individual without losing sight of the significance for social life of the experience of the individual; it simultaneously rejected all environmental determinisms without losing sight of the influence the social environment exerted upon human behavior. It was this conception of the interaction between individual and society that was at the center of the Chicago ethos. Its central themes were formulated by the Chicago humanists and reformers. Many of these themes were taken up in the empirically oriented sociology of the Chicago school. It was a point of view that Shaw introduced to the field of delinquency. In the next two chapters we will examine how he fared in his endeavor to introduce the classical synthesis into his work both as researcher and applied social scientist.

NOTES

1. William A. Healy was born in England in 1869 and received his B.A. from Harvard in 1899 and his M.D. from Rush Medical College in Chicago in 1900. He was professor of nervous and mental disorders at the Chicago Polyclinic from 1903 to 1916. This work brought him into contact with many young patients. In 1909, under the leadership of the Juvenile Protective League of Chicago, the Juvenile Psychopathic Institute was established for the psychological study of cases appearing before the Chicago juvenile court. Upon the recommendation of William James, Healy was appointed the director of the clinic. His tenure there led to his important work *The Individual Delinquent* (1915), based upon an analysis of the cases of 1,000 repeat juvenile offenders. He was one of the leaders in developing clinical psychiatric procedures for the diagnosis and treatment of emotionally disturbed children. His major contribution to criminology in America was his insistence upon the intensive study of the individual offender. In 1919 he moved from Chicago to Boston to become director of the Judge Baker Foundation.

2. William Healy, *The Individual Delinquent* (Boston: Little, Brown, 1917), p. 4.

3. Cesare Lombroso (1835-1909), an Italian by birth, was trained as a physician and psychiatrist; he early became interested in the problem of explaining criminal behavior. He was influential in establishing the principle that it was the criminal and not the crime who should be studied. His reputation was established by the publication of his book, *The Criminal Man*, in 1876. Here he contended that criminals were distinguished from noncriminals by various physical anomalies such as deviations in head size and shape. The criminal was a special type or subspecies of human being who had reverted to an earlier stage of evolution.

4. Roy Lubove, *The Professional Altruist: The Emergence of Social Work as Career, 1880-1930* (Cambridge: Harvard University Press, 1965), p. 65.

5. Ibid.

6. W. I. Thomas and Dorothy S. Thomas, *The Child in America* (New York, 1928), p. 144.

7. William Healy, *Twenty-five Years of Child Guidance*, Studies from the Institute for Juvenile Research, Series C, Number 256 (Illinois Department of Public Welfare, 1934), pp. 14-15.

8. William Healy and Augusta F. Bronner, *Delinquents and Criminals: Their Making and Unmaking* (New York: Macmillan, 1926), p. 211.

9. Ibid., p. 215.

10. Ibid., p. 12.

11. Ibid., p. 17.

12. Ibid., pp. 205-206.

13. Ibid., p. 219.

14. Shaw's work and career will be discussed in greater detail in a later chapter.

15. Clifford R. Shaw, *The Jack-Roller* (Chicago: University of Chicago Press, 1930), p. 1.

16. Ray Ginger, *Altgeld's America* (New York: Funk & Wagnalls Co., 1958), pp. 331-352.

17. Merle Curti, "Human Nature in American Thought: The Retreat from Reason in the Age of Science," in *Probing Our Past* (Gloucester, Massachusetts: Peter Smith, 1962), p. 153.

18. Ginger, *Altgeld's America*, p. 5.

19. Cited by ibid., p. 167.

20. Jane Addams, *The Spirit of Youth and the City Streets* (1909; reprint ed., Urbana, Illinois: University of Illinois Press, 1972).

21. Ibid., p. 45.

22. William I. Thomas, *The Unadjusted Girl* (Boston: Little, Brown, 1923), pp. 255-256.

23. Ralph H. Turner, ed., *Robert E. Park: On Social Control and Collective Behavior* (Chicago: The University of Chicago Press, 1967), p. xvii.

24. Robert E. Park, "The Sociological Methods of William Graham Sumner, and of William I. Thomas and Florian Znaniecki," in Stuart A. Rice, ed., *Methods in Social Science* (Chicago: University of Chicago Press, 1931), p. 164.

25. Thomas, *The Unadjusted Girl*, pp. 256-257.

26. Robert E. Park, "Community Organization and Juvenile Delinquency," in Everett C. Hughes and others, eds., *Human Communities: The City and Human Ecology* (Glencoe, Illinois: The Free Press, 1952), p. 58.

27. Ibid., p. 61.

28. Ibid., p. 62.

29. Ibid., p. 63.

chapter 5

The contribution of Clifford R. Shaw and Henry D. McKay

In the early 1920s in the favorable setting provided by the Chicago school, the sociology of the juvenile delinquency problem came of age. The methodological and theoretical themes that have since been central to the field first received explicit statement in the work of Shaw and McKay. It would not be inaccurate to view their contributions as the classical statement of the central problems of the field. Almost every major subsequent development in research, theory, and practice elaborates on themes that they first explored. The importance of their contribution to the discipline of sociology as a whole was expressed in a tribute by their teacher and colleague, E. W. Burgess: "Empirical American sociology was perhaps popularized and transmitted to all corners of the world by the Shaw monographs more than by any other examples of this brand of social research."[1]

The collaboration between Shaw and McKay began in the late 1920s when both were young sociologists, fresh from their training at the University of Chicago; it encompassed the working careers of both men. Jointly, and sometimes with others, they published *Delinquency Areas* in 1929, *Social Factors in Juvenile Delinquency* in 1931, *Brothers in Crime* in 1938, and *Juvenile Delinquency in Urban Areas* in 1942. Both Shaw and McKay held research positions in the sociology department of the Illinois Institute of Juvenile Research, and both also provided leadership to the Area Projects, a program of community organization in the inner city areas of Chicago. They differed considerably in temperament: McKay was detached and analytical; Shaw, dynamic and emotional. The latter was the more visible of the two, and his personality exerted the greater impact upon the Chicago Area Projects. Nevertheless, the Shaw-McKay cooperation was so close and enduring that it now is difficult to distinguish their individual contributions. Accordingly, it is solely for the sake of ease in presentation that the following discussion refers to Shaw alone. In all cases I could have substituted Shaw-McKay.

When Shaw began working in 1919, the momentum that had been imparted by the Chicago reformers at the turn of the twentieth century to societal efforts to prevent juvenile delinquency had begun to diminish. Social agencies, whether their services were directed to the individual, the group, or the community, had tended to become institutionalized in a manner that left the delinquent isolated and unreached. The social workers, responding to the powerful influence of psychoanalysis, were abandoning environmental manipulation and were turning increasingly to modes of clinical treatment of intrapsychic factors. This ideological change in professional orientation was accompanied by a shift in interest from the lower-class delinquent to the middle-class emotionally disturbed child. Empirical evidence beginning to become available on community-oriented agencies, such as the settlement houses and the boys' clubs, indicated that they had not succeeded in reaching delinquents and including them in their programs. Under such conditions, the empirically oriented sociological perspective Shaw and McKay introduced revitalized public interest in the problem and gave new impetus to programs of delinquency prevention and control.

Shaw's Entry to the Field

After some preliminary training in medicine, Clifford R. Shaw (1895-1957) became a graduate student in the department of sociology at the University of Chicago.

Here he first became interested in juvenile delinquency, as a result of courses offered by Professor Ernest W. Burgess. It was customary for graduate students of sociology to engage in specific activities related to the problems discussed in the classroom, which might also provide material for use in the preparation of theses. Hence, the author procured work as a probation officer in the city courts, and thus took the first step in his professional career.[2]

Shaw worked as a probation officer from 1919 to 1923, when he became research sociologist at the Institute for Juvenile Research, Chicago, and in 1927 he began his lifelong collaboration with Henry D. McKay. His varied experience during this early period appears to have played a determining role in his professional development. It was then that he began to ask the questions and to achieve the crucial insights that he later pursued in his research. Probation work, with its emphasis upon the supervision of individual cases, demanded that he concern himself with the process of becoming delinquent. "The work itself required the constant formulation and the solution of problems concerning sequences of experience and behavior in the life of *individual* delinquent boys."[3] From the evidence contained in Shaw's published volumes of case studies, it is obvious that his personal relationships with particular delinquents, which eventuated in these studies, were all established during his years of service as a probation officer.

At the same time, as the practical demands of his work led him to explore the processes through which individuals become delinquent, Shaw began to make observations about the community and group aspects of delinquency. He noted that his cases were not distributed in the city at random but tended to cluster in certain localities; moreover, such clusters tended to be characterized by single types of delinquent behavior. "There were little 'shoplifting' areas, little 'jackrolling' areas, little areas of homosexual perversion, etc."[4] Shaw also discovered that shared delinquent activity provided the basis for an extensive network of personal relationships. "An initial interview with one boy gave him eventually the names of more than two hundred and sixty others, all delinquent, and all directly or indirectly related in their delinquency to the first."[5]

Rice records that such observations soon led Shaw to conceive of delinquent behavior as group-supported behavior patterns based upon shared understandings that could be transmitted or "diffused" to others:

Among hypotheses developed by the author from early observations and inference ... one has been of particular value in reconciling evidence, and for explanation and prediction. While it was not so termed in his own thinking, it may be designated by an expression borrowed from the field of cultural anthropology and called the "diffusion" of delinquent habit patterns.[6]

The hypothesis itself may be described as follows: Delinquency among boys usually consists of group behavior, the pattern of which is learned by the individual delinquent.[7]

Shaw had achieved an important breakthrough. He had succeeded in discovering a sociological idiom for the depiction of delinquent behavior. The issue for sociological research was no longer that of searching for the causes of some nebulous behavioral entity called delinquency, but of describing and accounting for certain distinctive patterns of group behavior.

Under the auspices of the Institute for Juvenile Research and collaborating with McKay, Shaw now entered upon an intensive period of productive research and publication. Together they gathered a truly monumental quantity of empirical data on the community, group, and personal aspects of juvenile delinquency. Among their publications were *Delinquency Areas* (1929), *The Jack-Roller* (1930), *Social Factors in Juvenile Delinquency* (1931), *The Natural History of a Delinquent Career* (1931), *Brothers in Crime* (1938), and *Juvenile Delinquency and Urban Areas* (1942).[8]

As a probation officer Shaw had been concerned with delinquency both in its epidemiological aspects and as a problem of specific individuals. In his research, human ecology provided the framework from which he approached the epidemiological aspects of the problem and the case study provided the vehicle through which he studied delinquency as the meaningful behavior of individuals.

Shaw's Approach to the Epidemiology of Delinquency

Delinquency Areas was Shaw's first major publication of his research findings on the epidemiology of delinquency in Chicago. His analysis was concerned with a number of distinct sets or series of officially recorded cases of delinquents and other categories of offenders. Two of these series consist of the male delinquents adjudicated by the juvenile court during two periods, 1900-1906 and 1917-1923. Other sets of cases are comprised of male school truants (1917-1927), male offenders brought to the boys' court on felony charges between 1924 and 1926, delinquent girls brought before the juvenile court between 1924 and 1926, and adult male offenders, 1920. From his analysis of these various series of cases, Shaw and his colleagues arrived at a number of findings; the following are of major importance:

> 1. The first and perhaps most striking findings of the study is that there are marked variations in the rate of school truants, juvenile delinquents, and adult criminals between areas in Chicago. Some areas are characterized by very high rates, while others show very low rates. . . .
> 2. A second major finding is that rates of truancy, delinquency, and adult crime tend to vary inversely in proportion to the distance from the center of the city. In general the nearer to the center of the city a given locality is, the higher will be its rates of delinquency and crime.
> 5. The main high rate areas of the city—those near the Loop, around the Stock Yards and the South Chicago steel mills— have been characterized by high rates over a long period. Our data are based on records that go back thirty years, and the early and late Juvenile Court series show conclusively that many of the areas have been characterized by high rates throughout the entire period. It should be remembered that relatively high rates have persisted in certain areas notwithstanding the fact that the composition of population has changed markedly.[9]

The fundamental issues concerning the epidemiology of delinquency, which were first suggested by the findings of *Delinquency Areas*, were pursued in far greater scope and depth in *Social Factors in Juvenile Delinquency*:

> The study of the distribution of juvenile delinquents . . . revealed wide variations in the rates of delinquents in the 113 areas of the city [Chicago]. Likewise it was found that the areas of low and high rates of delinquents assume a typical configuration with regard to the center of the city and also that this con-

figuration of low and high rate areas has remained relatively unchanged over a long period of time. In attempting to interpret these findings, certain questions invariably arise: (1) What are the characteristics of these areas of high rates and how may they be differentiated from the areas with low rates? (2) Why do the low and high rate areas assume this configuration in relation to the center of the city? (3) Why have the rates in most of the areas of the city remained relatively constant over a long period of time? Any attempt to answer these questions must take into consideration the organic nature of the city and the processes of segregation and differentiation that take place in its growth and expansion.[10]

Shaw's application of human ecology to the epidemiology of juvenile delinquency was deeply influenced by Burgess's concentric zone hypothesis of urban growth. According to this hypothesis urban expansion occurred radially outward from the center of the city. As the city grew it tended to become spatially differentiated into a pattern of concentric zones, which were designated successively as the central business district, the zone in transition, the zone of independent workingmen's homes, the zone of better residences, and the commuters' zone. This concept implied that as such differentiation in space utilization proceeded, further growth of individual zones could occur only by encroaching upon the territory of those zones adjoining their outer boundaries. Because the center of the city with its concentration of business and industry was expanding most rapidly, the consequences of such encroachment would be experienced in their most intensified form in the zone immediately adjoining the center of the city. It is for this reason that Burgess called it the "zone of transition":

> Surrounding the central business district are areas of residential deterioration caused by the encroaching of business and industry from Zone I.
> Thus it may therefore be called a zone in transition, with a factory district for its inner belt and an outer ring of retrogressing neighborhoods, of first-settlement immigrant colonies, of rooming-house districts, of homeless men areas, of resorts of gambling, bootlegging, sexual vice, and of breeding places of crime. In this area of physical deterioration and social disorga-

nization our studies show the greatest concentration of cases of poverty, bad housing, juvenile delinquency, family disintegration, physical and mental disease. As families and individuals prosper, they escape from this area into Zone III beyond, leaving behind as marooned a residuum of the defeated, leaderless, and helpless. [11]

Shaw and McKay applied Burgess's hypothesis by searching for factors reflecting the processes and consequences of the spatial growth of the city. Their objective was to demonstrate the similarities between the radial patterns assumed by such indexes and that of the rates of delinquents. Almost as though they were drawing the curtain on a drama with the whole city for its stage, they directed attention to a base map of Chicago, which showed the areas zoned for industry and commerce during the 1920s:

When the maps showing the distribution of delinquents in Chicago are compared with this industrial map, it will be noted that most of the concentrations of delinquents and most of the high-rate areas of delinquents are either included in or are adjacent to the districts zoned for industry and commerce. . . .

From the foregoing it may be said that, in general, proximity to industry and commerce is an index of the areas of Chicago in which high rates of delinquents are found. It is not assumed that this relationship exists because industry and commerce are in themselves causes of delinquency. But it is assumed that the areas adjacent to industry and commerce have certain characteristics which result from this proximity and which serve to differentiate them from the areas with low rates of delinquents. . . . [12]

Shaw and McKay then presented a number of indexes derived from the conception of the zone in transition as constantly subject to the encroachment of business and industry from the center of the city. It is here, for example, that exisitng residential buildings are allowed to deteriorate in anticipation of the expansion of industry—and it is here that Shaw and McKay found a relative concentration of the "dilapidated and dangerous buildings, which were condemned by the building department of the city either to be destroyed or repaired (March,

1929)." [13] An additional consequence of the proximity of industry is to reduce the desirability of adjacent areas for residential purposes.

In view of the actual or anticipated displacement of residence by industry, the population of the inner-city areas tends to decline. This observation suggests that the percentage decrease in residential population may be associated with relatively high rates of delinquents:

> Most of the heavy concentrations of delinquents and most of the high-rate areas are included in those sections of the city which show a decreasing population. Likewise, the areas that are slowly increasing in population tend to be the areas with medium rates of delinquents, while the areas of more rapid increases tend to be the low-rate areas. [14]

The next factor that concerned Shaw and McKay was economic dependency, which also refers to one of the consequences of the expansion of business and industry into the adjacent residential areas. Their specific concern was with the processes that tend to select low-income families into such areas: "The areas adjacent to industry and commerce are also characterized by low rents and low family income. These are complementary characteristics. The rents in old, dilapidated buildings in deteriorated neighborhoods are naturally low and these low rents attract the population group of the lowest economic status." [15]

Shaw and McKay employ three indexes of economic dependency: (1) the percentage of the families in each local community who received financial aid from the United Charities and the Jewish Charities during a given year; (2) the distribution of children brought before the juvenile court on dependency petitions; and (3) the number of children in families who received financial aid under the provisions of the Mother's Pension Act. The geographic distribution of all three of these indexes was found to parallel closely that of the rates of juvenile delinquents.

The factors that attracted low-income residents to the inner city also attracted a high percentage of foreigners and Negroes, who tended to be of low economic status. Shaw and McKay commented on the connection between inner-city areas, Negro and foreign-born population, and relatively high rates of delinquents:

It is significant to note that the presence of a large Negro and foreign-born population in the areas having high rates of delinquents was not a unique situation in 1920. A study of the distribution of racial and national groups in both the school census of 1898 and the Federal census of 1910 showed that the highest percentage of the Negro and foreign born was in the areas having the highest rates of delinquents in the 1900-1906 juvenile court series. [16]

Having revealed a close association between foreign-born and Negro groups and high rates of delinquents, Shaw and McKay then proceeded to demonstrate the contingent and historically limited nature of this relationship. Their data on the nationality composition of boys known to the juvenile court since 1900, when combined with their knowledge of the changing settlement patterns of specific nationality groups over this period, enabled them to show that the representation of specific groups in the total delinquent population, in relation to the total number of each group, tends to go through typical stages. When immigrant groups first arrive in a city, their area of first settlement tends to be in the zone of transition, and they tend to contribute a disproportionate number of delinquents. As they succeed in moving to more desirable residential areas farther removed from the center of the city, the proportion of delinquents they contribute declines. During any given historical period the proportion of delinquents contributed by each group tends to be a function of its relative length of residence in the city. Relative rates of delinquents of specific nationality groups can then be viewed as a transitional phenomenon closely associated with the relative degree of urbanization attained by each immigrant group.

The movement of the German, Irish, English, and Scandinavian groups out of the areas of first settlement into the areas of second settlement has been paralleled by a corresponding decrease in the parentage of delinquent boys in these nationalities in the Cook County Juvenile Court. Likewise, the increase of Italians, Polish, Lithuanians, and Negroes in the areas of first settlement has been paralleled by an increase in the percentage of boys in these groups in the juvenile court. This fact is indicated both in the nationality classification of the delinquents in our two series

of court delinquents and in the nationality classification published in the annual reports of the juvenile court. [17]

At this point in his analysis Shaw took stock of his accumulated
findings and attempted to organize them into a single theoretical perspective. These findings may be summarized as follows:

1. Delinquency was to be viewed as a group-supported set of understandings, which could be transmitted to new individuals.

2. The rates of delinquents in a metropolis such as Chicago tended
to assume a characteristic pattern in relation to the overall spatial
organization of the city. The highest rates of delinquents were to be
found in the residential communities closest to the center of the city
and tended to decline in each outer layer of residential communities
as one moved towards the city's periphery.

3. While the spatial pattern manifested by rates of delinquents had
remained relatively stable and unchanging for several decades since
the start of the twentieth century (the period for which data from the
juvenile court were available), the ethnic composition of the areas with
highest rates had undergone profound changes during the same historical period.

It is to be noted that while some of these findings are primarily ecological in import (that is, they refer exclusively to spatial aspects of delinquency), others, like the group-supported delinquency heritage,
tend to be exclusively cultural in character; finally, the third
finding—that showing the relationship between ethnic group, pattern
of settlement in the city, and rates of delinquents—suggests the operation of a combination of ecological and cultural processes. Accordingly, Shaw's central problem was to develop a theoretical conception
that would account for both his ecological and his cultural data.

In this endeavor as in many other aspects of his work, Shaw was influenced by Burgess, who had postulated that the social institutions
and the solidarity of community life in the zones of transition would
be particularly subject to social disorganization under the impact of
imminent invasion by the industry and commerce of the center of the
city. Shaw now undertook to convert the idea of social disorganization
into a specific explanation of delinquency. This task was complicated
by the dual orientation of human ecology. One direction led to concern with the overall pattern of rates in the city and sought to explain
them in terms of the organic, interrelated nature of ecological pro-

cesses, such as succession, segregation, and dominance. This was the macrosocial approach to the problem. The alternative direction led to a concern, ethnographic in character, with the social life of specific natural areas of the city. As applied to the problem of juvenile delinquency, this direction led to concern with the distinctive nature of personal and primary group relationships in those communities differentially associated with high or low rates of delinquents. This was the microsocial approach to the problem. Shaw's data on the group nature of delinquency, with its emphasis upon the salience of personal relationships, and perhaps other factors as well, influenced him to give priority to the microsocial approach. This orientation is made especially clear in some of the introductory statements to *Social Factors in Juvenile Delinquency*:

> The subject matter of the report is limited to data concerning the community, the play group and gang, and the family, in their relation to the problem of delinquency among boys. [18]

> In this investigation delinquency has been studied in its relation to the social and cultural situation in which it occurs. The materials of the study pertain particularly to such primary social groups as the family, the play group, and the neighborhood. [19]

In this emphasis upon personal relations as the heart of culture and society, Shaw was following in the footsteps of those two giants of the Chicago school, Park and Thomas. As the Hinkles have observed concerning Park's point of view:

> Meanings of cultural forms are thus to be sought in the sphere of individual personalities. Accordingly, Park's comments about communication, convention, consensus, and moral order, which are characteristic of cultural areas, attest the cruciality of *individual* intent, will, and design in meanings. Orderliness on the cultural level is volitional and individualistic. And "social relations are finally and fundamentally personal relations" governed by attitudes and wishes. . . .
>
> In this perspective urban social structure is a constellation of individuals each of whom occupies a definite position with reference to the others. . . . [20]

In elaborating the implications of the concept of social disorganization for the understanding of juvenile delinquency, Shaw was indebted to the work of Thomas and Znaniecki. The latter had tended to view social disorganization as a process associated with the urbanization of immigrants of peasant origin. It had two manifestations: the breakdown of the kinship group as indicated by the loss of control of parents over their children and a decline in the capacity of the immigrants to act collectively.

> If we contrast now the conditions at home with those which the emigrants meet in America, we see that a loss of control over the child is inevitable if the parents do not develop new means as substitutes for the old ones. First, there is in America no family in the traditional sense; the married couple and the children are almost completely isolated, and the parental authority has no background. . . .
>
> Again, if there is something equivalent to the community of the old country—i.e., the parish—it is much less closed and concentrated and can hardly have the same influence. . . .[21]

Shaw and McKay thus saw juvenile delinquency as the result of the breakdown of social controls among the traditional primary groups such as the family and the neighborhood. Social disorganization as thus formulated represents a synthesis of both ecological and cultural processes:

> In the areas close to the central business district, and to a less extent to the areas close to industrial developments, the neighborhood organization tends to disintegrate. For in these areas the mobility of population is so great that there is little opportunity for the development of common attitudes and interests.[22]

> The neighborhood disorganization in the areas outside of the central business district is probably common to all rapidly growing American cities. However, in northern industrial cities, such as Chicago, the disorganization is intensified by the fact that the population in these areas is made up largely of foreign immigrants who are making their first adjustment to the complex life of the modern city. This adjustment involves profound and far-

reaching modification of the whole structure of the cultural organization of the immigrant group.[23]

It is to be noted that there is considerable determinism implicit in this application of social disorganization. The ecological and cultural processes referred to are regarded as unidirectional and inevitable. The effect of the ecological processes, in particular, is viewed as irreversible because of the continued expansion of the center of the city.

Social disorganization as so interpreted provided a plausible account of the various factors and indexes that were statistically correlated with rates of delinquency and of the changes undergone by newly arrived immigrant groups. Ironically, however, it did not provide a clear and unambiguous interpretation of delinquency as a cultural and group phenomenon. Two quite contrasting interpretations were possible—one derived from Thomas and the other from Shaw's own experience. The first would follow Thomas in his contention that juvenile delinquency was attributable to the inadequacy of the socialization experience of the second generation:

But an entirely new side of the whole question is disclosed when we ask ourselves not how the young generation loses a life organization that it has acquired but how it ever acquires a life organization at all. For then it proves that, while in relatively organized and isolated Polish-American communities—particularly in provincial towns—the economically most settled and socially most active part of the population can still impart to the growing youth a certain minimum of normal and vital principles of behavior, there is a large proportion of immigrant children—particularly in large cities—whose home and community conditions are such that their behavior is never socially regulated, no life organization worthy of the name is ever imposed upon them. Their status is, exactly speaking, not that of demoralization—for demoralization presupposes the loss of a moral system, and they never had any moral system to lose—it is simple and plain amorality. If personal character is the product of social education acting upon a given temperamental foundation, such individuals in the most radical cases have no character, good or bad. They are originally in a condition similar to that which . . . even socially formed individuals can reach if left outside of any orga-

nized social group and subjected to destructive influences—a
condition of passive or active wildness in which behavior is not
controlled by social customs and beliefs but directly conditioned
by temperamental tendencies and swayed by momentary
moods.[24]

However, this view of the delinquent as wild and untrammeled in his
behavior was contrary to Shaw's conception of the group-supported
nature of the heritage of delinquency. According to the second interpretation delinquent behavior was attributed not so much to inadequate socialization as to an alternative mode of socialization.

Shaw's treatment of delinquency in *Social Factors in Juvenile Delinquency* reflects this fundamental ambiguity. In the crucial chapter,
"The Spirit of Delinquency Areas," he presented two distinct images
of the delinquent. One image referred to "the random, uncontrolled,
unguided character of the activity of the delinquent children in these
areas. . . ."[25] The second suggested that delinquency tends to be a relatively well-organized group activity, which is controlled by the older,
established offenders:

> The presence of a large number of older offenders in a neighbor-
> hood is a fact of great significance for the understanding of the
> problem of juvenile delinquency. It indicates, in the first place,
> that the possibility of contact between the children and hard-
> ened offenders is very great. These older offenders, who are well
> known and have prestige in the neighborhood, tend to set the
> standards and patterns of behavior for the younger boys, who
> idolize and emulate them. In many cases the "big shot" repre-
> sents for the young delinquent an ideal around which his own
> hopes and ambitions are crystallized. His attainment of this
> coveted ideal means recognition in his group and the esteem of
> his fellows.[26]

From Process to Social Structure

The underlying premise of the social disorganization perspective on
juvenile delinquency was social change. As a premise, it suited well
the nature of the inner-city communities during the 1920s. Davis

noted its impact upon the residents of Chicago's inner-city residents: "Old neighborhoods were changing; the prosperity of the twenties gave many families the opportunity to move to better sections of the city or to the suburbs. They were replaced by Negroes, Latin Americans, and other groups. . . ."[27]

The coming of the depression reduced such residential mobility and gave salience to the issues of poverty and unemployment. Social change began to appear a less cogent premise for sociological theory than stable and structural features of society, such as social stratification. Subtly but surely a movement from the primacy of concern with *process* to that with *status* began to be reflected in Shaw's work. It is a shift that perhaps first became evident in the description of the local community in *Brothers in Crime* (1938), a volume of the case studies of five brothers.[28]

> The community in question is adjacent to a center of heavy industry located along one of the branches of the Chicago River—a drab, unattractive, and deteriorated community. When the Martin family established their home here, the community was inhabited almost exclusively by persons of their own nationality. Since that time despite the great population changes that have taken place in many other similar areas in the city, the population in this community has undergone little change as regards its nationality. It is a community of first immigrant settlement with the physical characteristics common to the so-called "blighted" or "slum" areas.[29]

> Three decades ago this community was characterized by a relatively great density of population with approximately one hundred thousand persons per square mile. Since that time the total population has decreased continuously to the extent that in 1930 the number of its inhabitants was less than half as great as it was in 1900. . . .[30]

> The obvious physical deterioration is suggestive of the low economic status of the population residing in this community. Rates of unemployment, poverty, and economic dependency have been relatively high for many years. For the most part the residents are unskilled laborers who have been forced to work at

those types of employment which are relatively unremunerative and provide little security. Even during periods of prosperity the standards of living have been generally low, while in times of depression a large segment of the population has been unemployed and dependent upon charity for subsistence.[31]

Shaw thus implied that the social life of the local residents was less influenced by the nature of their local community than it was by their position in the economy and occupational structure of the larger society. Their residence in the inner-city community was less a reflection of the relative newness of their arrival and their lack of acculturation to American institutions than it was a function of their class position in society. Such a realization turned Shaw's and McKay's attention increasingly from explanations that centered upon the nature of personal relationships within the local neighborhood to those that viewed the local community in relation to the larger urban community. Hitherto, such relationships between the part and the whole had been conceived in ecological terms. It now became clear that such connections needed to be construed in cultural and social terms as well as ecological. Ecological processes, such as succession and segregation, by emphasizing the relative isolation of the natural areas into which the city was differentiated did not suggest the variety of influence exerted by the linkages between the local community and the larger society.

Certain aspects of their data also resisted analysis in terms of social change and social disorganization. The highly stable spatial pattern manifested in the rates of delinquents, with the highest rates appearing in the inner-city areas decade after decade, could not itself be interpreted as an instance of social change. The central theoretical problem confronting Shaw and McKay had now subtly changed. Instead of seeking to relate juvenile delinquency to the processes of social change in the inner-city areas, it had become that of accounting for a relatively stable structural feature of these areas—the pattern of rates of delinquents. Not surprisingly, the new emphasis upon the role played by structural forces originating in the larger society was accompanied by a reduced emphasis upon the etiological significance of processes occurring in the local community. The most relevant feature of inner-city areas was no longer that they constituted the locus of processes of social change but that they comprised the local communities of lowest socioeconomic status in the city. Turning their attention increasingly to the societal factors involved in delinquency, Shaw and McKay tended to attribute less and less theoretical significance to the interpersonal process through which individuals became delinquent.

The line of thinking that led Shaw and McKay from a primary emphasis upon the processes of social disorganization to a social structural explanation, according to which delinquency became a product of differential access to the legitimate means to attain the common success goals of society, attained its culminating statement in *Juvenile Delinquency and Urban Areas*:

> Despite ... marked differences in ... [income and status] ... in different communities, children and young people in all areas, both rich and poor, are exposed to the luxury values and success patterns of our culture. In school and elsewhere they are also exposed to ideas of equality, freedom, and individual enterprise. Among children and young people residing in low-income areas, interests in acquiring material goods and enhancing personal status are developed which are often difficult to realize by legitimate means because of limited access to the necessary facilities and opportunities. [32]

The counterpart of a differential opportunity structure as a property of the urban community as a whole was a conflict of values in the local communities, as some local residents embraced illegitimate values and others remained conventional in their orientation.

The shifts that had occurred in Shaw's and McKay's position can be summarized as follows. From an emphasis upon social change and social process they had moved to an emphasis upon social structure. From stress upon personal and primary group relationships—that is, upon the local milieu—they had moved to attribute priority to the impersonal pressures originating in the larger social system. The conceptual primacy of the local community was replaced by that of social class. The process of city growth that had been phrased in terms of such ecological processes as invasion, succession, and segregation was now rephrased as social differentiation. The urban community was conceived of as a social system and the epidemiology of delinquency interpreted in functional terms.

Shaw's Use of the Case Study

Shaw's name and reputation are undoubtedly more intimately identified with his published case histories than his contribution to the epidemiology of delinquency. To a generation of readers who had been deeply influenced by genetic theories of criminality, he brought the actual voice of the offender presenting his own version of his origins, his growth, and his orientation to the world. A more forceful mode of presenting the force of circumstances in the molding of human lives would have been difficult to devise. The result was a highly compelling insider's view of criminality, made available to a public of readers and students normally far removed from the situations that produce confirmed criminal offenders. Shaw's interest in these documents was never restricted to their humanistic or pedagogic value; he used them in his research and for treatment. As a researcher he devoted himself unstintingly to seeking to understand the processes through which individuals became delinquent, and he was particularly interested in the conditions that accompanied recidivism. Suspicious of premature generalization, he patiently collected and encouraged others to collect hundreds upon hundreds of case studies of offenders. "An intensive study of the detailed life-histories of more than two hundred young repeated offenders on parole from the St. Charles School for Boys indicates rather clearly the great importance of dealing with the intimate personal aspects of the delinquent's situation."[33] One of the key enigmas of his life, and an issue that challenges any attempt to understand his work, is to account for the reasons why he made such little theoretical use of these case studies.

If we include within our purview Rice's report on the evolution of Shaw's early point of view, as well as the evidence of his published case studies, I believe he traversed three stages in his theoretical orientation to the case study. In the first of these, the early apprenticeship period when he was beginning to work as a probation officer, he was deeply influenced by the multiple factor approach. This was followed by a period when his interpretation of life histories was influenced by the symbolic interactionist perspective. In the third stage he relied largely upon a cultural interpretation of the life history.

THE MULTIPLE FACTOR APPROACH

Rice provides us with some insight into Shaw's manner of proceeding during this initial phase of his work as a probation officer:

Confronted with evidence concerning a particular delinquent, the author consciously or unconsciously sought among the apparent factors in the case one or more which seemed to have causal significance. . . . For example, Shaw relates that among the factors involved in one case was the separation of the delinquent's parents. He immediately classified this in his mind as a "broken-home case."[34]

According to Rice, Shaw was soon led to abandon the multiple-factor approach.

An illustration of the manner in which the author revised his explanatory concepts is given by him as follows: In a certain family there were two brothers whose ages did not greatly differ. One was delinquent, the other not. The social worker who interviewed the delinquent boy diagnosed the delinquency of the first as "a case of bad companions." When a thorough case study of the family and its social environment was made, it was discovered that the brothers had the same companions. Moreover, the author points out, they lived in the same family, had the same immediate heredity, and shared the same community environment. Hence the causal explanation first assigned appeared deficient. Other traditional explanations had similarly to be abandoned when an effort was made to apply them to individual cases of delinquency.[35]

THE SYMBOLIC INTERACTIONIST APPROACH

Shaw's discouraging experience with the application of the multiple-factor approach rendered problematic the issue of how to conceive of the process of becoming delinquent. As is suggested in "Benny's" case, he then began to interpret his cases from a social psychological perspective.

It was observed that the customary *simple* explanations of delinquent behavior had little meaning except when they were related to a total situation. . . .

For example: Undernourishment and slight stature have often been naively regarded as "causes" of delinquency. On the surface this explanation seemed to fit the case of "Benny":

When Benny was about ten years of age, he accompanied a gang of boys who were planning to rob a butcher-shop. Unexpectedly, the door which they wished to enter was locked and Benny was the only boy small enough to be pushed through the transom. In a playful mood, the older boys gave him a loaded revolver. This was the proudest moment of his life and gave delineation to his delinquent career. Thus the important factor antecedent to delinquency in this case was neither "undernourishment" nor "slight stature." It was rather this complex situation: boy in gang with certain set of group values and attitudes; attempt to rob butcher-shop; door unexpectedly found locked; only member of gang sufficiently small to enter through transom; ego enhanced by praise and award of loaded revolver by older boys; variety of other factors and sequences not stated. [36]

A group of boys was trying to break into a butcher shop. Their attainment of this objective was blocked. This unanticipated turn of events led to a group redefinition of Benny's potential role. His small stature and relative youthfulness, previously viewed as disadvantages, now became a potential asset to the group because they suggested an alternative means of entry. The "situation was redefined." The activity of the group, including Benny's part in it, presupposed a communicative process that allowed them to cope with the blocked act.

It was just such insights into the relation between the individual and group activity that had been formulated by G. H. Mead, W. I. Thomas, R. E. Park, and others who contributed to the symbolic interaction point of view. There is substantial evidence that Shaw was familiar with this approach. His first published life history, *The Jack-Roller*, includes extensive citations from W. I. Thomas in which the latter elaborated upon the symbolic interactionist perspective. The life-history method itself had been introduced by W. I. Thomas in order to provide data amenable to analysis from this point of view. Symbolic interactionism provided the framework for Burgess's discussion of delinquent behavior in his paper, "The Study of the Delinquent as a Person." [37]

It can be conjectured, then, that after rejecting the multiple-factor approach, Shaw entertained the possibility of applying the symbolic interactionist perspective to the interpretation of his case studies. It was a position that did not require ignoring the role played by various factors in delinquent conduct, but such factors were to be viewed as influencing behavior through a process of social definition. The conception of the delinquent shifted from one who responded immediately and automatically to certain factors or combinations of factors to one who delayed his response and guided his action by the symbolic organization of the factors which he regarded as relevant into a meaningful situation. His conduct was viewed as being mediated by a verbal process in which he communicated with himself and others.

THE CULTURAL APPROACH

Although Shaw may have been influenced by symbolic interactionism, his publications of case studies largely reflect a cultural interpretation. It appears that during the mid-1920s he began to be strongly influenced by the cultural interpretation of social life. He first explicitly stated this perspective in *Delinquency Areas* (1929) where he acknowledged his indebtedness to the anthropologists:

> The cultural anthropologists have emphasized the importance of understanding the cultural background—the customs, codes, taboos, and traditions of a group—in the study of the behavior of any group. They have pointed out that many differences in behavior of peoples are based on differences in culture rather than on differences in biological inheritance.
>
> These customs, traditions, folkways, mores are thought of as results of the experiences of the group which have become common and habitual in the group. These are passed on from generation to generation and are accepted more or less unconsciously. A part of any study of behavior, therefore, must consist of an understanding of this culture setting of the person or group whose behavior is studied.[38]

Shaw found the concept of culture very useful. Through its application he sought to interpret the differences between communities with high and low rates of delinquents, the group-supported nature of delinquency, and the process through which the individual became delinquent.

The manner in which the nature of the community could be illuminated by the concept of culture was stated as follows: "We have used community or community situation in a broad sense to include both the combination of Old World and New World heritages and all other conditions which might be related to the development of delinquent behavior."[39] An instance of the application of this cultural view of the local community to the interpretation of a specific case of delinquency is presented in the first chapter of *Social Factors in Juvenile Delinquency*. The presentation of this case concluded with the following summary:

> It is clear that the parents had very little appreciation of the nature of Nick's problems and the sort of social world in which he was living. Although his behavior was, for the most part, strictly in conformity with the socially approved standards of the play group and neighborhood, it was a violation of the family tradition and expectations. He was torn between the demands and expectations of two conflicting social groups. On the one hand, we have in the family background a persistence of an Old World family pattern, the outstanding features of which consist in the exercise of paternal authority, rigorous discipline, and the subordination of the individual member to the ideals of economic security. In accordance with this tradition the boy must go to work at an early age and contribute his wages to the family budget. On the other hand, the boy has grown up in an American community; his attitudes and interests have been defined in terms of the activities and values of a more or less typical American group. His interests are centered chiefly in sports and high-school attendance, both of which are in direct conflict with family expectations. This conflict is made more acute because the boy was conscious of the economic and social inferiority of his family and had accepted the contemptuous and superior attitudes of the neighbors toward his family. It is in this conflict of values, attitudes, and interests that the boy's temper tantrums, stubbornness, and open defiance of authority occurred. From this point of view it may be assumed that his behavior problems were incidental to the larger cultural conflict between the family and the prevailing social values of the neighborhood.[40]

Second, the delinquent group was viewed as being characterized by its own distinctive cultural standards. Indeed, so salient is the concept of culture in this context that Short was led to remark:"Some may wonder that Shaw and McKay did not hit upon the notion of 'delinquent subcultures,' since, with Thrasher, they were responsible for a large portion of the data upon which contemporary formulations rest."[41] Third, the process of becoming delinquent was viewed as a process through which individuals came to learn such standards.

It should be noted that the idea of culture and the perspective of symbolic interactionism are far from antithetical. From the point of view of symbolic interactionism, the traditional shared understandings to which culture refers are to be viewed as contributing elements in given social situations but not as coercing the definitions of behavior with which people respond to such situations. For reasons that will become evident, Shaw, and Burgess who was his colleague in the interpretation of the life histories, chose to maximize the cultural elements in delinquency. Indeed, they moved increasingly toward a cultural deterministic approach, that is one in which cultural elements have primacy in the definition of specific situations of which delinquent behavior is the outcome.

The trend toward cultural determinism became increasingly marked with each succeeding publication of Shaw's case studies. It was a tendency that had first become explicit in Burgess's discussion of *The Jack-Roller*:

> For the first time in the field of delinquency this volume provides adequate material for description and analysis from the standpoint of explanation in terms of the cultural factors in behavior. In penetrating beneath the external behavior of the delinquent boy it reveals the intimate interplay between his impulses and the effective stimuli of the environment. It shows how the cultural patterns, of his home, of his associates in the neighborhood, of the delinquent and criminal groups outside and especially inside correctional and penal institutions, define his wishes and attitudes and so control, almost in a deterministic fashion, his behavior. His account also discloses how certain changes in his social environment, by affording contact in an intimate and sympathetic way with the cultural patterns of normal society, redefine his impulses and direct his conduct into fields of socially approved behavior.[42]

The Jack-Roller contains inconsistencies that become intelligible if
we assume some tension in Shaw's mind between the cultural and
symbolic interaction points of view. In the first chapter he quoted with
approval Thomas's proposal that it is in large part the very subjectiv-
ity of the case study, its disclosure of the idiosyncratic aspects of the
subject's experience, that endows the case study with its special value:

> There may be, and is, doubt as to the objectivity and veracity of
> the record, but even the highly subjective record has a value for
> behavior study. A document prepared by one compensating for
> a feeling of inferiority or elaborating a delusion of persecution is
> as far as possible from objective reality, but the subject's view of
> the situation, how he regards it, may be the most important ele-
> ment for interpretation. For his immediate behavior is closely
> related to his definition of the situation, which may be in terms
> of objective reality, or in terms of a subjective appreciation—"as
> if" it were so. Very often it is the wide discrepancy between the
> situation as it seems to others and the situation as it seems to the
> individual that brings about the overt behavior difficulty. To
> take an extreme example, the warden of Dannemora Prison
> recently refused to honor the order of the Court to send an in-
> mate outside the prison walls for some specific purpose. He ex-
> cused himself on the ground that the man was too dangerous.
> He had killed several persons who had the unfortunate habit of
> talking to themselves on the street. From the movement of their
> lips he imagined that they were calling him vile names and he
> behaved as if this were true. If men define situations as real, they
> are real in their consequences. [43]

Shaw further acknowledged his commitment to this view in his own
statement about the uses of the life history or "own story":

> In our study and treatment of delinquent boys in Chicago, we
> have found that the "own story" reveals useful information con-
> cerning at least three important aspects of delinquent conduct:
> (1) the point of view of the delinquent; (2) the social and cultural
> situation to which the delinquent is responsive; and (3) the se-
> quence of past experiences and situations in the life of the de-
> linquent. [44]

Despite this statement, Shaw made no attempt to pursue the implications of *The Jack-Roller*'s idiosyncratic point of view for an understanding of his involvement in delinquent conduct. On the contrary, Burgess, in his discussion of the case, emphasized its representativeness as a social type at the expense of any attention to its individual distinctiveness. Dollard has commented on this characteristic of the case as an insider's view of the delinquent world rather than a portrayal of how a specific individual became delinquent:

> The overwhelming power of the delinquent situation is clearly presented and the writer of the autobiography is seen by himself, as well as his social analysts, as a "function" of the collective life into which he chanced to come. Indeed, it strikes the discriminating reader of the document that it is less a life history in the sense of an account of the socialization of a person than it is an inside view of the gangland culture. [45]

Dollard makes a second observation, which suggests that Shaw and Burgess were not particularly interested in pursuing the theoretical implications of the idiosyncratic aspect of *The Jack-Roller*'s experience. They apparently did not view as problematic one of the most salient features of the jack-roller's personal experience with delinquency: his failure to attain success as a criminal offender.

> For some reason, we cannot help noting, the highest and most dangerous standards of criminal practice did not take on with Stanley since he never rose higher in the criminal hierarchy than jack-rolling; if he had really been thoroughly accessible to the gangland culture, he had certainly some opportunity to go after big money before he was twenty. We can only assume that this limitation of accessibility to the highest values of the criminal world was due to personality difficulties of his own, not adequately specified in his autobiography. [46]

One factor that appears to have been influential in giving a deterministic cast to the cultural interpretation of the case studies was Burgess's distinction between personality pattern and social type and the consequences that followed from it:

In analyzing this and other life-histories, a basic distinction must be made between personality pattern and social type. . . . We have been describing the personality pattern which may be defined as the sum and integration of those traits which characterize the typical reactions of one person toward other persons. The personality pattern, according to our tentative hypothesis, is formed in infancy and early childhood through a conjunction of constitutional and experiential factors and persists with some modification and elaboration as a relatively constant factor through later childhood, youth, and maturity. . . .

The term "social type" does not refer to the mechanisms of personality reactions but to attitudes, values, and philosophy of life derived from copies presented by society.[47]

The perhaps unintended effect of this analytical distinction was to relegate subjective factors to the childhood period. By implication, patterns of personal relationships henceforth tended to be fixed. The framework did not allow for the possibility that the individual could generate new meanings in his responses to changes in his experience once his personality pattern was set. The only sources of changes in the meanings of his behavior tended to be restricted to the external cultural influences to which he was exposed. Burgess's distinction had one other undesirable consequence: it fit all too neatly into the polemic between sociology and psychology as to which discipline encompassed the more important causes of delinquent behavior. The personality pattern was viewed as belonging to the domain of psychology and that of the social type to that of sociology. Determining the causes of delinquent behavior became a matter of demonstrating which of the two factors was the more important in the behavior of specific cases. In partitioning the individual into two mutually exclusive spheres, this analytic distinction eliminated the possibility of viewing the person as a whole interacting with others. Unfortunately, it was a distinction that remained central to the interpretation of all Shaw's life histories of delinquents.

Although Shaw did not place much emphasis upon the idiosyncratic aspects of The Jack-Roller's experience in his theoretical discussion of the case, he revealed considerable sensitivity to these aspects of the case in his mode of treatment:

The case-study revealed certain aspects of Stanley's [The Jack-

Roller] personality which greatly complicated his adjustment to other persons. Among the more outstanding of these aspects of personality were his attitudes of persecution, suspicion, resistance to discipline and authority, self-justification, and a definite tendency to excuse his misconduct by means of self-pity, fatalism, and by placing the blame on other persons.

In the light of the foregoing interpretation of the case, it was decided to place Stanley in an entirely new social situation, and to initiate a plan of treatment adapted, as far as possible, to his particular attitudes and personality. The first step was to secure a foster-home in one of the non-delinquent communities of the city. Because of his egocentric personality, it was thought necessary to select a family in which the relationships were sympathetic and informal. . . .

The second step in the process of treatment was in connection with the problem of vocational guidance. Here again our problem was greatly complicated by Stanley's personality difficulties. He was constantly in conflict with his employers and fellow-employees. Furthermore, at the time of his release from the House of Correction he was devoid of any specialized occupational training and definitely resistive to unskilled labor. During the first two years of the period of treatment, we placed him in a great variety of positions. We observed that his most favorable reactions occurred in positions which gave him a sense of superiority and in which he was not under the direct control of a person of superior rank. This observation, along with the fact that he was able to express himself vividly and convincingly, led to the assumption that he might make an adjustment in the field of salesmanship. A position in salesmanship was secured for him two years ago, and since that time he has made a fairly satisfactory adjustment in that field. [48]

The Jack-Roller suggested that there was considerable discrepancy between the image of man implicit in Shaw's theory and the one implicit in his practice. In his practice he revealed himself as extraordinarily sensitive to the role of idiosyncratic meanings in the experience of the individual, viewing cultural elements as these are reflected in the individual's personal experience. In his theory he appears to have gone along with Burgess in emphasizing the patterned nature, rather than the distinctiveness, of the individual's experience. It was a distinction with considerable methodological implications. From the symbolic interactionist perspective, personal relationships are at the center of concern because they are believed to manifest a degree of autonomy in relation to all elements in the social situation, including the cultural elements. All elements are studied in terms of their meaning within the interaction among persons involved in group behavior. In contrast, a culturally oriented approach tends to view social situations as being defined primarily in cultural terms. Personal relationships lose their theoretical autonomy and become little more than a neutral medium for the transmission of cultural meanings.

The full implications of cultural determinism became evident in *Social Factors in Juvenile Delinquency*, which appeared in 1931, a year after the publication of *The Jack-Roller*. [49] In it Shaw presented a statement of the process of becoming delinquent as one of "culture transmission." He succeeded in demonstrating how sharing in the experience of delinquent groups acts as a vehicle through which patterns of delinquent behavior are transmitted to the individual. The following conclusions are drawn from an intensive analysis of the case of "Sidney":

Sidney was arrested at least sixteen times, was brought to court on petitions alleging truancy or delinquency ten times, and received seven commitments to four different correctional institutions. . . .

In the course of his career in juvenile delinquency, from 7 to 17 years of age, he was officially known to have been involved in delinquency with 11 different companions, although the number implicated with him in any given offense was never more than 3. He was apprehended as a lone offender in only two instances; one of these was for fighting and the other was for larceny of merchandise from his employer. His 11 companions represented three distinct groups, whose activities and traditions were clearly of a delinquent character. Furthermore, the successive types of delinquent activity in which Sidney engaged, beginning with pilfering in the neighborhood and progressing to larceny of automobiles and robbery with a gun, show a close correspondence with the delinquent patterns prevailing in the successive groups with which he had contact. The materials presented . . . along with the official records of the 11 boys, suggest very strongly that Sidney acquired the early patterns of pilfering, burglary, and shoplifting from his first play groups, and the later patterns of larceny of automobiles and robbery with a gun from the adult criminal gang with which he had contact after the age of 15.[50]

Shaw's subsequent publications of case histories, *The Natural History of a Delinquent Career* and *Brothers in Crime*, presented no significantly new ideas about the process of becoming delinquent.[51] Juveniles who became delinquent, said Shaw, went through a process in which they became increasingly committed to delinquent standards of conduct. This development assumed the form of a sequence of stages characterized by the individual's progression from less serious to more serious types of offenses. Once introduced to delinquent contacts, he was perceived as moving inexorably from stage to stage. The temporal pattern manifested by these successive changes in modes of law violation was called the "natural history" of the delinquent career.

This line of analysis reached its culmination in Burgess's discussion of *Brothers in Crime*. In contrast to the previously published case studies, each of which dealt with individuals, this volume presented the life histories of five brothers. Despite considerable variation in personality types, all five brothers had become involved in delinquent careers. For them, at least, the data suggested that social factors had been more influential than personality factors in the determination of their delinquent behavior.

The life-histories of the five brothers make it possible to give a preliminary answer to the crucial question: To what extent is a criminal career a result of personality traits and to what extent is it a product of the situation in which the person is born and reared?

With each of the five brothers social factors are much more important than personality traits in influencing their behavior. The entrance and progress of each brother in a delinquent career appears to be almost a direct outcome of the residence of a poverty-stricken immigrant family in a neighborhood of boys' gangs and criminal traditions. Counteracting factors, it is true, were present, such as parental concern over the behavior of the boys and opportunity for them to follow law-abiding careers in school and at work. But the appeal to the boys of conventional patterns of behavior was weak in comparison with the thrill of adventure and the easy rewards of stealing. . . .

The psychogenetic traits of the person and his cultural characteristics are to be considered as separate and independent. The five brothers might have widely divergent psychogenetic traits and yet each be inducted into the same criminal culture and exhibit apparently uniform criminal behavior. Such, in fact, was the case. The cultural traits of the five brothers are, as demonstrated by their life-histories, practically identical.[52]

If the contentions made during the preceding discussion are correct, then certain implications appear to follow. It becomes clear why Shaw never pursued studies in which he attempted to determine the conditions under which individuals remained nondelinquent in local communities with high rates of delinquency. With his conception of the cultural determinism operative in such areas, there could be no systematic sociological influences leading to nondelinquency. As Dollard observed, Shaw had succeeded in depicting the overwhelming nature of the pressures leading to delinquency in slum communities. If this view was valid, then interindividual differences were indeed irrelevant to the understanding of the entry of individuals into delinquency in such areas. Such an acknowledgment, however, is not tantamount to a recognition that every individual in such areas was fated to recapitulate all phases of a delinquent career. It is quite feasible to assume that idiosyncratic factors could play a significant role in determining the nature and extent of the individual's subsequent involvement in delinquent behavior. Shaw and Burgess appear to have applied their cultural determinism not only to the genesis of delinquency but to the inevitability of its unfolding as well. Their theoretical scheme allowed no place for possible contingencies and turning points during which individuals might abandon deviant pursuits. Because of this fatalistic conception of the delinquent career, they failed to ask some of the significant questions suggested by the individually distinctive features of their cases. They did not ask why the jack-roller did not proceed to more sophisticated types of criminality but confined himself to rolling drunks, an offense of low prestige in the world of the offender. They did not ask why some of the five brothers continued in criminality after their imprisonment, and why others became lawabiding. If they had used a more flexible scheme of the life career they might have found a way to connect idiosyncratic factors with the delinquent career. Ultimately, it may be conjectured, it was Shaw's inability to find a place for interindividual differences in his theoretical scheme that discouraged him from making additional use of the life history after the publication of *Brothers in Crime.*

Attempted Synthesis

Shaw from the beginning was committed to the task of synthesizing his statistical and case study findings. Rice has commented on this aspect of his methodology:

> Certain groups of social scientists have been contrasted by the statement that one exemplifies the use of statistical method while the other upholds the use of case methods. In such a comparison, Shaw would doubtless be classified with the exemplars of case method. The statement itself implies divergence between the objectives of the groups compared.
>
> The author, however, would object to being classified within either of the categories mentioned, as he would also object to the principle of the classification itself. He feels the need of no such distinction in method or objectives with respect to his own research problems. He views his methodological procedure as an alternation, without defined termination, of case method and statistical method. [53]

In undertaking to integrate his findings on both the epidemiological and the individual aspects of the problem, Shaw was not only striving to attain a comprehensive theoretical perspective on the nature of juvenile delinquency, but was also responding to an intellectual challenge inherited from the nineteenth century. The moralistic approach to the problem of delinquency that had dominated the early part of the nineteenth century had been followed, in its latter half, by an environmental emphasis. It was one of the major contributions of the Chicago humanists to have proposed a view of human nature that espoused the role of the social environment without nullifying the contribution of the individual. This fundamentally social psychological view of society, with its attempt to balance the needs of the individual with the pressures of society, had been rendered explicit in the writings of Jane Addams.[54]

Following this lead, Healy, in his clinical work with delinquents during the early decades of the twentieth century, had arrived at an increasing appreciation of the role of community influences upon the conduct of the young. Apparently, however, his ability to make use of this insight was limited by his individualistic orientation:

> Healy conceived his task to be a search for all the influences, factors, and forces which determine behavior. . . . His own special training was in psychiatry and psychology. Accordingly his technique was highly developed in the individual aspects of the behavior of the delinquent, namely, in the physical examination, anthropometric measurements, and mental tests. . . . His search for the concrete materials of the mental life of the individual led necessarily to some appreciation of social influences. Secondly, through the use of the case-study method he could not if he would ignore the play of social forces. Healy quite naturally recognized the value of the experience of the social worker in securing facts about the family history and social environment, but apparently perceived no place for the technique of the sociologist and sociological research. His appreciation of the role of social factors went little farther than common sense.[55]

Shaw inherited the challenge of synthesizing the epidemiological and the individual aspects of juvenile delinquency. It was not an easy task. Unlike Jane Addams he could not be content with merely presenting a point of view. Unlike Healy he had the standards of a social scientist. His commitment to a synthesis led him to seek to integrate the findings derived from two quite distinct and contrasting methodologies. His findings on the epidemiology of delinquency had been derived from applying the perspective and techniques of human ecology. His findings on the process of becoming delinquent had been derived from case studies that emphasized the life history of the delinquent as told in his own words. The presuppositions of each of these research techniques were diametrically opposed.

Hawley has presented the presuppositions of the ecological framework as follows:

The subject of ecological enquiry is therefore the community, the form and development of which are studied with particular reference to the limiting and supporting factors of the environment. Ecology, in other words, is a study of the morphology of collective life in both its static and its dynamic aspects. It attempts to determine the nature of community structure in general, the types of communities that appear in different habitats, and the specific sequence of change in community development.

The unit of observation, it should be emphasized, is not the individual but the aggregate which is either organized or in process of becoming organized. The individual enters into ecological studies, on the theoretical side, as a postulate, and, on the practical side, as a unit of measurement. As something to be investigated in and of itself, however, the individual is subject matter for other disciplines. [56]

Perhaps the most succinct statement of the presuppositions of the case study is included in Blumer's definition of the human document, of which the case study is one type: "The human document is an account of individual experience which reveals the individual's actions as a human agent and as a participant in social life." [57]

From a slightly different perspective, the task that confronted Shaw was to formulate a unitary point of view that would bridge the ecological and cultural levels of his data. Park formulated his conception of these two analytical levels of society and the nature of their interdependence:

The fact seems to be . . . that human society, as distinguished from plant and animal society, is organized on two levels, the biotic and the cultural. There is a symbiotic society based on competition and a cultural society based on communication and consensus. As a matter of fact the two societies are merely different aspects of one society, which, in the vicissitudes and changes to which they are subject remain, nevertheless, in some sort of mutual dependence each upon the other. The cultural superstructure rests on the basis of the symbiotic substructure, and the emergent energies that manifest themselves on the biotic level in movements and actions reveal themselves on the higher social level in more subtle and sublimated forms. [58]

Confronted by the task of synthesis Shaw proceeded in a tentative pragmatic manner. His fundamental concept in this endeavor was that of social disorganization. As a concept it referred to the cultural level of social life where it connoted the breakdown of traditional forms of social control. The conditions under which such breakdown occurred, however, were both ecological and cultural. From the eco-logical perspective, the spatial expansion of the business and industry located in the center of the city outward into the adjacent zone of transition greatly reduced the stability and effectiveness of the social institutions that organized the social life of the residential commu-nities located in these inner-city areas. The weakening of these social institutions resulting from the ecological pressures was intensified by concomitant culture conflicts experienced by the most recently ar-rived immigrant groups as they sought to find their place in the urban economy and social structure. A third source of social disorganization was attributable to the conflicts inescapably associated with the cul-tural diversity of the inner-city areas.

According to Shaw these various forms of social disorganization were irreversible. Because growth was postulated as an inherent qual-ity of modern industrial city, it was unavoidable that the center of the city should be constantly expanding. The urbanization of groups of peasant origin was an unavoidable phase through which all immi-grant groups had to pass. The social disorganization attributable to the diversity of cultures was also unavoidable. The convergence of these various unidirectional processes rendered social disorganiza-tion an inevitable response of residents in the zone of transition.

The environmental determinism inherent in Shaw's conception of social disorganization as a framework for the explanation of juvenile delinquency had definite implications for the type of synthesis that he was able to attain between his ecological and his case study data. The assumption of environmental determinism prohibited the possibility of taking into account differences in the personal experiences of his case studies. Such data were used solely to provide the reader with data on the subjective aspects of the delinquency areas as contrasted with the formal indexes constituted by his data.

While such formal indices as increasing and decreasing popula-tion, percentage of families owning their homes, percentage of foreign born, rate of dependency, and rate of adult crime, may serve as a basis for making rough distinctions between areas of the city, they do not disclose the more subtle and intangible processes which constitute the very essence of the social and moral life in the community. More important than the external realities of the area are the traditions, standards, and moral sentiments which characterize the neighborhood life. While these more intangible factors are difficult to ascertain and do not readily lend themselves to objective analysis, they are nevertheless important aspects of the moral world to which the growing child must make an adjustment.[59]

When he used his case study for such purposes, Shaw was always careful to specify that it was being used for illustrative purposes only. In this manner—by the combination of rigorous presentation of his ecological data and their analysis in combination with illustrations from his case studies—Shaw succeeded in presenting a highly effective portrayal of the problem of delinquency in the most salient forms that it assumed in his era. He tended to avoid the methodological issues of how to synthesize his ecological and his case study data. The equally difficult task of integrating the ecological and the cultural levels of analysis was overcome by giving priority to the ecological processes with their implication of environmental determinism and by placing his cultural interpretation, too, within a deterministic context. His resolution, his attempted synthesis, provided a valuable and influential descriptive account of delinquency.

Perhaps because it was limited to a given historical era, Shaw's attempted synthesis was bound to be unstable. His conceptualization of the local community proved to be inadequate. His conception of the slum community as the scene of irreversible processes of social disorganization prevented him from conceptualizing the indigenous processes of social reorganization that tended to occur in such communities, particularly in the form of rackets and politics. It remained for William F. Whyte to make this contribution toward the reconceptualization of the inner-city community. Implicit in such a reconceptualization was a reduction in the role played by ecological processes. Shaw attempted to reconceptualize the slum community in terms of the conflict of values, but the social disorganization perspective was never entirely displaced.

Shaw's attempted synthesis also broke down because of his inability to bridge the gap between the ecological and the cultural analytical levels. The reasons for this become clearer when we look at the methodological means that he had available. He sought to advance a view of delinquency as the provision of group support for delinquent cultural patterns within the context of the slum community. However, he did not have the data available to present a realistic depiction of this community. On the one hand, he had the ecological data, which he never ceased to regard solely as indexes of culture and social organization. His data for the cultural level of the local community were entirely restricted to his case studies of delinquents. Such case studies provided indispensable sources of information of the social organization of the local community, but they were inadequate in themselves to provide the data from which the social organization of the local community could be constructed. Specifically, they did not provide adequate cultural data for the interpretation of the ecological indexes. Shaw did not possess data adequate to the task of presenting a realistic depiction of the local community. Fuller data on the local community were required if the gap between the ecological and the cultural levels was to be bridged.

After attaining his seminal insight into the group-supported nature of delinquency, Shaw never succeeded in raising the cogent theoretical questions that its existence implied. It is clear that he sought to relate it in some way to processes associated with the local community. However, he did not succeed in stating this relationship unambiguously in terms of the social disorganization perspective. To have done so would have required that he work out some conception of the relationship between social disorganization and personal disorganization. If social disorganization was inevitably accompanied by some degree of personal disorganization, then the group character of delinquency would tend to assume one form. One would not, for example, expect personally disorganized individuals to be capable of forming groups with a relatively high degree of organization. If it was assumed that social disorganization had no necessary connection with personal disorganization, one might have expected relatively well-organized delinquent groups. Since Shaw avoided this issue, it is difficult to decide what the implications of the social disorganization perspective are relative to the group nature of delinquency.

Finally, Shaw's attempted synthesis did not succeed because of the inadequate use he made of his case-study data. Clinically, he was committed to their value. From the perspective of research he tended to accept the prevalent judgment of his era that such data were inferior in scientific usefulness to quantitative data and served primarily an exploratory function:

> There are those who, while granting the importance of the personal document for diagnosis and treatment, seriously question its value for the purpose of scientific generalization because of its subjective and non-quantitative character. While this is indeed a limitation, nevertheless, it seems to be true that there are many aspects of delinquency which are not, for the present at least, susceptible to treatment by formal statistical methods. While quantitative methods are applicable to a wide range of the more formal aspects of delinquent conduct, some more discerning, though perhaps less exact, method is necessary to disclose the underlying processes involved in the formation of delinquent-behavior trends. Perhaps with the further refinement of such techniques as the questionnaire and personality rating scales, many aspects of delinquent behavior which we now study by means of personal documents will be subject to more objective analysis. [60]

NOTES

1. Ernest W. Burgess and Donald J. Bogue, *Contributions to Urban Sociology* (Chicago: University of Chicago Press, 1964), p. 591.

2. Stuart A. Rice, "Hypotheses and Verifications in Clifford R. Shaw's Studies of Juvenile Delinquency," in Stuart A. Rice, ed., *Methods in Social Science: A Case Book* (Chicago: University of Chicago Press, 1931), p. 550.

3. Ibid.

4. Ibid., p. 553.

5. Ibid., p. 552.

6. Ibid., p. 554.

7. Ibid., p. 556.

8. Clifford R. Shaw, *Delinquency Areas* (Chicago: University of Chicago Press, 1929). Clifford R. Shaw, *The Jack-Roller* (Chicago: University of Chicago Press, 1930). Clifford R. Shaw and Henry D. McKay, *Social Factors in Juvenile Delinquency*, Report on the Causes of Crime, vol. II (Washington, D.C.: National Commission on Law Observance and Enforcement, 1931). Clifford R. Shaw and Maurice E. Moore, *The Natural History of a Delinquent Career* (Chicago: University of Chicago Press, 1931).

Clifford R. Shaw, Henry D. McKay, and James F. McDonald, *Brothers in Crime* (Chicago: University of Chicago Press, 1938). Clifford R. Shaw and Henry D. McKay, *Juvenile Delinquency and Urban Areas* (Chicago: University of Chicago Press, 1942).

9. Clifford R. Shaw et al., *Delinquency Areas* (Chicago: University of Chicago Press, 1929), pp. 198-203.

10. Shaw and McKay. *Social Factors*, p. 60.

11. E. W. Burgess, "Urban Areas in Chicago: An Experiment inSocial Science Research," in ibid., p. 62. Originally published in T. V. Smith and L. D. White, eds., *Chicago: An Experiment in Social Science Research* (Chicago: University of Chicago Press, 1929), pp. 114-117.

12. Shaw and McKay, *Social Factors*, pp. 68-69.

13. Ibid., p. 69.

14. Ibid., p. 71.

15. Ibid., p. 74.

16. Ibid., p. 82

17. Ibid., p. 94.

18. Ibid., p. v.

19. Ibid., p. 4.

20. Roscoe C. Hinkle, Jr., and Gisela J. Hinkle, *The Development of Modern Sociology: Its Nature and Growth in the United States* (Garden City, New York: Doubleday and Company, 1954), p. 36.

21. William I. Thomas and Florian Znaniecki, *The Polish Peasant in Europe and America* (New York: Alfred A. Knopf, 1927), 1: 710-711.

22. Shaw and McKay, *Social Factors*, pp. 99-100.

23. Ibid., p. 103.

24. Thomas and Znaniecki, *The Polish Peasant*, 2: 1777.

25. Shaw and McKay, *Social Factors*, p. 117.

26. Ibid., p. 127.

27. Allen F. Davis, *Spearheads for Reform* (New York: Oxford University Press, 1967).

28. Shaw, McKay, and McDonald, *Brothers in Crime.*

29. Ibid., p. 98.

30. Ibid., p. 99.

31. Ibid.

32. Shaw and McKay, *Juvenile Delinquency*, p. 438. Cited by Solomon Kobrin, "The Formal Logical Properties of the Shaw-McKay Delinquency Theory," in Harwin L. Voss and David M. Petersen, eds., *Ecology, Crime, and Delinquency* (New York: Appleton-Century-Crofts, 1971), p. 111.

33. Shaw, *The Jack-Roller*, pp. 17-18.

34. Rice, *Methods in Social Science*, pp. 550-551.

35. Ibid., p. 551.

36. Ibid., p. 553.

37. E. W. Burgess, "The Study of the Delinquent as a Person," *American Journal of Sociology* 28 (May 1923): 657-680.

38. Shaw, *Delinquency Areas*, pp. 1-2.

39. Clifford R. Shaw and Henry D. McKay, "Rejoinder," *American Sociological*

Review 14 (October 1949): 615, to Christen T. Jonassen, "A Re-evaluation and Critique of the Logic and Some Methods of Shaw and McKay," ibid., 608-614.

40. Shaw and McKay, *Social Factors*, pp. 19-20.

41. James F. Short, Jr., Introduction to *Juvenile Delinquency and Urban Areas*, rev. ed., by Clifford R. Shaw and Henry D. McKay (Chicago: University of Chicago Press, 1969), p. xli.

42. E. W. Burgess, "Discussion," in Shaw, *The Jack-Roller*, p. 197.

43. W. I. Thomas and Dorothy Swaine Thomas, *The Child in America* (New York: Alfred A. Knopf, 1928), pp. 571-572.

44. Shaw, *The Jack-Roller*, p. 3.

45. John Dollard, *Criteria for the Life History* (New Haven: Yale University Press, 1935), p. 189.

46. Ibid., p. 193.

47. Shaw, *The Jack-Roller*, p. 193.

48. Ibid., pp. 165-166.

49. Shaw and McKay, *Social Factors in Juvenile Delinquency*.

50. Ibid., pp. 204, 220-221.

51. Clifford R. Shaw and Maurice E. Moore, *The Natural History of a Delinquent Career* (Chicago: University of Chicago Press, 1931). Shaw, McKay, and McDonald, *Brothers in Crime*.

52. Shaw, McKay, and McDonald, *Brothers in Crime*, pp. 326-328.

53. Rice, *Methods in Social Science*, p. 563.

54. Jane Addams, *The Spirit of Youth and the City Streets* (1909; reprint ed., Urbana, Illinois: University of Illinois Press, 1972).

55. Burgess, "The Study of the Delinquent as a Person," p. 662.

56. Amos H. Hawley, *Human Ecology* (New York: Ronald Press, 1950). Reprinted in part in Walter L. Wallace, ed., *Sociological Theory* (Chicago: Aldine Press, 1969), pp. 64-65.

57. Herbert Blumer, "An Appraisal of Thomas and Znaniecki's *The Polish Peasant in Europe and America,*" *Social Science Council Bulletin* 44 (New York: Social Science Research Council, 1939), p. 29.

58. Robert E. Park, "Human Ecology," in *Human Communities*, ed. E. C. Hughes et al., (Glencoe, Illinois: Free Press, 1952), p. 157. Originally published in *American Journal of Sociology* 42 (July 1936): 1-15.

59. Shaw and McKay, *Social Factors*, p. 109.

60. Shaw, *The Jack-Roller*, p. 21.

chapter 6

The Chicago Area Projects

As a man of ideas who was also a man of action Shaw lived with irony. The originator of the Chicago Area Project, whose primary goals were the prevention and treatment of delinquency, he devoted his life to the exposition of the point of view of the delinquent. From this point of view the delinquent was normal. In insisting on this view Shaw was seeking to remove what he regarded as the incubus of morality from society's response to the delinquent. Nevertheless, Shaw was a very moral man. As long as he lived, his sense of justice was continually outraged by the treatment that the existing correctional system and other social agencies accorded the delinquent. It was, however, an outrage that he scrupulously sought to harness within the impersonal disciplines of social science and rational analysis. It was this fundamental ambiguity, this ceaseless tension between his heart and his head, his moral judgment, and his striving for the objectivity of the scientist, that rendered him so complex and vital a person. One wonders, however, if even Shaw was able to confront with equanimity what was perhaps the fundamental irony resulting from his life work. A novel and exciting approach to the issue of delinquency in the inner-city areas had as one of its most important consequences the provision of an avenue of upward mobility for many of the most conventional and respectable people of these same areas. There was irony in the contrast between his ability to inspire others with his vision of the projects while at the same time being quite limited in his ability to influence their actual course of development. Of course, this limited control was inherent in the very idea of the Chicago Area Project, but it did mean that in many cases the projects inevitably became something other than Shaw would have wished.

Shaw's and McKay's Critique of the Correctional System

The findings of Shaw's research, as interpreted from his distinctive point of view, provided an empirical basis for his critique of the existing correctional system. This critique also posed the challenge to which the Chicago Area Project was a response. In fact, Shaw's deep concern with evaluating the existing system and with seeking to improve it is implicit in the very types of cases that he selected as subjects for his published life histories. These were all identified as recidivists, who had had repeated contacts with the whole gamut of official correctional agencies.

The various criticisms that Shaw and McKay made of the existing delinquency control system derived from the dual features of their perspective. In the first place they sought to view the delinquent as an individual in his own right with his own kind of personal makeup. In the second place they sought to view his behavior as intimately related to his situation in the community. Various features of the existing system were viewed as violating this organic conception of the delinquent, either because they ignored his integrity as a person or the intimate nature of his bonds to his milieu. The fundamental note of criticism is sounded early in Shaw's introduction to *The Jack-Roller*.

An intensive study of the detailed life-histories of more than two hundred young repeated offenders on parole from the St. Charles School for Boys indicates rather clearly the great importance of dealing with the intimate personal aspects of the delinquent's situation. The large amount of failure in probation and parole work is not at all surprising, since the worker is forced, under the pressure of a heavy case load, to deal primarily with the more formal and external aspects of his cases. An essential preliminary step in the effective treatment of any case of

delinquency is to secure a knowledge of the delinquent's personal attitudes and intimate situations as revealed in his "own
story." In many cases this knowledge is to be secured only after
painstaking study and prolonged contact with the delinquent.
In the absence of such knowledge, the worker's relation to his
case is necessarily more or less formal, and the treatment consists chiefly of attempts to gain control and effect judgment
through threats of arrest and punishment.[1]

His criticism, here, was directed against the formality of the relationship between the probation and parole officer and the delinquent.
He thought that the parole officer had too little knowledge about his
cases to permit him to look at the world from the delinquent's point of
view. In such a situation the correctional agent's efforts to control the
conduct of the delinquent assumed the form of threats, the technique
of control that Thomas and Znaniecki had earlier called "ordering
and forbidding." This was in Shaw's eyes the most profound criticism
he made of the existing system because formality and its consequences
violated the individual's integrity as well as forced the system to
operate in ways that virtually ignored his background.

Burgess formulated a similar criticism but in a somewhat different
manner. He was concerned with the implications of the casework approach of his era, which tended to view the individual, rather than the
group and the community, as the target of change:

The life-history of Stanley, taken in conjunction with the facts
on the concentration of delinquency presented in *Delinquency
Areas* and the analysis of boy gang life and organization in
Thrasher's *The Gang*, provide a foundation for new modes of
attack upon the problem of the delinquent and the criminal. Attention has largely been centered upon case work with the individual, but that is only a partial approach. An all-round program will require, in addition, research upon the social factors
in delinquency and the development of techniques of group and
community treatment. This volume is a notable pioneer contribution to that end. . . .

To them [the readers] this autobiography will point the way to
a basic attack on the conditions of boy life in deteriorating
neighborhoods in Chicago. They will become convinced that the

problem of the gangster and the gunman will be to get back to first causes in the neighborhood where traditions teach delinquency and where crime is the most interesting play of children. They will demand a thoroughgoing program of community prevention in place of the present emphasis upon institutional correction, the futility of which is so clearly shown by this volume.[2]

In the *Natural History of the Delinquent Career* Shaw elaborated his criticism of the correctional system, emphasizing the limitations of the legal view of criminality. He recognized that in order to determine the guilt or innocence of the alleged offender that it was necessary to focus upon the criminal act as abstracted from all other considerations of his personal history. He also felt, however, that the legal approach precluded attention to the causal factors involved, the identification of which required that the criminal act be viewed within the context of the individual's life history. It is here that Shaw came closest to a clear statement of his positivism. He commented on *the case* of Sidney, the subject of the *Natural History*, as follows:

It is important to note that in accordance with accepted legal procedure attention was limited, throughout the apprehension, trial, and disposition of this case, to a consideration of evidence bearing strictly upon the question of the innocence or guilt of the defendants. The offense was regarded as an act which was entirely isolated from everything except the defendants' intent and those formal definitions of law which pertain to the type of offense charged in the case. We recognize that it is necessary, in order to prove the innocence or guilt of an offender, to view his delinquency as an isolated act. Furthermore, it is obvious that society must protect itself from the criminal, must deal with instances of crime as they occur, and must devise methods for their repression. It is to this end that laws have been enacted, courts of justice established, and methods of discipline instituted. However, since our accepted legal procedure in cases of adult offenders, as illustrated in the present case, is largely limited to matters bearing directly upon the question of the innocence or guilt of the offender, any consideration of the causal factors involved in the crime is obviously beyond the scope of its inquiry. . . .

The case study of Sidney is presented as a specific illustration
of the need for taking into consideration the whole process of
behavior of the offender in our efforts to understand his specific
offenses. From this standpoint delinquency is viewed, not as an
isolated act, but in its relation to the mental and physical condition of the offender, the whole sequence of events in his life, and
the social and cultural situations in which his delinquent behavior occurred. A delinquent act is part of a dynamic life process,
and it is artificial to view it except as an integral part of that process. Until the delinquency is viewed in relation to its context in
the life-history of the individual, it is not intelligible. Until it is
made intelligible it cannot be effectively treated.[3]

The implication of this criticism is that the legalistic approach alone
could not provide an effective basis for the social response to criminal
behavior. The legal approach, although indispensable, had of necessity to disregard what Shaw viewed as fundamental to his own perspective.

The third target of Shaw's criticism was directed toward institutionalization as a response to delinquency. In addition to the disadvantages of formality, he questioned the efficacy of any kind of institutionalization that gave priority to treatment; Shaw believed that the
priority should be prevention. Shaw was also concerned with the relationship between institutionalization and the tradition of delinquency. Instead of combating the delinquency tradition his life histories
suggested that it tended to nurture it. Institutionalization exerted this
influence through various mechanisms. Most obviously, by bringing
together delinquents of varying degrees of sophistication it facilitated
the transmission of the delinquency heritage. Equally important, because of its emphasis upon the exercise of coercive formal authority, it
tended to generate attitudes of hostility, which found expression in increased identification with the heritage of delinquency.

The findings of Shaw's and McKay's ecological studies provided
documentation for the importance of giving special attention to the
community background of delinquency. Their interpretation of these
data suggested the compelling nature of the pro-delinquency forces in
the local community. Their findings and interpretation cast the
gravest kinds of doubt upon any social response (such as institutionalization) that sent the delinquent back to the setting that had produced
him.

There was one final criticism that Shaw was to direct against the existing delinquency control system. It was advanced during the course of a discussion of the Chicago Area Project, in which he expressed his hopes that it would be able to avoid becoming institutionalized. By implication the established system's ineffectiveness was attributed to its tendency to become preoccupied with its own survival at the cost of remaining detached and critical towards its own functioning:

Unless the Area Project is able to withstand the institutionalizing attitudes which prevail throughout our society, it will in time become as ineffective as all other forms of treatment and prevention machinery. The Area Project will be institutionalized when its interest is focused upon its own reputation and perpetuation and thus becomes protective rather than critical of its methods and achievements.[4]

Shaw was also concerned with the various social agencies, such as the settlement houses, child guidance clinics, and casework agencies, that attempted to do preventive and treatment work among the youth of the inner-city areas. All of these agencies were undergoing significant changes during the early 1920s.

From the time of their origin in the closing decades of the nineteenth century, the settlement houses had sought to distinguish themselves from the casework agencies. They had regarded themselves as serving the neighborhood rather than individuals. However, World War I had made serious inroads into their ability to support themselves financially. After the war they were under great pressure to sacrifice their independence in order to obtain support from community funds, and the lines separating them from other social agencies became increasingly blurred. During the same period settlement house workers began to look at themselves not as social reformers but as professionally trained social workers:

Even more important than the failure to attract financial support was the failure after the war to attract large numbers of dedicated reformers. In general, most of those who chose to become settlement workers in the 'twenties thought of themselves as social workers rather than social reformers, and many were graduates of professional schools of social work. They thus came trained as case workers or recreation experts, and they gradually began to speak of the people they were helping not so much as their neighbors as their clients. . . . They were interested neither in living in a working-class neighborhood nor in remaining at the settlement in the evening to attend meetings of labor unions or reform organizations. They often wanted a home in the suburbs and other trappings of status that earlier residents had taken for granted. Looking at settlement work as a job, they tried consciously to make their work professional. By stripping away much of the sentimental and emotional tradition that had developed in the movement, they lost in the process some of the crusading zeal of the progressive era.[5]

It also became increasingly evident that, despite the impressive contributions that settlement house leaders had made to major social reforms between 1900 and 1915, the potential contribution of the settlement house to its own neighborhood was severely limited.

It [the settlement house] was also, even at its best, an institution of limited success. Its resources were never adequate, depending, as it did, wholly on voluntary giving. In addition, the relations with their own neighborhoods were always tenuous because the social and economic gap between the settlement workers and the local residents was immense and not easily bridged. . . .[6]

Despite everything they did in the neighborhood, the settlement workers remained outsiders. "No one but a member of our own race can really understand us," one immigrant remarked. "No outside agency can undertake to tell my people what to do." . . . The settlement workers, most of them unmarried, had their own life, their own fellowship within the settlement. This meant that they were only artifically a part of the neighborhood.[7]

The most serious gap of all was that between the settlement workers and the men of the neighborhood. Here they succeeded only with the select few who pursued intellectual interests and ambitions:

Perhaps the most serious limitation of all was that the settlements failed to attract the men in the neighborhood; the women and children came, but the men, who were the dominant force in most immigrant families, stayed away. "The social settlement here meant nothing to us men," one immigrant remembered, "we went there for an occasional shower, that was all." . . .

The settlements especially played a part in developing leaders; they influenced only a small number but sometimes the few could be crucial. They helped inspire many young men and women to get an education or to break the dreary pattern of their lives.[8]

Shaw was fully aware of these limitations of the settlement house, limitations that were most marked in its inability to offer conventional activities that would attract delinquents. He was also extremely critical of the individual-oriented social casework agencies. He objected to their focus upon the individual to the point of neglecting the role social environments played. He also objected to their disposition to abandon the problem of the inner-city delinquent. Writing in the middle 1930s and perceptively noting these trends, Healy commented:

In recent years the definite shift away from attempting to deal extensively with the problems of delinquency is due principally to the fact that the clinic cannot have control enough over the individual or over his social situation. Aside from the individuals who become delinquent mainly because of inner conflicts and frustrations, it is plainly discernible that in the complex of factors which make for delinquency there are many social elements, deprivations and pressures that cannot possibly be bettered by clinical effort alone.

The conception that the guidance clinic may be of great aid in a program for the prevention of delinquency remains thoroughly valid, but indispensable for any such program is well-conceived, cooperative, social effort. . . . Whatever is undertaken, I am convinced that any project for the prevention of delinquency will be confronted with the necessity for modification of the spirit or ideology of the community life. . . . As it stands at present in most large communities, it is impossible for child guidance clinics, through their work with individual cases, to be playing any very important part in the prevention of delinquent and criminal careers.[9]

It is possible to summarize Shaw's critique of existing methods for dealing with the delinquent as follows:

1. The relationships between the official control agents and delinquents tended to be distant and impersonal. Attempts to control the latters' behavior consisted primarily of threats, orders, and other coercive measures, which respected neither the distinctive personal makeup of the individual delinquent nor the nature of his ties to his social world.

2. Existing techniques of assisting the delinquent tended to deal with him as an isolated individual in abstraction from his group and community background. The target of change was the individual and not the setting that had produced him and that he would return to.

3. The existing system of delinquency control had hardened into a set of institutionalized practices performed by functionaries whose primary objective was to perpetuate the organizations that employed them.

The common theme running through all of these criticisms is that of social distance or mutual isolation between the control agents and the delinquents. The reasons for this state of affairs varied in different correctional settings. In the case of the probation officer, it was attributed at least partially to the size of his case load. In the case of the social worker, it was attributed to a complex of factors: the individualistic bent of the ideas with which he worked, the professionalism that required that he view himself as providing a service for his client and that required also that he adopt a somewhat paternalistic stance, and the bureaucratization that removed him so completely from the setting of the delinquent. In the case of the correctional institution, the constraints of confinement themselves were regarded as inevitably leading to the isolation of delinquents from staff.

The theme of social distance also runs through the conceptual framework with which Shaw approached and analyzed his data. The concept of social disorganization implied in a very immediate and direct way the breakdown of key social and personal relationships. W. I. Thomas had emphasized the breakdown of relationships among members of the kinship group. Park and Burgess had emphasized the cumulative effect of ecological and social processes, which resulted in the relative isolation of the most recently arrived immigrant groups in the inner-city areas of the city.

Not surprisingly Shaw regarded all these various processes of isolation as being cumulative in their impact upon the young person in the inner-city area. It was out of such processes that he contructed his fundamental image of the delinquent as "disaffiliated," which McKay elaborated on:

> If . . . disruption associated with change is associated with high rates of delinquents, the degree of disruption should be high in the inner-city areas. . . . The proposition presented here is that as a result of this disruption in the inner city most of the basic social institutions are so weak, inadequate, and inconsistent that they do not furnish an adequate framework for the control of the conduct of children. . . .
>
> In extreme form this absence of stabilizing influence is seen among the adolescent males who do not only have the freedom which comes from weak institutional structure, but tend also to be detached from whatever basic institutions there are. For this group, ties with family and church tend to be weak and only the school represents the thread which ties them to respectability.
>
> When the boy finishes school, or leaves school because he cannot get along there, this last thread is broken. . . .
>
> These boys without institutional ties tend, in the inner-city areas, to become identified with one another in groupings often called gangs. . . .
>
> These corner groups and the social-athletic clubs into which some of them develop may be regarded as natural institutions which came into existence to meet the needs of the detached adolescent males.[10]

This analysis suggested that both in the local community and in his contact with correctional institutions, the delinquent as an individual person tended to get lost. Under such conditions the high rate of recidivism was inevitable. Only through personal relationships, it was believed, could effective control be exerted. Shaw and his colleagues thus had to ask themselves how a correctional format could be devised that would be conducive to personal relationships between control agents and delinquents and that would incorporate the latter within a web or network of informal social control.

If the isolation of the young person in the inner city was to be overcome, two kinds of symbolic bridges had to be built: bridges between the adults and young people within the local community and bridges between the local residents and the institutions of the larger community. Each bridge would be contructed out of informal social and personal relationships.

Shaw's response to these criticisms was to inaugurate the Chicago Area Project in 1934. This consisted of a central staff of sociologists and community organizers, whose salaries were paid by the state of Illinois, and several local organizations to which the community organizers were assigned. The policy of the Area Project was arrived at in consultation with a board of directors, who were predominantly businessmen with an interest in innovative approaches to the problems of social welfare. The directors assisted in fund raising, acted as spokesmen to the welfare establishment, and sponsored a number of research projects in juvenile delinquency, adult criminality, and drug addiction. The sociologists on the central staff carried on research and consulted with the various community projects when requested. The contribution of the state to the local projects was restricted to the salaries of the community organizers. Occasionally, some supplemental funds were provided by the central board of directors, but for the most part each community financed its own program.

The local projects were organizations of the residents in the areas of the city with the highest rates of delinquents. Shaw and his colleagues considered it essential to recruit local leaders who would initiate and support indigenous community organizations to promote youth welfare. All residents of a community could become members, but project leaders made a special effort to involve those who played important roles in the formal and informal structures of local community life, regardless of the moral or legal standing of such persons from an outsider's perspective. They hoped that the structure of the projects would provide these new organizations with a solid base of support among the local residents. Each project had a community committee, which was composed of local residents who ideally joined it both as representatives of other community groups as well as an expression of their own personal commitment.

Each of these community committees was an independent unit operated under the guidance of a board of directors chosen from the general membership of local community residents. Each project was also a cooperative venture with the state of Illinois, which made available trained staff and initial financial assistance. At first the responsible state agency was the Illinois Department of Welfare working through the Institute for Juvenile Research; later it was the the Illinois Youth Commission; and most recently it has been the Department of Corrections. The staff organization of these community committees included one program director recruited from the local residents, whose salary was paid by the state, and additional community workers employed either full time or part time, who were remunerated from private sources. Much of the work of the community committees was also done by volunteers. To assist in the work of the various community committees, the Chicago Area Project was organized to provide funds from private sources to supplement those of the state and those raised by the committees themselves. Is also acted as sponsor for a number of research projects carried out by a professional staff working at the central office.

The first projects were initiated in three areas: South Chicago, the Near North Side, and Near West Side. The number of such projects has since continued to grow, and today twenty community committees continue to function in Chicago. In addition numerous groups in many other urban and smaller communities of the state have taken the projects as the model for the organization of their own delinquency control programs.

Such organizations had three goals. First, they were to provide a forum in which the local residents could become acquainted with new scientific perspectives on such topics as child rearing, child welfare, and juvenile delinquency. Second, they were to take the initiative in opening up new channels of communication between local residents and the many institutional representatives of the larger world who played such an influential part in determining the life chances of the local youth. Overtures were to be made to such significant authority figures as schoolteachers and principals, playground directors, juvenile court judges, probation officers, and employers. The third goal was to bring adults into contact with the youth of their own community and particularly the delinquent youth.

It was in the third area of social action that the most imaginative experimentation occurred. In the search for modes of approach to which the local youngsters would be responsive, the members of the various community committees experimented with a great variety of ideas. Some attempted to work directly with gangs. In some instances, ex-offenders were used as youth workers. The development of ties with individual offenders led to supportive efforts on their behalf in court appearances. Some communities began to work with institutionalized offenders. Others provided summer camping and other recreational facilities. Such a broad range of programs gave scope to the varied talents seeking to cope with the myriad forms assumed by youth problems. Through such kinds of intervention it was hoped to reestablish the bonds between youth and adults and to improve the access of young people to the educational, recreational, and occupational structures of the larger society. This whole range of imaginative initiatives represented an effort to revivify the reality of community in the experience of young people.

The spirit and temper in which the area projects were conceived is well reflected in a report Shaw made in 1944:

> The Chicago Area Project was inaugurated . . . for the purpose of developing an experimental program for the treatment and prevention of delinquency in a limited number of low-income communities which for many years had been characterized by disproportionately high rates of delinquency and crime despite the ever growing number of programs, agencies, and institutions established to cope with the problem. Even in low-income communities of Chicago and other large cities, where especially concentrated effort has been made to treat and prevent delinquency, juvenile delinquency and crime among youth have continued in undiminished volume through the years. Without experimentation and critical evaluation of methods, there was little prospect of discovering more effective means of coping with this social problem. It was for the purpose of testing new methods of treatment and prevention that *The Chicago Area Project* was established.
>
> It is our hope that *The Chicago Area Project* may continue to operate in the spirit of experimentation and inquiry. If

we operate in this spirit, we should be as willing to record and accept our failures as we are our successes. In fact, we are not truly scientific unless we are willing to face complete and absolute failure in our attempt to deal with the problem of delinquency. It is my profound conviction that experimentation is necessary to discover the most fruitful way to serve the interests of delinquent children and offers the greatest prospect for discovering methods or procedures by which the volume of delinquency may be reduced. [11]

The Area Projects and the Urban Political Machine: An Analogy

The area projects, I would like to argue, followed the urban political machine as their organizational model. Each political machine was organized around the personality of its boss and was known by his name. It was a personal creation. In accounts such as one finds in the autobiography of Lincoln Steffens the essential framework of leadership was provided by the boss and his lieutenants. [12] There was total trust between them primarily because of their total dependence upon him. Shaw's field lieutenants were the "indigenous workers." They were selected, typically, from among the people whom they were to serve. They were also required to have additional qualifications— organizational ability, a profound interest in people, an equally profound knowledge of the local society, and the ability to live comfortably with moral and legal diversity. The indigenous worker was Shaw's answer to the professionally trained social worker. He believed that one of the reasons the social workers of this era were unable to enter into personal relationships with delinquents was because of the attitudes of expertise and superiority that they had absorbed during the course of their higher education. He was not opposed to education but he was concerned with what he regarded as its unfortunate by-products. Accordingly, with some exceptions, the individuals whom he selected were not college educated, although not a few of them were subsequently to obtain such an education. The unanticipated result of recruiting individuals with such qualifications was, of course, to intensify their dependence upon him. No boss's lieutenant was ever more dependent upon his leader than were Shaw's indigenous workers upon him.

It has been argued that the special development of the political machine in America was closely tied to the process of immigration. The machine, an organizational form in which votes were exchanged for services, was adapted to the ethnic differences among the newly arrived immigrants and to the variety of experiences of these different groups. It provided a framework through which ethnic groups could find a basis of integration within their own community and with the larger community. The Chicago Area Project, like the political machine, tended to be organized around ethnic communities. There were projects that were predominantly, if not exclusively, Italian, Polish, Mexican, and black. Shaw pragmatically turned this feature of the city into one of the key assets of his organization. Aside from its parallelism with the political machine, this development would not be particularly noteworthy except for the fact that in all their research Shaw and McKay scrupulously avoided making any reference to ethnicity as a factor with any revelance for delinquency.

So far the parallels between the political machine and the area projects may appear to be relatively obvious. Others are less obvious. I would also like to argue that there was a resemblance in the amorality that became an integral part of the projects. Shaw approached the problem of delinquency from a peculiar angle of vision. By regarding it as a normal response of persons to the situation of the inner city, he was able to avoid making any moral judgment about the local residents. Those who participated in illegitimate activities were not viewed as necessarily being committed to illegitimate values. People did what they had to do in order to survive and get ahead in the world, but this was not an indication of their true beliefs and commitments. Underlying it was a belief that all people fundamentally shared a common consensus concerning conventional values. If this were the case, then it should be possible to mobilize all types of people in the "delinquency area" to support youth welfare and juvenile delinquency prevention programs—hence, Shaw's capacity to envisage men with records as fit individuals to work in such programs. It was a position that exalted the common humanity of individuals.

The Project: Idea and Practice

On the face of it the Chicago Area Project appeared to be an unassailable idea. Because delinquency was fundamentally a process that occurred in the local milieu, it was a process that could be brought under control by the people of the local milieu. To individuals moving away from the fatalistic attitudes of their peasant background toward American attitudes of seeking to bring about change through voluntary association, the idea must have appeared as a revelation. No matter how appealing the idea in practice, however, it would not have taken root among various segments of people living in the inner-city areas of Chicago unless conditions were favorable to the idea.

In understanding why the idea worked as well as it did the historical timing of the development must be carefully noted. The idea of the area project was introduced and became established during the 1930s when the second generation of such ethnic groups as the Italians and Poles were passing through adolescence and attaining adulthood and becoming an increasingly important factor in the social organization of these communities. Indeed, William F. Whyte's description of the Italian ethnic community in Boston in the 1930's can easily be construed as a situation in which the social organization of this community was substantially under the control of the second generation. [13] As Whyte also points out, it was a generation that felt keenly the cleavage separating it from the mainstream of the American community. How was this cleavage to be overcome? Upward mobility through education involved great costs for the individual. The other route upward led through the rackets. The significant majority who were neither college trained nor in the rackets thus had to grope for some channel toward greater participation in American life without betraying their ethnic fellows. The difficulties of their position were aggravated by the coming of the depression itself, with its reduction in the opportunities for upward mobility.

By the 1930s immigration had declined to a trickle for several years. This drying up the sources of new recruits for the ethnic communities, it can be conjectured, led to certain significant changes in the social organization of inner-city ethnic communities. It has frequently been noted that the vitality of ethnic institutions, such as the churches, lodges, mutual insurance, and various cultural activities, are greatly dependent upon newcomers. With the slackening in the numbers of such arrivals, the vitality of such institutions tends to undergo decline. The same decline should also affect the unquestioning support of ethnic group members for the political machines. Greater sophistication, particularly on the part of the second generation, would tend to loosen the ties of dependence upon the political boss, particularly if he was identified with another ethnic group. The old paternalistic relationship would tend to decline. The import of such trends is that there was some degree of slack in the social organization of the ethnic community. There would be a deficiency in institutional channels through which the second generation of males might attain status and develop collective means for dealing with their problems. This gap would be felt particularly acutely by those not involved in the rackets.

The area project idea took hold as well as it did because it provided an organizational form for a whole segment of the local population who were without adequate institutional resources and who felt intensely their exclusion from the life of the wider society. It follows from this analysis that the motivation to organize provided by the delinquency problem itself was only secondary.

The Project as Social Movement

Several commentators on the Chicago Area Project have suggested that it could be appropriately interpreted as a social movement. According to Gusfield social movements are "socially shared activities and beliefs directed toward the demand for change in some aspect of the social order."[14] If we accept this definition, then the question is suggested as to what aspects of the social order the project was directed against. We believe that it may be interpreted as a protest movement against the impersonality of the city. It was in some sense also a movement of liberation, but in a very general sense as indicated by Park, who wrote about the oppressiveness of the larger formal institutions in the urban community. By seeking to humanize the delinquent, it sought also to humanize all of the residents within the inner-city area.

Another indication of its character as a social movement was that it had a distinctive rhetoric, composed primarily of some frequently reiterated phrases and slogans, which comprised a rudimentary yet nevertheless quite effective ideology. These phrases were: "indigenous institutions versus imposed institutions," "indigenous worker," and "local residents" or the "community." The reference in each case is toward a strong polarization between in-group and out-group, which presupposes that the in-group is characterized by some shared identity or other bond that clearly demarcates it from the members of the out-group. The line between in-group and out-group, however, was never made clear. In some contexts it appeared to refer to a specific locality, although in practice such boundaries were never clearly designated. The reference of the "imposed institution" was not solely to locality. It actually referred to a class institution. Settlement houses and schools, for example, were imposed institutions because in defining policy they did not involve the constituencies whom they served. Another reason was that their management was in the hands of people from a different social class. Imposed institutions were those run by outsiders ("outsiders" referred to some vague combination of a different locality, class, and ethnic group). Conversely, the reference of "indigenous institutions" was equally vague. For example, would local rackets be indigenous institutions? What is important, however, is not the precision in the denotation of these terms but their utility as rhetoric. Here the idea of the imposed institution became a shorthand phrase for a complex of feelings on the part of the local people: protest because their wishes on policy and operation were being ignored by powerful outsiders, resentment at the lack of understanding they received in such settings, and a feeling of resignation that at best not much could be expected from such organizations. Indigenous groups referred to spheres of understanding, participation, and warm personal relations.

Both the denotations and connotations of the community worker are much easier to specify. He was a man from the people who also kept the common touch. If he were college educated or in the midst of obtaining such an education, he was careful not to make any public show of his intellectuality. The distinctive forte of the indigenous worker was his understanding of the people he worked with and his easy accessibility. In the competence of his performance he suggested the substantial capacity of the in-group for providing their own leadership and organizing to meet their own needs. Since they typically made some contribution toward his financial support he was also testimony to the responsible manner in which they approached community problems.

The Functioning Projects

Bright Shadows in Bronzetown, written by the Southside Community Committee, provides a description of how a community committee, the Southside Community Committee, came to be organized.[15] The various stages involved in organizing the local residents was more or less typical.

In the early 1940s the Southside area exhibited one of the highest rates of delinquency in the city of Chicago, which made it a prime target for the Chicago Area Project. The moment appeared to be propitious: a group of prominent residents from the area was interested in the project, and a sympathetic governor in the state capital was willing to draw upon special sources of funds in order to provide financial support.

The first stage was one of consultation with the professional staff members of the area projects. Local residents were encouraged and assisted to inform themselves about the nature of the problem of juvenile delinquency in the locality. They also examined the existing structure of services to youth by the police, the correctional system, and the social agencies. The severity of the problem, its many ramified and symbiotic linkages with the life of the local community, and the inadequacies of existing delinquency control policies were explored. Area project ideas on the important role local adults could play were also explored. Finally a group of interested leaders agreed to organize as the Southside Community Committee. Funds for the operation, including the support for the community workers were obtained, and the first operation was set up operating out of a storefront in a large apartment building.

The conception of social intervention that underlay the area projects was that which Diesing has called "working within the system." This is the type of intervention that is based upon intensive knowledge of the "system," whether a person or a community. It is the type of knowledge that Diesing indicates takes the form of the case study:

> "Working within the system" may take a great variety of forms. Essentially the worker brings his personal resources into the system and uses them there; and there can be great variation in the resources brought in, the roles in which they are used, and the problems on which they are used. The worker may take an ordinary role or a leadership role; he may provide emotional support or intellectual challenge; he may act like a politician, mediating conflicts and interpreting conflicting parties to each other, or he may take an agitator's role, championing and stir-

ring up some oppressed or forgotten part of the system; he may work internally, interpreting the system to itself and bringing unrecognized parts to public attention; or he may work externally as an interpreter and a liaison between a system and its environing systems.

To work effectively within a system in any of these ways, a worker needs knowledge: knowledge of the main problems of the system, its resources for dealing with these problems, and by inference, what additional resources would be helpful. [16]

Working within the system permitted the community workers to adjust their techniques to the situation in which they worked. This adaptability is illustrated in the following comparison of the techniques they used as they attempted to assist adult parolees returning to the Italian and Polish communities. Note particularly the varying approach to the family of the offender in each case.

> Italian community workers would only tend to become involved in the case of an offender after the latter's family had solicited their assistance. Thereafter, all work with the offender was done in co-operation with the offender's family and, as far as possible, through reliance upon its resources. Commonly, contact with the offender through visits and correspondence was initiated while he was still in prison. Either the community worker himself, or some associate, frequently the "chairman of the adult parole committee" of the local community organization, sought to establish a personal relationship with the offender as a peer. Such a bond would conform to a pattern long familiar to Italian offenders. Its novelty in this particular context lay in the purposive and controlled manner in which it was utilized so as to provide channels of re-entry to conventional roles in the free community for the offender.

> . . . It [the program] presupposed the centrality of the family as a key resource and exploited to the full the importance of peer-group relationships among adult males. . . . Taking cognizance of the role played by familial relationships in the Italian community also contributes to an understanding of the mechanism through which an interest in reforming criminal offenders,

tenuous as it was, could be generated. The selection of indigenous "volunteers," and in particular of those adult males who consented to serve in the office of "chairman of the adult parole committee," was not a random process. Some familial experience, such as a familial tie to the prisoner, or perhaps the occurrence of similar types of problems within their own families, appeared to be necessary to stimulate a reformative interest in Italian males.

In taking for granted that under appropriate conditions Italian offenders would find the work role quite attractive, the program was on solid ground. One gathers that, over the long haul, the heroes of the illegitimate opportunity structure had to compete against the glory and esteem which accrued to another type of culture hero, the workingman who was also a family man. One of the Italian informants gave the following description of such an exemplar, his brother: "When I look at it today I see it ——'s way. ———, in fact, is one of the most impressive guys in the neighborhood today. He got married and settled down, he's got a trade, he drives a new car, he's got two good sons, and when he goes into the neighborhood everybody is real glad to see him. He is really respected in the sense that he is a man."

The techniques employed by the Polish community workers were perhaps ideologically similar but actually quite different in practical application. The initiative in working with a case was generally taken by the worker and only rarely by the offender's family. In all cases, the community worker would attempt to interest family members in assisting the offender. The key relationship, however, was that between the worker and the offender. Indeed, not infrequently the community worker's job was as much to protect the offender from his familial relationships as it was to use the family as a resource. . . .[17]

Evaluation of the Project

The conception of the Chicago Area Project as a social movement needs to be balanced by recognition of its tendencies toward institutionalization. To the extent that it did so, of course, it represented the very kind of development that Shaw was trying to prevent.

There was a tendency for some of the community committees to distance themselves from the problem of juvenile delinquency. True, in some communities the problem of juvenile misbehavior was so pervasive and intractable that it would have swamped the resources of the community committee if it had attempted to confront the problem in all of its dimensions. Confronted with this issue, however, some of the committees merely carved out a segment of the problem with which the members felt more competent and able to deal with. Others tended to avoid the problem completely. In such communities, in effect, the work of the projects was unable to overcome the stigma that attached locally to association in any capacity with those who had juvenile or adult records. In such cases even the community worker, because of his intimacy with such individuals as part of his work, came to share in the stigma. The conflict over this matter was intensified by the concern with upward mobility manifested by many committee members.

The second feature that was conducive to institutionalization is to be attributed to the community workers themselves. Because of the criteria according to which they had been selected, they had difficulties in conforming to any conventional notion of career. They were qualified, and in many instances superbly qualified, to do their jobs as community workers. Any advancement beyond this status became quite problematic. Several obtained college educations and moved on to other types of work. Those who did not found that their marginality increased as they advanced. Some, understandably, felt uneasy in the role of aging boys' worker. Given this insecurity in their position there was a strong tendency for them to attain a kind of vested interest in their local organization. They took steps to mold the organization around themselves. Concomitantly they tended to become protective and defensive about their local organizations. They directed and channeled them into safe types of activities at which they could succeed. They cultivated support for themselves from the people of the locality, and they sought to make the organization completely dependent upon themselves. It was for this reason, among others, that it became increasingly difficult to evaluate these projects in any comprehensive and rigorous fashion as time went on. As Kobrin has indicated, these were not, of course, the only reasons:

The Chicago Area Project shares with other delinquency prevention programs the difficulty of measuring its success in a
simple and direct manner. At bottom this difficulty rests on the
fact that such programs, as efforts to intervene in the life of a
person, a group, or a community, cannot by their very nature
constitute more than a subsidiary element in changing the fundamental and sweeping forces which create the problems of
groups and of persons or which shape human personality. Declines in rates of delinquents—the only conclusive way to evaluate a delinquency prevention program—may reflect influences
unconnected with those of organized programs and are difficult
to define and measure.[18]

In contrast to the obstacles associated with the use of rates of delinquents, the functioning of the community committees has permitted
more confident judgments to be made. Perhaps the most balanced
general evaluation of the Chicago Area Project was made by Witmer
and Tufts in a study for the U.S. Children's Bureau';

 1. Residents of low income areas can and have organized
 themselves into effective working units for promoting and con-
 ducting welfare programs.
 2. These community organizations have been stable and enduring. They raise funds, administer them well, and adapt the
 programs to local needs.
 3. Local talent, otherwise untapped, has been discovered and
 utilized. Local leadership has been mobilized in the interest of
 children's welfare.[19]

It is desirable to go beyond the summary impressions of competent
observers to seek to identify the specific conditions that tend to favor
or to limit the relative effectiveness of the area project approach to
community organization. Such questions as the following are suggested for inquiry: What are the criteria of an effectively functioning
community committee? Are all types of local community equally
hospitable to the development of effective community committees? If
not, is it possible to specify the types of community settings that are
more or less amenable to the development of such committees?
  It is possible to throw some light on these matters by drawing upon

a report prepared in 1962 by a governor's survey committee to survey the Illinois Youth Commission. [20] As part of its investigation a consultant was employed to visit a representative sample of the community committees operating in the Chicago area. His observations were sufficiently detailed to permit a comparison of some aspects of the functioning of the various community committees. The first task of analysis was to establish criteria of the relative effectiveness of the community committee operations. Perhaps the basic notion upon which such operations were based was that inner-city areas possessed many resources, hitherto unutilized, which could be mobilized to cope with delinquency. Specifically, the reference was to such things as the capacity to supply leadership and raise funds, and to the existence of indigenous organizations and groups with some potential for making a contribution to the cause of youth welfare. Starting from such premises, it was possible to formulate the following criteria:

1. *The relative capacity of the organization of local residents to raise funds.* To the various allusions already made to the capacity of inner-city residents to contribute toward the financing of their own welfare enterprises may be added the following statement from a report of the Illinois Youth Commission for the biennial period 1959-1960: "It seems highly significant that, through the years, the funds expended by the Youth Commission and the services rendered by its staff members have been more than matched on a statewide basis by funds raised locally and by volunteer services donated toward community programs of youth welfare." [21]

2. *The relative degree of autonomy of the community committee.* It was reasoned that the greater the autonomy and initiative in evidence in the operation of the community committee, the greater the likelihood that important human resources in the local community were being mobilized to deal with the problem of delinquency.

3. *The motivations of local residents for joining the organization.* One of the assumptions underlying the project was that it would be possible to recruit local residents who were sufficiently well organized as individuals to be able to contribute to the reconstruction of community life. To the extent that community committees were comprised of members who joined primarily to seek assistance for their own problems, they would tend to have a less solid and competent membership base.

4. *The relative degree of integration of the members of the commu-*

nity committee into the local social structures. One of the goals of the Chicago Area Project was to develop voluntary associations that would be linked to the local networks of social relationships by seeking to recruit committee members who were integral parts of such networks. To the extent that it succeeded in doing so, it would be able to open up channels of communication within the local community, which would serve to enhance the influence of the community committee. In contrast, a community committee whose membership was restricted to relatively isolated unaffiliated individuals would be quite limited in the scope of its local influence.

When these various criteria were applied to the materials available in the reports, it became evident that they all tended to classify the various community committees in the same way. The results suggested the existence of two types of community committees, one of which was consistently capable of mobilizing more, and more varied, types of human and financial resources than the other. The analysis, then, appeared to have uncovered two types of community organizations, which, for purposes of reference, were designated the strong and weak community committees. In what follows the evidence for this classification is presented under each of the four evaluative criteria.

1. *The relative capacity of the organization of local residents to raise funds.* The various community committees were able to raise the following amounts of funds during 1959:

Strong Community Committees

Near Northwest Civic Committee	$13,500
Hegewisch Community Committee	6,350
Rolling Meadows Police Juvenile Advisory Commission (not available)	

Weak Community Committees

North Central Community Committee	$ 400
Lawndale Community Committee	1,200
Midwest Youth and Community Committee	8,000
Beatrice Caffrey Youth Service	
North Side Community Committee	50
South East Community Committee	600

Ida B. Wells Community Committee	500
East Englewood Community Committee	—
St. Andrews Community Committee	400
Altgeld Gardens Community Committee	—
Mid South Side Community Committee	1,200

On the whole, these data suggest that the financial argument advanced in a blanket fashion to justify the project approach should realistically be qualified in the light of differences among local communities.

2. *The relative degree of autonomy of the community organization.* One of the basic premises underlying the Chicago Area Project was that the local residents should be encouraged to assume responsibility for their own youth welfare enterprises. The staff worker assigned by the state was to act solely as a consultant and resource person. The clarity with which these standards and goals were formulated was, in part, a reaction against the subordinate role in which the local residents had been assigned in the traditional welfare and youth-serving agencies. A number of indexes suggest that the goal of local autonomy was much closer to realization in the strong as contrasted with the weak organizations.

In the first place, each of the strong organizations had an independent facility—a storefront or some similar location—as a base for its operations, which provided a setting within which the organization could promote its youth welfare endeavor with a maximum of flexibility and freedom from outside interference. Independent facilities are perhaps equally important as a visible symbol of the autonomy of the local residents and of their freedom from dependence upon specific persons, institutions, or power groups. A facility located in the basement of a housing project or in a police station may be the location for some excellent work by local residents, but it is not either in reality or symbol a manifestation of the autonomy of the local residents. All the weak organizations, with one exception, were without an independent base of operation.

A second index of autonomy is the degree of dependence of the local organization upon the staff worker assigned by the state. Each of the strong community organizations appeared to have sufficient momentum, structure, and general awareness of the value of their youth welfare enterprise to assure their own continuity despite the loss of their present state worker. It is quite apparent that the weak organizations would collapse immediately upon the departure of the present worker. Conversely, the state worker in a strong organization is free to turn his attention to broader objectives such as delinquency prevention, community projects, and cooperative relationships with other private and public agencies. In a weak organization, such an excessive proportion of the state worker's energies is taken up with merely attempting to maintain the local enterprise that he has little time to promote the broader objectives of youth welfare.

A third index of autonomy is provided by the extent to which the members of the community committee assume initiative and responsibility for managing the program and determining policy. Evidence that they are dependent upon outsiders in these respects suggests that paternalism rather than autonomy tends to prevail in the local organization.

3. *The motivations of local residents for joining the organization.* The consultant's observations suggest that there were three types of motivation to account for persons' willingness to participate in community committees.

a. A personal commitment to the value of youth welfare.

b. A desire to maintain or improve their social status or a wish to promote other interests, such as business, politics, or the goodwill of the local community. What such motivations share in common is that they are quite distinct from any interest in youth welfare or delinquency prevention.

c. The use of the local organization as a means of coping with a personal problem; for example, an individual might join the community committee in order to seek assistance for a relative or friend in a correctional institution, seeking parole, or who perhaps is in legal difficulty.

The strong and the weak community organizations appeared to differ in the distribution of the types of motivation characteristic of their memberships. The strong organizations appeared to attract a membership with all three motivations. The persons of higher socioeconomic standing, mainly local businessmen, who provided the leadership and the major part of the financial support, tended to participate for status reasons or because of their interest in youth welfare. The persons of lower socioeconomic standing, the members of the working class, tended to join in order to receive support and assistance in coping with the problem of some family member. The weak community organizations tended to be built rather exclusively around the latter type of member. An individual who joins with the primary purpose of obtaining assistance for a relative may, through participation, come to broaden his perspective and make a valuable contribution. Nevertheless, it appears that a group comprised of a high proportion of such persons will have difficulty in developing into a stable and active community organization.

4. *The relative degree of integration of the members of the community committee into the local social structures.* It is important that the local organization be linked by channels of communication and overlapping membership with other important groupings in the community. The inclusion of at least some such members in the group gives the organization of local residents a representative character. If strategically placed within the social structure of the local community, it does not itself need to be a large and unwieldy group. But such placement does give it a much larger public and constituency to which it can turn for financial and political support. The strong community organizations tended thus to ramify beyond their own immediate boundaries. The weak community organizations tended to be isolated groupings.

Since the application of the area project ideas appears to have generated two distinct types of community committee and since such committees are regarded as a precondition of any effective attempt to deal with delinquency, it becomes relevant to inquire into the conditions under which each has tended to develop. On the whole the stronger community committees have been in existence considerably longer—for more than twenty years in the case of the Near Northwest Civic and Hegewisch community committees. Although the Rolling Meadows operation was much more recently initiated, all of the residents are homeowners. Each of these communities appears to be relatively stabilized. Each appears, moreover, to have an adequate supply of persons sufficiently knowledgeable, experienced, economically secure, and motivated to seek status and recognition through involvement in community projects. For the most part such persons tend to come from the business and professional groups where their business, political, or social interests tend to focus their attention upon the local community and its conditions. It is, therefore, an advantage for indigenous community organizations if the local population has some di-

versity in socioeconomic composition. Finally, each of these commu-
nites manifests a high level of morale as exhibited by their commitment to the value of attacking local problems cooperatively.

The weaker organizations are found either in rapidly changing
neighborhoods where a general disorder in social life is prevalent or in
housing projects where population tends to be exceedingly homogeneous, clustered at the lower end of the income scale, and relatively
isolated from the rest of the community. In such situations it cannot
be routinely expected that the leadership for taking hold of indigenous welfare enterprises will be readily forthcoming.

Perhaps the most important factor that differentiates between the
strong and weak community committees is the relative level of rates of
delinquents of the communities in which they are situated. From the
data presented in table 1, it is evident that as contrasted with the weak
community committees, which tend to be located in communities with
high rates of delinquents, the strong community committees tend to
be located in communities with *substantially lower rates*. On the basis
of this relationship it is possible to conclude that those local communities where the problem of juvenile delinquency is comparatively
greater are less amenable to the development of indigenous community organizations. It is also apparent that community committees in
such areas are placed under considerable strain in attempting to
achieve the goals of the area project. Confronted on one hand by the
local concentration of all forms of juvenile violative behavior and on
the other by the considerable difficulty of organizing and maintaining
an indigenous community committee, the community worker is likely
to be overwhelmed by the varied demands of his task.

Indeed, in seeking to cope with the problem of delinquency, community committees in the high-rate areas are likely to find themselves
caught on the horns of a dilemma. If they define the scope of their concern as encompassing the total volume of delinquency in the local
area, their impact is likely to be quite superficial. Alternatively, the
community committee may seek to scale down its objectives by carving out a limited domain in relation to the more manageable aspects
of youth problems. Regardless of how the dilemma of confronting
youth problems on a local community basis with limited resources is
resolved, the conclusion is strongly suggested that the Chicago Area
Project has not provided a method of coping with the problem of delinquency in its most serious form in the areas of the city with the
highest rates.

The present study suggests some of the limitations encountered by the area project in its practical application. If one crucial measure of its effectiveness is the quality and quantity of human resources that can be mobilized within a local community to cope with the problem of delinquency, it is evident that inner-city communities differ considerably in such a capacity. Particularly at a disadvantage are those areas associated with the problem of delinquency in its most aggravated form in the contemporary metropolis.

The Contribution of the Chicago Area Projects

In his article "Community Organization and Juvenile Delinquency" (1925), Park anticipated an era in which advances in delinquency control would develop from the collaboration of experimentally oriented social agencies and the new social science. [22] What he had envisioned was never better realized than through the medium of the Chicago Area Projects. Indeed, the whole conception of these projects reflects his views of the problems of social control in the city. For Park, the modern world reached its epitome in the social contrasts of the large city. City communities, in his view, confronted a paradoxical situation in attempting to establish effective modes of social control. While the impersonal world of the city became increasingly dependent upon the law as a form of social control, the only effective agency of social control continued to be the primary group with its basis in personal relationships. Park viewed juvenile delinquency as arising out of the discrepancy between the distant formal demands of the law and the institutions that enforced it and the spontaneous life of the primary group. If social control among youth was to be effective some means would have to be found to align the support of the primary group world within which youth lived in favor of conformity with the law and its institutions.

It was this idea that informed the Chicago Area Projects. The instruments for making it work were the adults of inner-city communities where the breakdown in the control exerted by the law was most severe—not adults as isolated individuals but adults as functioning members of the various groupings and institutions located in the inner-city. The idea that through organization they could make an impact upon the youth problem in their communities was an attractive and deceptively simple one. It proved, however, to be effective

TABLE 1

Community Area Number, Rate of Delinquents, and Percentile Rank of Strong and Weak Community Committees, 1958-1962

	COMMUNITY AREA NUMBER	RATE OF DELINQUENTS*	PERCENTILE RANK
Strong Community Committees			
Near Northwest Civic Committee	24	11.6	68.2
Hegewisch Community Committee	55	5.9	41.2
Rolling Meadows	—	—	—
Weak Community Committees			
North Central Community Committee	8	25.0	95.3
Lawndale Community Committee	29	28.1	96.6
Midwest Youth and Community Committee	27	24.9	93.3
Beatrice Caffrey Youth Service, Community Area	35	22.3	86.5
Beatrice Caffrey Youth Service, Community Area	38	30.3	98.0
	40	20.7	83.1

*The rates of delinquents published in this table were taken from a mimeographed release published by Henry D. McKay, Chief, Division of Social Relations, Institute for Juvenile Research, Chicago, Illinois, April 1962, with the title "Rates of Delinquents by Communities in Chicago 1958-61." This release included the following comments on the sources of data from which these rates were constructed.

The attached rates of male delinquents for Chicago's seventy-five communities are based on the number of male individuals brought before the Family Court of Cook County on delinquency petition during the four year period 1958-61, and the aged 12-16 male population as reported in the 1960 United States Census of Population. . . .

These rates of delinquents by communities in Chicago represent the seventh series of such rates released by the Sociology Department of the Institute for Juvenile Research. The first five of these series were based on juvenile males who appeared in Court on delinquency petition for the first time during seven year periods at selected intervals during the first fifty years of the Court's history. The population base used in the calculations was the number of males 10-16 years of age at the mid-year of the series. The rates presented here, as well as those in the 1954-57 series, are based on cross section studies, that is, they are based on enumeration of all boys (not just first offenders) who came to court on delinquency petition during a four year period. For these two series the population base used in the calculation was changed to include only males 12-16 years of age. In all instances the rates have been based on a count of individuals and not on court appearances.

These and previous rates of delinquents have been computed primarily to indicate the differences in rates among communities, and to establish the relative rather than the absolute magnitude of the rates in the different areas. For such purposes one method of collecting data, one age base, and one method of calculating rates, is about as good as another.

Source: Division of Social Relations, Institute for Juvenile Research, Chicago, Illinois, April 1962.

only in special historical and social situations. It presupposed a type of community in which disorder and the breakdown of controls were juxtaposed with elements of stability and organization. It also presupposed the existence of a coherent primary group system supported by functioning institutional structures. Wherever the area project was effective it was able to call upon institutional strengths rooted in the local community, such as the church, the kinship group, and sometimes the rackets. Where the disorder characterizing a community was so great as to preclude the existence of such established institutions with a stake in the area, the area project idea tended to become more form than substance. In retrospect it is unrealistic to have expected the area projects to be able to develop effective community organizations out of whole cloth.

Recognition that the area project idea can thrive only in certain restricted types of settings may provide a reason why in its original form it did not spread beyond Chicago. The highest rates of delinquency have typically tended to occur in the most severely disorganized communities, those most deprived of institutional resources. The situation might be phrased as follows: If a community has a high rate of delinquents, the organization of an area project will not make much difference; if it has a low rate of delinquents it does not need the area project.

It is such factors that probably help to account for the kind of influence that the Chicago Area Projects actually exercised. It was not its original design but some of its component ideas that were subsequently to prove so influential. Separate themes, such as those of the "indigenous worker," "street gang worker," "reaching out," and the use of "ex-cons," were each picked up and utilized widely in other contexts during the post-World War II era. Such ideas had been generated by the area project in response to the rigidities and lack of responsiveness to the legitimate needs and aspirations of the residents of inner-city areas shown by the social agencies of the 1920s, 1930s, and 1940s. The post-World War II era experienced the rapid growth and bureaucratization of both the private and public agencies serving the residents of the inner-city areas. These developments were intensified by the immense growth of the welfare state, on the one hand, and the expansion of disorganized communities, on the other. The implications of the bureaucratization and rigidities of the social service agencies again had to be confronted. The seminal ideas of the Chicago

Area Project were revived in all their force and relevance in response to a parallel in situations. It is noteworthy that these themes of the indigenous worker and the others all imply an attempt to reduce the impersonality of the situation in which services are provided to people in slum communities. Park's insight continued to remain valid.

NOTES

1. Clifford R. Shaw, *The Jack-Roller* (Chicago: University of Chicago Press, 1930), pp. 17-18.

2. Ernest W. Burgess, "Discussion," in ibid., p. 196.

3. Clifford R. Shaw and Maurice E. Moore, *The Natural History of a Delinquent Career* (Chicago: University of Chicago Press, 1931), pp. 7-8.

4. "Methods, Accomplishments, and Problems of the Chicago Area Project: A Report to the Board of Directors of the Chicago Area Project," 1944 (mimeo.).

5. Allen F. Davis, *Spearheads for Reform: The Social Settlements and the Progressive Movement, 1890-1914* (New York: Oxford University Press, 1967), p. 231.

6. Ibid., p. viii.

7. Ibid., p. 87.

8. Ibid., p. 88.

9. William Healy, *Twenty-five Years of Child Guidance*, Studies from the Institute for Juvenile Research, Series C, No. 256 (Illinois Department of Public Welfare, 1934), pp. 14-15.

10. Henry D. McKay, *Testimony at Hearings Before the Subcommittee to Investigate Juvenile Delinquency of the Committee on the Judiciary United States Senate*, 86th Cong., 1st sess., 1959.

11. "Methods, Accomplishments, and Problems of the Chicago Area Project."

12. Joseph Lincoln Steffens, *The Autobiography of Lincoln Steffens* (New York: Harcourt, Brace, 1931).

13. William F. Whyte, *Street Corner Society* (Chicago: University of Chicago Press, 1943).

14. Joseph R. Gusfield, ed., Introduction to *Protest, Reform, and Revolt: A Reader in Social Movements* (New York: John Wiley, 1970), p. 2.

15. Southside Community Committee, *Bright Shadows in Bronzetown: The Story of the Southside Community Committee* (Chicago, 1949).

16. Paul Diesing, *Patterns of Discovery in the Social Sciences* (Chicago: Aldine-Atherton, 1971), pp. 264-265.

17. Harold Finestone, "Reformation and Recidivism Among Italian and Polish Criminal Offenders," *American Journal of Sociology* 72 (May 1967): 587-588.

18. Solomon Kobrin, "The Chicago Area Project—A Twenty-five-Year Assessment," *The Annals of the American Academy of Political and Social Science* 322 (March 1959): 20.

19. Helen L. Witmer and Edith Tufts, *The Effectiveness of Delinquency Prevention Programs*, Children's Bureau, U.S. Department of Health, Education, and Welfare (Washington, D.C.: U.S. Government Printing Office, 1954), p. 15.

20. The following section is taken from Harold Finestone, "The Chicago Area Project in Theory and Practice," in Irving A. Spergel, ed., *Community Organization: Studies in Constraint* (Beverly Hills: Sage Publications, 1972), pp. 149-186.

21. *Illinois Youth Commission Biennial Report for 1959-60* (Chicago, n.d.).

22. Robert E. Park, "Community Organization and Juvenile Delinquency," in Everett C. Hughes and others, eds., *Human Communities: The City and Human Ecology* (Glencoe, Illinois: Free Press, 1952), pp. 52-63.

chapter 7

Antiestablishment subcultures: the functionalist theory of delinquency

In his capacity as both researcher and practitioner Shaw faced a number of dilemmas, which centered upon the importance that he initially assigned to primary group relationships in his theoretical and practical approaches to delinquency. In his research, however, he had moved increasingly toward a cultural interpretation of delinquency (that it represents a constancy of pattern) in which primary group relationships were merely a neutral medium for the transmission of the heritage of delinquency. Moreover, as practitioner he was becoming increasingly aware that he needed to take more account of the structural constraints and the organizational contexts within which the area projects were operating. It was not so easy to turn back the tide. Yet what was distinctive about the Chicago Area Projects was this emphasis upon the primary group, and he was hardly prepared by temperament or experience to abandon his faith in personal relationships in dealing with juvenile delinquents. The projects had been based upon a fundamental critique of the existing juvenile correctional system and social agencies as too distant and impersonal in their treatment of delinquents. To the impersonality of the existing juvenile delinquency control system they offered, by contrast, the example of a program based upon personal relationships. To the abstraction of the individual from his natural setting they offered the alternative of working with the delinquent within his natural group and community setting. The problem that Shaw now confronted was how to take account of these structural and cultural factors involved in delinquency without transforming the personal relationships of delinquents into mere epiphenomena.

By the time of World War II Shaw and his colleagues were well aware that the area projects worked far better in some community settings than in others. Among the most stable and effective of the community committees were those founded in the three original areas: the Near West Side, the South Side, and the Near North Side. These were all well-established ethnic communities dating back in their origins to the late nineteenth and early twentieth centuries. In each of these areas the predominant ethnic groups had remained unusually loyal to their localities, had become home owners, and had developed stable communities. In each the second generation was coming to maturity during the 1930s and was seeking modes of entry into the mainstream of American life. Under such conditions the ideas of the primary group and personal relationships could work because they were buttressed by a local network of social institutions. Such a favorable organizational context was not to be found in all inner-city communities. Equally difficult to confront was the development in which specific area projects assumed an institutionalized form quite inconsistent with area project philosophy. For example, some of them began to turn away from concern with the problem of juvenile delinquents, believing it to be personally stigmatizing to be too closely associated with delinquents or adult offenders. This tendency could well have been intensified by the mobility aspirations common to many members of the community committees. In other instances the projects were converted into organizations for advancing the self-serving social and political interests of the residents and community workers. Indeed, the area projects proved to be a fine training ground for leadership in community enterprises, in this way helping to expedite the upward mobility of many of its members out of the inner-city areas. Finally, the projects encountered difficulties in meeting the legitimate aspirations of its community workers for careers and advancement. The institutional channels that social agencies provided social workers for moving ahead as they gained professional proficiency were lacking in the projects. Consequently although many able "indigenous workers" were attracted to employment in the projects, the latter never succeeded in transforming their mode of work into a recognized occupation with opportunities for advancement and a career.

If the projects were to remain true to the experimental spirit in which they had been inaugurated, they required new theoretical formulations more congruent with the emerging findings and lessons of both research and practice. New conceptualizations were required in different areas: the nature of the social structure of the inner-city areas, the manner in which the area projects articulated with the political and social interests of the local residents, and an explicit statement of the role social stratification played in the functioning of the projects. The theory of social disorganization upon which the projects had been founded was inadequate to these purposes. The focus of this approach, as Whyte pointed out, was to overemphasize the disorganizing processes and to ignore the social reconstruction that occurred in the slum community, particularly when such reconstruction occurred through the medium of politics and the rackets.[1] Moreover, the only systematic data available to Shaw on the local communities were ecological, data that remained tied, for the most part, to theories of social disorganization.

In attempting to modify his theoretical formulations so as to be more consistent with the structural aspects of the urban community, Shaw found little assistance in his major intellectual influences, Park and Thomas. According to Turner, "Park took no substantial steps toward developing a theory of stratification."[2] According to Parenti, Thomas had tended to slight the role of institutions in his analysis of human behavior: "Thomas gives too little attention to institutional analysis: for him, the crucial effects of macrocosmic social changes on individual lives can best be seen through the personal documents; the wider forces which play such a disruptive and creative role are themselves given no direct detailed consideration."[3]

From both Park and Thomas, Shaw had inherited a priority of emphasis upon process rather than structure. Moreover, as Shaw interpreted it, the social process entailed an optimistic view of the prospects of resolving the problem of juvenile delinquency. As Kobrin has observed: "From the beginning the Area Project program rested on a conception of human nature which was optimistic concerning the prevention of delinquency and the rehabilitation of the delinquent. Delinquency was regarded as, for the most part, a reversible accident of the person's social experience."[4]

There was in addition a deeper optimism underlying Shaw's whole conceptual scheme. Much of the strength of his argument for the important degree of influence exerted upon delinquency by the social environment of the inner-city areas was based upon the dramatic contrast between the stability of the structure of rates of delinquents among the various areas of the city and the constantly changing ethnic composition of the inner-city areas. This scheme presupposed a relatively open society in which the progression from lower class to middle class as measured by spatial mobility operated in an orderly, almost inevitable, fashion. Such a progression implied that delinquency was a more or less transient aspect of the experience of the ethnic group during the process of urbanization. The area projects then could be viewed as working with the grain of urban growth. A structural approach would have had to regard delinquency more pessimistically as a permanent product deeply rooted in the stable features of the society. The color line provided one instance of such a structural feature, and the rate of delinquency among blacks always required special interpretation within the ecological framework. Discrimination against the free spatial movement of blacks within the city resulted in a basic change in their settlement pattern. Shaw chose to emphasize the parallels between the blacks and earlier ethnic groups in the patterns that they manifested in the spatial distribution of rates of delinquents. In so doing he tended to view discrimination as an intrusive factor in the regularity of the ecological pattern rather than as a possible causal factor of delinquent behavior in its own right. Again his emphasis upon social processes belied the role structural factors played.

Shaw did make serious efforts in such works as *Juvenile Delinquency in Urban Areas* to replace social disorganization theory with a functionalist theory in which the concept of social stratification was central. He never, however, made the attempt to apply this theory as a rationale for the area projects. Perhaps he resisted doing so because it would have required a shift from *community* to *social class* as the central organizing concept of the projects. In summary, Shaw did not succeed in reconciling the dilemmas generated by either his research or his practice. In moving increasingly toward a cultural interpretation of delinquency he was forced to abandon his original wish to study the individual delinquent from the social psychological perspective of his personal relationships. In contrast, in the intellectual leadership that he provided to the area projects, he continued to insist upon the priority of such personal relationships. The ultimate result was a profound disparity between the general tenor of his research and the philosophy underlying the area projects. His interpretation of his research underwent change; the fundamental rhetoric of the projects did not change.

Shaw did modify his conceptualization of the local community in a way that was to prove highly significant for the subsequent theoretical development of American criminology. His primary objective as a sociologist had been to interpret delinquency as an aspect of the social life of the local community and, more specifically, of those inner-city communities in which it tended to be concentrated. In order to do so he had applied the perspective of human ecology, which permitted the social life of the slum community to be viewed in two diametrically opposed ways. As a natural area characterized by a distinctive culture, it could be approached as a separate and distinct social unit, relatively separate from the remainder of the urban community. As an area subject to ecological processes such as invasion and succession, which characterized a growing city, it could be viewed as part of a larger interdependent ecological system. The perspective of the natural area was conducive to viewing the local community as a constellation of primary groups and primary group relationships. From the view of the city as an ecological system the local community could be approached as a status area, and various ecological data could be utilized as indexes of its relative position within the socioeconomic structure of the city. However, there were profound methodological difficulties in the way of making inferences about social structure on the basis of ecological indexes. As Shaw's interest in the relationship between social status and rates of delinquents increased, there was a tendency on his part to reduce the relative importance of ecological processes and to recast his conception of the inner-city community in more exclusively sociological terms. This transition was facilitated by viewing the inner city as the locus of a conflict of values rather than as the scene of social disorganization. The explanation for the presence of such conflicting value systems within these areas required that they be viewed in relation to the social structure of the larger city; that is, it required a functional explanation in which the social attributes of the slum areas were viewed as part of a larger social system. The functionalist approach replaced both the view which regarded the inner-city community as an isolated cultural unit and that which viewed its integration into the larger city solely in ecological terms.

Viewing the slum community as the locus of a conflict of values was a prelude to the formulation of new theoretical perspectives on the central problems of the sociology of delinquency. How did individuals become delinquents in situations characterized by a conflict between conventional and criminal value systems? How did the inner-city communities become the locus of criminal value systems? Each of these questions became the starting point of new theories. E. H. Sutherland came to grips with the process of becoming delinquent in his theory of differential association.[5] The functionalist interpretation of delinquent patterns, which Shaw himself had initiated was continued and elaborated in the work of the subcultural theorists such as Cohen and Cloward and Ohlin. The competing value systems now required more rigorous definition and specification. As long as Shaw had regarded the social heritage of delinquency as an integral part of the local community and its culture, it did not require special definition. However, once the inner-city community came to be viewed as the setting for competing value systems, it would ultimately become important for theory to specify their nature. Accordingly, postulating a conflict of values paved the way for the introduction of the concept of the delinquent subculture.

Sutherland's Contribution

Sutherland's formulation of differential association theory began a new era in American criminology. Shaw had been concerned with identifying the social causes of delinquency and with applying the scientific method; however, from the evidence of his published work, he did not conceive of the construction of theory as a separate operation. He had tended to view it as a conceptual framework, which could guide the gathering and the analysis of the data on delinquency. The empirical emphasis and the data, however, remained primary. Sutherland, in contrast, attempted to state his theory in a series of propositions that would have universal application. In this effort to state a theory as a set of abstract interrelated propositions, Sutherland was the first theoretically oriented American criminologist.[6] It should also be noted that Sutherland's formulation appeared during the late 1930s, a period in which the relative importance of sociological theory was being given a new emphasis:

The great Depression and World War II have had a major role in shaping contemporary American sociology.[7] The painstakingly descriptive data collected in the 1920s proved to be inadequate to meet the demands of the Depression crisis. Recognizing this predicament, many sociologists reconsidered their orientation and attempted to make sociology more useful by employing theory or theories to organize and to interrelate the mass of discrete studies. Moreover, some sociologists welcomed this more favorable attitude toward theory, especially the increasing acceptance of logical systems used to order, articulate, and accumulate research as a major advance in scientific sociology.[8]

Sutherland viewed the process of becoming delinquent as a type of acculturation. What was distinctive about his point of view was that he saw it occurring in two value systems simultaneously. It was an original conception and one well suited to the pluralistic nature of American society. He assumed that for those individuals who did not engage in criminal behavior, acculturation to conventional values assumed primacy; for those who did engage in such behavior, the acculturation to criminal values predominated. There was no precedent in American sociology for the conceptualization of socialization in situations of such complexity. In his search for propositions that could be formulated as objectively as possible he solved his problem by resort to a quantitative metaphor. According to Sutherland, conventional and criminal value systems were composed of elementary units called "definitions." Each of these units could be weighted by a number of modalities, such as frequency, priority, duration, and intensity of contact. Criminality or noncriminality was determined by the algebraic sum of these weighted units. "A person becomes delinquent because of an excess of definitions favorable to violation of law over definitions unfavorable to violation of law."[9] Despite the lack of a clear empirical reference for such ideas, Sutherland's general conception that individuals become delinquent through a process of learning criminal techniques and motives in personal relationships was to prove immensely influential.

Sutherland's originality also lay in the rigor with which he pursued the implications of criminal behavior as an expression of value conflict. He quickly realized that it was an idea that emancipated the criminologist from viewing the phenomena of criminal behavior as restricted to inner-city communities:

> *Cultural conflict is the underlying cause of differential association and therefore of systematic criminal behavior.* Differential association is possible because society is composed of various groups with varied cultures. These differences in culture are found in respect to many values and are generally regarded as desirable. They exist, also, with reference to the values which the laws are designed to protect, and in that form are generally regarded as undesirable. This criminal culture is as real as lawful culture and is much more prevalent than is usually believed. It is not confined to the hoodlums in slums or to professional criminals. Prisoners frequently state and undoubtedly believe that they are no worse than the majority of people on the outside. The more intricate manipulations of business and professional men may be kept within the letter of the law as interpreted but be identical in logic and effects with the criminal behavior which results in imprisonment. These practices, even if they do not result in public condemnation as crimes, are a part of the criminal culture.[10]

The Concept of Subculture and Social Stratification

In contrast to Sutherland who strove to formulate a theory of criminal behavior that would transcend its conventional stereotyped linkage with lower-class status, the subculture theorists made the linkage between delinquent subcultures and lower-class status the cornerstone of their theories. On closer inspection, this apparent contradiction is perhaps not as great as it seems. Sutherland was concerned with formulating a general theory of criminality. His work was in the tradition of the grand European theorists of criminal behavior such as Lombroso, Ferri, Tarde, and Bonger. The subcultural theorists had a more limited objective—accounting for the culture of delinquent gangs—and they had persuasive reasons to suspect that such gangs were concentrated in the lower classes. First, they were strongly influenced by Shaw and McKay's massive documentation that delinquency as a group-supported phenomenon tended to be concentrated in the inner-city communities:

> The conclusions of students who have been more specifically concerned with delinquency as a subculture tend . . . to localize subcultural delinquency in the lower socio-economic strata of our society. The principal conclusion of a monumental series of works by Shaw and McKay is that delinquency is a subcultural tradition in the areas of the city inhabited by the lower socio-economic classes. [11]

Second, the post-World War II era, during which trends that had started during the depression gained momentum, gave special poignancy to the problems of youth of low social status. It was during this era that the symbolic line, however vague, that demarcated the lower classes from the mainstream of American society became increasingly a color line. During the 1950s the elements of color differences, poverty, and adolescence all coalesced to create a situation in which the contingents of minority group youth dammed up in the ghettos of large cities found their life chances and their position in the community severely undermined.

This historical context of the depression and the post-World War II era within which they worked helps to render intelligible the work of the subcultural theorists. Indeed, according to Rainwater the concept of subculture itself gained currency during the 1930s as social scientists once again "discovered" the issue of "how the other half lives":

> Because almost all of them have until very recently been poor, conceptions of the poor and of the black have had a natural kinship. The enterprising historian can match almost every statement made about the European-American poor with a comparable statement about the Afro-Americans.
>
> In the 1930's these two streams of social observation began to come together in the work of social scientists concerned with social stratification in the United States. Out of their work has grown the most influential concept of the past two decades for trying to make sense out of the situation of the American poor in general and the Negro American poor in particular. This is the concept of the lower-class subculture. [12]

The concept of subculture as employed by sociologists was closely akin in both meaning and purpose to the anthropologists' usage of the concept of culture. Just as the concept of culture had served the anthropologist as a means of studying the differences evidenced in the ways of life of primitive people in a relativistic mode and without implying invidious judgment, similarly the concept of subculture served as an entree for the social scientist to the differences in the ways of life of the poor in a spirit that assumed their common humanity.

Although it is not possible to make definite assertions about the degree to which upward mobility declined during the years of the depression, incontestably it did have the effect of diverting attention to the various rigidities in the social class system and by the same token to the structural features of American society: ". . . The depression of the thirties brought into a new focus the significance of many new factors in American life for the restriction of social mobility and the rise of a more rigid stratification of social classes."[13]

One of the consequences of analyzing American society in terms of social stratification was a new interest in the relationship between social classes and the basic values of American society: Certain contradictions in the American social system became apparent:

The American social system . . . is permeated with two conflicting social principles: The first says that all men are equal before God and man. . . . The second, contradictory to the first, more often found in act than in words . . . declares that men are of unequal worth, that a few are superior to the many, that a large residue of lowly ones are inferior to all others.[14]

The two constitute the realities of American democracy. The democracy of the American Dream is true only because of the social gradation on the ladder where successful men are permitted to realize their ambitions. The social-class system is true only because the precepts of the Dream provide the moral code which enforces the rules of social mobility by insisting that all able men who obey the rules of the game have "the right" to climb.[15]

Perhaps the most telling insight into the nature of American society came from Myrdal's analysis of racial stratification within American society in *An American Dilemma*.[16] Here Myrdal contended that there was a fundamental contradiction between the American adherence to the value of equality and the actual mode of discriminating against the black American population.

Impact of Urbanization on the New Migrants

Before analyzing further the consequences of the large-scale urbanization of the black for his position in American society during the period under consideration, it will be helpful to have a more concrete idea of the actual numbers of migrants involved. Most blacks migrated largely to the cities of the North and West; and while they predominated among the urban newcomers, the movement also included substantial numbers of Puerto Ricans and Mexicans. Between 1940 and 1950 the nonwhite population more than doubled in thirty metropolitan areas of the United States, all but one of these being in the North or West rather than the South, the historical region of Negro concentration. In many instances these large proportional increases in nonwhite population involved rather small absolute numbers, but this was by no means uniformly true. The Detroit metropolitan area, with 173,000 nonwhites in 1940, experienced an increase of 109.5 percent to 362,000 in 1950. The Chicago metropolitan area showed a nonwhite increase of 80.8 percent, from 335,000 to 605,000 during the decade. Smaller, but still large, percentage increases were involved in the growth of the nonwhite population from 669,000 to 1,046,000 in the New York metropolitan area; from 337,000 to 485,000 in the Philadelphia metropolitan area; and from 151,000 to 216,000 in the St. Louis metropolitan area. In all these instances of rapid growth of nonwhite population, the corresponding increases of white population were only moderate.[17]

The newcomers swelled the lower classes of the cities in which they settled. From the poverty-stricken rural areas of the South they streamed into the inner-city ghettos of the North and West where they experienced considerable suffering and misery. Nevertheless, after a careful assessment of the varied problems that accompanied their urbanization, Weaver provided the following overall sanguine assessment:

... The transfer of disadvantaged Negroes to the areas where people have more advantages represents a gain. It brings the problems they face to light, forcing the attention of society to the contrasts they represent and causes acute discomfort. It is quite natural that society should choose to think that it is the transfer which creates the problems. It is important to recognize, however, that the transfer merely exposes the problems to view. In a word, the urbanization of the rural Southern Negroes has created a situation which has more potential for growth and improvement than their continued isolation from the mainstream of society.[18]

Some idea of the harshness with which the whole gamut of problems confronting the Negro migrants impinged upon youth is expressed by Marris and Rein:

The issues raised in the late 1950's—the sluggish economic growth, the unrelenting rise in unemployment, racial disparity, the implications of automation, the neglect of education, the assimilation of more and more young people into the labor force, immigration and depressed areas—were all related, and converged especially in the plight of Negro boys growing up in the city slums. A third of them were soon to be out of school and out of work—a whole generation of misfits, driven from the poverty of the South to the more humiliating frustrations of an urban ghetto.[19]

Under these conditions the disadvantages of lower-class status were compounded by the disadvantages of subordinate racial position. Blumer has clarified this connection between race relations and social structure in his conception of race prejudice as a sense of group position: "It is the *sense of social position* emerging from this collective process of characterization which provides the basis of race prejudice."[20]

One of the classical controversies among social scientists has dealt with the degree to which the urbanization of the black, the Puerto Rican, and the Mexican groups has tended to resemble that undergone by the various European immigrant groups. In *The Newcomers*, a book dealing with the blacks and Puerto Ricans in New York City, Handlin argued that there were significant differences between the urban experience of the new arrivals and those of the earlier immigrant groups. [21] For most of the earlier immigrants such as the Italians and the Poles, the movement to America had represented a decisive break with their past; they had accordingly set about to adjust their institutions and their community life to the new situation. For the blacks and Puerto Ricans moving to New York, however, the break with their past was not so decisive. The blacks had migrated from the South and retained close contact with their roots there. The Puerto Ricans, similarly, remained within easy access of Puerto Rico. Under such circumstances, Handlin argued, neither group evidenced much momentum to elaborate the social organization of their communities in the new urban setting. As a consequence, the latter tended to remain rudimentary. According to Handlin, other dispositions shared by the two groups tended to be conducive to the same end. Unlike other immigrant groups who had manifested a distrust of government because of their experiences in their European homelands, each of these groups was disposed to turn to the government for assistance in dealing with their problems. Another factor that mitigated against deliberate organization on an ethnic basis was the influence of relatively new media, such as television. By providing direct access to the models of behavior esteemed by the larger society, these media reduced the need for the orientation that would have been provided by ethnic institutions.

This lack of voluntary associations by no means implies that the new minority groups were without social organization. Such organization, however, remained on an extremely informal and noninstitutionalized level. One of the most distinctive features of contemporary social organization, for example, has been the development of various institutions for the differentiation of adolescence as a distinctive social category. Short's and Strodtbeck's observations of the lower-class Negro community in Chicago suggest that it is characterized by a minimum of such age differentiation:

> . . . In lower class Negro communities where petty crime, small-time "professional" burglary and robbery, drug traffic, and policy are rampant, neither legitimate nor criminal local adults are powerful politically, and economic affluence is illusive and undependable. Here the institutional structures for separating adults and adolescents appear to have broken down

or never to have existed. There is competition among all age levels for excitement wherever it may be found—from a bottle, a battle, or a broad. Poolhalls are habituated by young and old alike, and it is hard to tell where life in the street leaves off and formal institutional life begins. In Homans' terms, a greater portion of behavior is "subinstitutional" than is the case in the white communities. We are inclined to attribute this to the lack of institutional organization and of formal institutionalized power. With Cloward and Ohlin, we expect this situation to change, as institutionalized power, both legitimate and illegitimate, increases in Negro communities. In the meantime, however, it is lacking, and the lack is compounded by fear and suspicion among themselves and of outsiders, both white and Negro, which is endemic among lower class Negroes. [22]

The new features that characterized the social organization of slum communities after World War II were not the results of a simple set of social forces. Rather they reflected a complex blending of historical, class, racial, economic, and technological factors. They reflected the social structure of the city as much as they did the distinctive historical traditions of race relations in America. It is not surprising that the variety and depth of such changes should be reflected in changes in the delinquency characteristic of such areas. Spergel observes that delinquency became more "aggressive":

During and after World War II, the character of delinquency changed, as lower class communities became more unstable or less strongly organized. Already crowded major city slums of the North were inundated with an influx mainly of southern Negroes, Puerto Ricans, and Mexicans, which created severe social problems. Delinquency increased in aggressiveness in direct proportion as routes to desired status which had been open to old time residents decreased for the newcomer. [23]

Such changes would sooner or later be reflected both in theories of delinquency and in the response that society would make to the problem.

It is instructive to compare Spergel's observations of slum communities made during the 1960s with those made approximately twenty years earlier during the early 1940s by William F. Whyte in his classical article, "Social Organization in the Slums." Whyte, who objected to the characterization of slum communities as disorganized, proposed a distinction between types of slum communities in order to advance conceptual clarification:

> The first essential is the establishment of clear distinctions between different types of slum districts. On the one hand we have the rooming house district. . . . Since members of the rooming house population have very little contact with one another, it is accurate to say that such a district is largely lacking in social organization. On the other hand, we have the area of immigrant settlement. . . . Here people live in family groups and have built up an elaborate social organization. These two areas resemble each other in congestion of population, poor quality of housing, and low income of the inhabitants, but such physical and economic indices do not provide us with the discriminations needed for sociological analysis. The social life differs so fundamentally from one district to the other that any attempt to lump the two together and make generalizations upon this basis is bound to be fruitless and misleading. [24]

Whyte argued that the slum family area tended to develop an indigenous social organization based upon politics and the rackets. Twenty years later it was becoming increasingly necessary to recognize that not all areas fit this pattern. Some conformed to the model Whyte formulated. Others had such social and institutional instability that they could no longer be characterized as organized in the same sense. Thus the concept of social disorganization was reintroduced.

Rainwater has suggested that it was during the course of attempts by social scientists to interpret the social life of the lower classes during the pre- and post-World War II eras that the concept of subculture was introduced. The subcultural theorists of delinquency such as Cohen and Cloward and Ohlin were working within a comparatively new tradition of research into the problems of social stratification. Rainwater goes on to indicate that the concept of subculture was compatible with two quite antithetical conceptions of the social context, which was relevant to the functioning of such subcultures:

> The concept of the lower-class subculture has been one of the

mainstays of professional attempts to comprehend the life, the motivations, and the problems of the least well off portion of the population. However, it has been interpreted in two different ways in the sociological and anthropological literature of the past 30 years dealing with the distinctiveness of lower-class norms and values from those of the larger, "conventional" society. The now classic views, fathered most directly by Allison Davis and further developed by Walter Miller, holds that there is a distinctive culture that characterizes those who are brought up in the lower class world. . . .

In apparent opposition are the views of such general theorists as Parsons and Merton, who seem to maintain that American society possesses a single system of values which is "morally integrated," shared by most actors in the society "in the sense that they approve the same basic normative patterns of conduct." This contrary view was developed by Merton in his well-known essay on social structure and anomie. . . .

It is an interesting and important issue, but its status in the sociological literature is curious. Neither of the sets of scholars whose views are presented above deal with the conceptual problems of maintaining that there does or does not exist a distinctive lower-class culture. . . . The relatively offhand way in which the competition between these two concepts developed has meant that the dialectic between them has never been fully explored or adequately tested against empirical research.

Both Davis and Merton are in fact seeking to come to terms with the adaptiveness of lower-class behavior, but their focus is different. Merton seeks to highlight the stratification system and the general social and cultural situation of the lower class by using the concept of anomie: he seeks to show that lower-class behavior can be regarded as arising from an effort to adapt to a disjunction between universal American goals and the lack of access lower class people have to these goals. His approach is macro-sociological. Davis' approach, however, involves microscopic examination of the exigencies of day-to-day life of lower class people. He seeks to show how they construct their adaptations to the lack of opportunities in their environment and how they selectively emphasize the opportunities that are available to them, primarily opportunities for "bodily pleasures" of various kinds. [25]

Functionalism and the Subcultural Theorists

In the preceding section I have sought to depict the changes in American society that occurred during the depression and World War II eras among the lower classes in American Society. In discussing the successive forms assumed historically by the problem of delinquency, I have suggested that new theoretical and practical approaches to this problem have tended to occur during periods of rapid urbanization and concomitant social change. Since World War II, however, although urbanization has once again become highly salient, the fundamental concept for the analysis of the delinquency problem has become social status rather than social change. The new movement of urbanization directed attention to the issues of social stratification, particularly as these were reflected in the behavior of the lower classes. It was in order to depict their way of life during this era that the concept of subculture was introduced. Social stratification is a feature of communities and societies viewed as wholes; accordingly, it tends to coincide historically with the emergence of functionalism as a highly influential sociological theory. As Martindale has indicated, functionalism is to be distinguished by its preference for relatively large-scale systems as the basic referents for theory, the central idea being that of "system": "Functionalism reaches its distinctive subject matter when it takes the organism-like *system* as its peculiar object of study and conceives of this as the primary subject matter of sociological analysis, studying all other items as system-determined and system-maintaining."[26] Furthermore, in his classification of functionalism as one of the social structural theories, Wallace gives centrality to the concept of status in such theories. He characterizes such viewpoints as seeking "to explain the social . . . mainly through reference to the socially generated, established (i.e., 'structured') statuses of participants."[27]

It was functionalist theory, particularly those influential versions associated with Parsons and Merton, that informed the work of such subcultural theorists of delinquency as Cohen and Cloward and Ohlin. Accordingly some of the central assumptions these functional theorists made in their work are indispensable to an understanding and assessment of the subcultural theories. Such assumptions profoundly influenced the questions they raised about group delinquency and the answers they proposed. And by the same token, the theoretical and empirical inadequacies, which were subsequently found in their work, are attributable in part to the functional assumptions that they accepted.

One of the implications of functionalism is that all social behavior should be viewed as constantly oriented toward the social system. Or, using Wallace's formulation, we might say that all social behavior can be interpreted as expressive of the status position of the relevant actors in the social structure constituting the system. For such a point of view to be feasible, mechanisms are required through which ultimately the system determines the behavior of its subcollectivities and its individual actors. Presupposed in the very idea that the social system determines behavior is the assumption that collectivities and individuals are integrated into the system. There were two mechanisms through which it was postulated that such integration was attained. The first was the concept of oversocialized man. The second was the view that the sphere of interpersonal relations or social milieu may be viewed as the social vehicle through which the social structure transmits its influence to the individual actor.

According to Wrong, who formulated the concept, there are two aspects to the concept of oversocialized man. The first is concerned with a distinctive conception of the process of socialization, according to which the individual becomes a member of a society by internalizing its norms. Such norms become constitutive of his human nature so that his conformity to them can be assumed. The individual is not conceived as having any detachment or psychological distance from the norms. The possibility of experiencing inner tension because of one's personal attitude toward them is eliminated:

> Thus when a norm is said to have been "internalized" by an individual, what is frequently meant is that he habitually both affirms it and conforms to it in his conduct. The whole stress on inner conflict—on the tension between powerful impulses and superego controls, the behavioral outcome of which cannot be prejudged—drops out of the picture. [28]

The second component of socialized man "is the view that man is essentially motivated by the desire to achieve a positive image of self by winning acceptance or status in the eyes of others." [29] Man guides all his actions to elicit positive reactions from others.

According to the conception of socialized man, the individual is integrated into the social system because his very human nature is a personal replica or microcosm of those aspects of the social structure to which his experience has exposed him. His integration into the social system is complete because he is totally a product of that system, and his normative integration into the social system is reinforced by his sensitivity to the responses of others who have internalized the societal norms to a degree equal to his own. Thus normative regulation of the individual actor's behavior plays a crucial role in his integration into the social system.

The second mechanism through which collectivities and individual actors become integrated into encompassing social systems deals with the relationship between the two analytical levels designated as the sociological and the social psychological. The sociological is concerned with the functioning of collectivities, the social psychological with interpersonal relationships. Sociological theory may abstract its subject matter from direct and explicit concern with social psychological factors such as interpersonal relationships, but even as it does so it cannot avoid making some assumptions about the relationship between sociological and social psychological realms, between the society and the individual. Consequently, one way of assessing the mechanisms through which the social system is conceived as determining behavior is to ask how the relationship between the sociological and the social psychological domains is viewed. In the following citation Merton is critical of tendencies in the field of delinquency study that have overemphasized the role of interpersonal relations or the "milieu" at the cost of the larger social structure. He argues that such an approach should be replaced by one that would give primacy to social structural factors. In elaborating his position he suggests that the milieu be regarded as a mediating or intervening structure through which the pressures originating in the larger structure are brought to bear upon the individual:

> There is . . . a tendency, in thinking about the social environment of individual behavior, to lay great emphasis on the milieu rather than on the larger social structure. By the milieu I mean the immediate environment in the form of the interpersonal relations and social relationships in which a particular individual is directly engaged. And for this, of course, there is a great deal to be said. Yet there seems to have developed an overemphasis

on the milieu, as contrasted with the larger social structure, in
dealing with the social environment of human behavior.

> . . . To relate the behavior of individuals to the larger social
> structure—the class structure or the political structure of a to-
> tal society—raises the problem of how this massive larger envi-
> ronment can have a direct impact upon individuals living in it;
> the emphasis therefore shifts to the intervening social struc-
> tures,namely, the milieu.
>
> Observation of the milieu is theoretically essential, but it is
> not sufficient. It is essential because the pressures of the larger
> social structure are mediated through the intervening structure.
> But useful as it is, the tendency to focus on the immediate milieu
> (the patterns of interpersonal relations in which individuals are
> directly involved) has led to relative neglect of the larger social
> structure.[30]

Merton's remarks suggest that interpersonal relations do not have independent or autonomous theoretical significance. They are the vehi-
cles for the processes originating in the larger social structure.

Cohen's Theory

Cohen pioneered in applying the functional approach to the problem of the delinquent subculture. He began by posing the issues that
he proposed to pursue (his own point of view is sharpened by contrasting it with the "cultural transmission" approach):

> Now we come to a curious gap in delinquency theory. Note the
> part that the existence of the delinquent subculture plays in the
> cultural-transmission theories. It is treated as a *datum*, that is,
> as something which already exists in the environment of the
> child. The problem with which these theories are concerned is to
> *explain how that subculture is taken over by the child*. Now we
> may ask: Why is there such a subculture? Why is it "there" to be
> "taken over"? Why does it have the particular content that it
> does and why is it distributed as it is within our social system?
> Why does it arise and persist, as it does, in such dependable

fashion in certain neighborhoods of our American cities? Why does it not "diffuse" to other areas and to other classes of our population? [31]

Cohen's goals are also clarified by his comments in a footnote in which he criticized Sutherland's theory of differential association as an oversimplification and distortion of the group processes associated with delinquent behavior:

"It is not necessary that there be bad boys inducing good boys to commit offenses. It is generally a mutual stimulation, as a result of which each of the boys commits delinquencies which he would not commit alone." Edwin H. Sutherland, *Principles of Criminology* (New York: J. B. Lippincott Company, 1947), p. 145. Having made the point, however, Sutherland failed to develop its implications, and in his general theory of criminal behavior the function of the group or the gang is not collectively to *contrive* delinquency but merely to *transmit* the delinquent tradition and to provide protection to the members of the group. [32]

Cohen's charge that Sutherland had paid no attention to the origin of criminal and delinquent values was wrong. In each edition of Sutherland's criminology there is considerable material on the origins of criminal values in American society, but these are discussed from a historical perspective as part of the development of American society. What Cohen meant is that Sutherland had not provided a functional interpretation of these values. But let us turn to a consideration of the first major problem that Cohen had set himself: how to explain the origin of the delinquent subculture. The challenge of the question that Cohen posed is intensified when placed within the context of functionalism. How was it possible for oversocialized man to deviate? Granting this possibility, how was it possible for him to construct a system of deviant values? The answer, of course, is that the functionalists never viewed society, and particularly American society, as fully integrated on the normative level. Accordingly, normative conflicts were possible. As already observed in the reference to Warner's work, it was because of its internal inconsistencies and contradictions that the social stratification of American society had come to claim the attention of social scientists.

For the functionalist, deviant behavior was a product of certain types of normative conflict. Cohen had to go beyond this to specify that such normative conflicts were differentially distributed in the social structure in such a manner that the emergence of a shared or group-supported subculture was possible. This could be accomplished by postulating that certain normative conflicts would be concentrated in certain status segments of the society. If the delinquent subculture was predominantly associated with lower-class boys, this meant that such boys were exposed to certain normative conflicts from which other segments of the society tended to be spared. Granting the localization of such conflicts in certain status segments, how did oversocialized man break through his own internalization of the conventional values and the potentially negative response of his significant others in order to give expression to a delinquent set of values that flouted the dominant conventional values of the social system? It required special conditions and a special type of group process.

From such general considerations the methodology of the subcultural theorists followed inevitably. Because all behavior is system determined, the status problem had to be some type of structural strain or inconsistency within the social system. What status problem was shared by lower-class boys? Cohen constructed a model of the social stratification system in which there is a single "measuring rod" of success—that of the middle classes. Moreover, there is a single "status universe" of competition so that no individual can escape measuring his attainments according to middle-class criteria. In competing for success under such rules lower-class boys are at a distinct disadvantage. Unlike middle-class boys who are exclusively socialized into the dominant middle-class system of values, lower-class boys are socialized into varying mixes of middle-class and lower-class values. Accordingly their own normative commitments are likely to be more or less ambivalent. However, regardless of their training and personal value commitments, they cannot avoid the competition with middle-class boys at school, at settlement houses, and in all institutional settings in which the "long arm" of the middle class is evident. In such competition they are perennially exposed to the risk of failure. They may reject this risk and rebel against the negative assessment of themselves constantly implied, and through interaction with like-minded fellows construct an alternative set of values according to which criteria they can succeed. It is at this juncture, the interactive process through which new values are constructed, that the group process Cohen postulated becomes crucial:

> The final product, to which we are jointly committed, is likely to be a compromise formation of all the participants to what we may call a cultural process, a formation perhaps unanticipated by any of them. Each actor may contribute something directly to the growing product, but he may also contribute indirectly by encouraging others to advance, inducing them to retreat, and suggesting new avenues to be explored. The product cannot be ascribed to any one of the participants; it is a real "emergent" on a group level.[33]

Cohen's theory was a contribution of the greatest importance to the development of criminology. As Matza indicated, the sociological vision implies placing a given social phenomenon within a larger context; thus, for sociologists, Cohen's work was a highly provocative example of such vision.[34] It gave form and substance to the burgeoning interest in gangs characteristic of the 1940s and 1950s. By linking up in such clear-cut fashion the relation between social class and delinquency, it offered many suggestive guides to social policy in dealing with gang problems. Perhaps its greatest contribution lay in the intellectual excitement and stimulation it produced. It made a major contribution to the research design and ideas utilized by Short and Strodtbeck in their empirical study of gangs.[35] It acted as an important stimulus to the work of subsequent subcultural theorists such as Cloward and Ohlin. Out of this variegated experience, including the empirical testing of the theory, have come a number of criticisms, issues, and controversies, which may be dealt with under two rubrics: theoretical issues and the issue of empirical validity.

Let us take up first Cohen's contention that the delinquent subculture as he depicted it represents an "emergent." If so, he could reasonably claim that he had improved upon Sutherland's statement of the group process involved in delinquency. The issue that has to be decided is whether a subcultural development can be both system determined, as required by the functionalist approach, and simultaneously a true "emergent." It is true that there is an emergence of new norms, but only boys who already share a given status problem can contribute to their emergence. Cohen's conception of interaction is that it makes explicit what had hitherto been implicit and latent in the dispositions of the individual boys. This is not a type of process during which new norms could be generated whose nature was unpredictable at the start. The process through which the subculture develops does not meet Sutherland's condition that "it is not necessary that there be bad boys inducing good boys to commit offenses," since only the "bad boys" are involved in the process.[36] Under such conditions the outcome of the boys' interaction would appear to be a foregone conclusion, predetermined if and when they engage in effective interaction. The process of interaction itself is neutral; it does not add anything to the content of the subculture except to facilitate its release. For a true "emergent" to occur one would have to conceive of Cohen's lower-class boys as possessing some degree of autonomy relative to the social class system. Gouldner has suggested that this relative autonomy could be attained within the scope of functional analysis by postulating individuals capable of membership in more than one social system:

> . . . Human beings are not invariably characterized by a total dependence upon any one social system. *Socialized* individuals have some measure of mobility, vertical and horizontal, among the social systems within their society, moving with varying degrees of ease or stress from one to another. They may and do also migrate to, or sojourn in, societies different from those in which they were originally socialized. They have, in our terms, considerable, if varying, degrees of functional autonomy in relation to any given social system.[37]

Cohen's way of phrasing his theory of the subculture was to view it as the product of a single problem of adjustment in relation to a single social system, that of social stratification. It is perhaps this circumstance that accounts for the special cast to subcultural theories Bordua noted: "Cohen's boys and Cloward and Ohlin's boys are driven by grim economic and psychic necessity into rebellion."[38]

The argument is clarified by Short's findings in his empirical study of gangs. He found that the gang delinquents that he studied participated in more than one social system. Their delinquent activity could not be understood by assuming that it was entirely a response to the status problems arising out of their position in the social class system:

> ... Particular behavior episodes suggest that . . . the conception of social structure . . . must be broadened to include situations which are more immediate to the boys, such as local community norms and opportunities, and normative and status considerations *within* the group, in addition to the abstract conceptions of opportunity structures and status deprivation which are stressed by Cohen and by Cloward and Ohlin.[39]

A theory of delinquent subcultures that would have postulated the theoretical relevance of more than one social system and more than a single problem of adjustment was never attempted. One of the reasons it was not is perhaps suggested by Short's findings. Some of the spheres of relations that he found relevant were those that encompassed interpersonal relationships or the milieu. The functionalist theory would have to be extended to include social psychological as well as sociological systems. What was involved was a challenge to the whole functionalist theory of society in which the milieu was to be viewed as merely an intervening structure between the larger social structures and the individual. Short's findings implied that the milieu itself would have to be viewed as an autonomous source of social behavior.

Cloward's and Ohlin's Theory

The culminating statement of the subcultural approach was presented in Cloward's and Ohlin's *Delinquency and Opportunity* (1960), an ambitious effort of synthesis.[40] It incorporated within a single formulation a typology of types of slum communities and a typology of gangs based upon variations in subcultural patterns of law-violative behavior. The most important theoretical contribution was Cloward's concept of the illegitimate opportunity structure. This is most appropriately viewed as a bridging concept between the larger social structure and the milieu. Cloward's and Ohlin's theory had forced them to explore the relationships between these two analytic levels because of the nature of their problem. They were trying to account for the emergence of three types of delinquent subcultures—criminal, conflict, and retreatist—each characterized by a distinctive set of norms:

The most crucial elements of the delinquent subculture are the prescriptions, norms, or rules of conduct that define the activities required of a full-fledged member. . . . What we have called the criminal subculture prescribes disciplined and utilitarian forms of theft; the conflict subculture prescribes the instrumental use of violence; the retreatist subculture prescribes participation in illicit consummatory experiences, such as drug use. Thus the delinquent norms that govern these activities are the primary identifying and organizing elements of delinquent subcultures. [41]

Since each of these subcultures was a response to an identical status problem viewed from the perspective of the larger social structure, additional mechanisms were required in order to account for the differentiation of the three types of delinquent subculture:

The pressures that lead to deviant patterns do not necessarily determine the particular pattern of deviance that results. A given problem of adjustment may result in any one of several solutions. In other words, we cannot predict the content of deviance simply from our knowledge of the problem of adjustment to which it is a response. In any situation, alternative responses are always possible. We must therefore explain each solution in its own right, identifying the new variables which arise to direct impulses toward deviance into one pattern rather than another and showing how these variables impinge upon actors in search of a solution to a problem of adjustment. [42]

Cloward and Ohlin used the concept of the milieu to subsume the new intervening variables required by their theory: "We shall suggest that the milieu in which actors find themselves has a crucial impact upon the types of adaptation which develop in response to pressures toward deviance." [43] Their conception of the social milieu proved to be the local community as Shaw had conceived it, that is, as a sphere of personal relationships. They went beyond Shaw, however, in assuming that there could be variation in the social structure of slum communities. Once they could make this assumption they could apply Merton's conception of the relationship between the larger social structure and the local social milieu. The local milieu could be viewed as a sphere of interpersonal relationships through which were transmitted the pressures that originated in the larger social structure. If the social structure of this milieu varied, these pressures from the larger social structure would be mediated differently and would lead to different types of delinquent subcultures.

What still remained unclear was the mechanism through which the larger social structure was to be articulated with the local milieu. This was accomplished by Cloward's notion of the differential opportunity structure. He pointed out that Merton's original formulation of social structure and anomie had assumed that individuals exposed to anomie could independently contrive innovative behavior. Cloward suggested that just as conventional achievement presupposed access to the legitimate opportunity systems, so did criminal achievement presuppose access to illegitimate opportunity systems. Drawing upon the work of Shaw and McKay and of Sutherland he showed that inner-city communities provided access to such opportunity systems. He called his theory one of differential opportunity systems. The conception of opportunity system operated as a "bridging" concept since it was applicable to both the social structure and social milieu level.

Remaining true to the methodology of functionalism, Cloward and Ohlin attempted to show that each step in their argument was system determined. This meant that each step would have to be related to the larger social structure or to the more immediate milieu: "The social milieu affects the nature of the deviant response whatever the motivation and social position (i.e., age, sex, socio-economic level) of the participants in the delinquent subculture."[44] They remain true to their methodology with one curious exception, their treatment of retreatism. The social milieu is only indirectly involved in retreatism. Here for the only time in their theory they were forced to incorporate the relevance of interindividual differences; for the difference between those who become retreatist and those who do not is primarily a matter of personal differences. The retreatists are the "double failures," those who cannot succeed in either the criminal or the conflict subculture.

Criticisms of Subcultural Theories

With the formulation of Cloward's and Ohlin's theory, subcultural theories of delinquency became the center of increasing controversy. The criticisms that will concern us here will deal primarily with the two assumptions of functionalism around which the previous discussion of Cohen's and of Cloward's and Ohlin's work has been organized. According to the first assumption behavior was normatively determined, that is, the members of a social system tended to interact with one another in conformity with the norms of that system. According to the second assumption, the milieu or the domain of interpersonal relationships acted as the vehicle for the transmission of forces and pressures originating in the larger social structures of the society; it was not conceived of as itself autonomously capable of generating such forces or pressures.

Matza in *Delinquency and Drift* attacked the subcultural theorists' notion that the acts of boys in delinquent gangs were determined by their socialization and therefore their commitment to delinquent norms.[45] He contended that the boys believed and acted as though other members of the gang were committed to such norms but that they were not themselves committed to such norms. As empirical evidence of this contention Matza advanced the results of a questionnaire administered to one hundred delinquents at a training school for boys:

> Each respondent was shown a series of pictures, each picture portraying a different offense. They were asked in a general way how they would feel about a boy who committed the particular offense being shown. The question was further clarified by adding, "Would you want to hang around with him or like him, more, less, the same, or what?"[46]

The offenses depicted included mugging, fighting with a weapon, armed robbery, auto theft, stealing from a warehouse, stealing from a car, vandalism, and stealing a bike. Matza commented on his findings as follows:

> The first thing of note in the distribution of judgments is the tiny proportion who approved of the act by suggesting in some way that they would admire, or like, or feel an affinity with the boy in the picture.... There are virtually no cases in which positive approval accrues to the perpetrator of these delinquent acts. Two per cent of the eight hundred judgments rendered by one hundred boys elicited positive approval. ...
>
> The reader must be reminded that in not a few instances these

were acts that had been committed by the respondent, so two-minded are the adherents of the subculture of delinquency.[47]

If the members of the subculture taken individually are not committed to its norms, how does it happen that they come to believe that others are? Matza attributed this fact to what he called "shared misunderstandings." Lack of communication about the nature of their real beliefs prohibits the individual members from penetrating the deceptions that they all are practicing. Matza pointed out that there are a variety of reasons to account for such inhibitions upon open and frank communication. As exemplified, for example, by the practice of "sounding" in which each boy is constantly subject to insult by the others, the situation of the gang boy is such as to induce considerable anxiety about his sense of adequacy in his masculine status. Furthermore, the norms that prevail in the delinquent gang exist solely within an oral tradition. They do not receive the publicity that they would if they were codified and available in some public document.

Matza is not denying the existence of norms that are conducive to delinquency, but he differs from the subcultural theorists in his conception of these norms and in the relation between them and delinquent behavior. In sharp contrast to the subcultural theorists, he attacks their assumption that norms can be rather sharply categorized as either conventional or delinquent. Instead of viewing the corpus of conventional values as a more or less unitary system with ascetic puritanism at their core, he views conventional values as comprised of many different streams. This stream is large and complex enough to include a number of subterranean traditions, which manifest a kind of chameleon character. In certain situations their expression is conventionally sanctioned; in others they assume the form of delinquent acts. Among the subterranean traditions are bohemianism, radicalism, and delinquency. Such a conception of the mainstream value system and of the manner in which it attains expression requires a drastic revision in the conception of the relationship between conventional and delinquent values. The subculturalists tended to view them as primarily oppositional. According to Matza they should more properly be conceived as overlapping and being interrelated in the most manifold ways.

From this conception of the nature of conventional and delinquent values, there follows a correspondingly different conception of the

nature of the relationship between the delinquent gang and delinquent acts. Instead of delinquent acts being conceived of as a direct
expression of delinquent norms and therefore as system determined,
they become situational. Under certain circumstances with certain
associates, delinquency may become the appropriate response. Delinquent acts accordingly become contingent. One has to take
account of the delinquent as a person and of the nature of his interpersonal relations. Indeed, one of the major implications of Matza's
work is to restore to the individual and his personal relationships
some degree of autonomy. Delinquency becomes not merely a response to a certain type of situation but a response to the "definition
of the situation." Methodologically, if one wishes to understand the
act one must pay attention both to the situation and to the manner
in which it is defined. In Matza's formulation the relation between
norms and delinquency had become problematic. Under such conditions Matza's work restimulated interest in the process through
which individuals became delinquent. Such a question was not very
salient as long as the assumption was made that delinquent behavior
was normatively regulated, but it did become of interest when the
relationship between norms and behavior became problematic. What
was common to the process through which individuals became delinquent?

Quite independently, Short had arrived at identical conclusions
concerning the problematic nature of norms on the basis of his empirical study of gangs in Chicago:

> These boys do not seem as committed to delinquent norms as
> Cohen, and Cloward and Ohlin suggest. Indeed, their commit-
> ment to delinquent norms seems quite tenuous except in spe-
> cific types of situations which involve the group, such as threat
> to the group from another gang, or, in some instances, threats
> to the status of boys individually. [48]

We turn now to a discussion of the second assumption of the subcultural theorists: that the influence of the milieu of the domain of interpersonal relationships is restricted to its role in mediating influences that originate in the larger social structures, such as social class
and political institutions. Here again, the implications of Short's
findings are relevant:

Clearly, there are important causal processes operating in the immediate situation to which a boy is oriented, as well as the nature of his orientation with respect to goals and the institutionally prescribed means of achieving these goals. Again, this is not a new theory. W. I. Thomas indicated the importance to one's behavior of his "definition of the situation". . . . What is added is theoretically oriented description of important situational elements. The reaction of gang boys to a variety of status threats is an example of the operation of group processes which have been neglected in the causal models of the theories examined. [49]

What is lacking in most models of gang behavior is precisely this type of Meadian act, in which behavior is seen as a process of *continuous adjustment* of actors to one another, rather than as a sort of mechanical reaction to some one factor or combination of factors in the situation, whether they be characteristics of actors, or subcultures, or other features. It is this conception, too, which is lacking in anomie theory. [50]

Short proposed that an adequate explanation of the behavior of delinquent gangs needs to view their milieu as a source of influences leading to delinquent behavior, independent of the influences originating in the larger social structure. Like Matza, he attributed a great deal of importance to the actual situation of the boys; moreover, he viewed this situation largely in terms of interpersonal relationships. Short had been led to this conclusion by his analysis of particular episodes of gang behavior. The active involvement of some gang members and the abstention of others from participation in these episodes tended to be contingent upon the status of individuals within their face-to-face groupings.

It is possible to interpret Miller's theory of delinquent gangs with its emphasis upon the formative influence of the lower-class milieu as a direct attack on the assumption of functionalist theories that the milieu is to be conceived as merely a medium for transmitting influences that originate in the larger social structure. Miller argued, instead, that what was alleged to be their delinquency was actually a response to the microsocial realities of their lives. [51] Implicit in Miller's formulation is an attack upon one of the central assumptions of the functionalist theorists: that the generation of the subcultural norms was a status-linked problem of adjustment to which the norms of the subculture were a response. The behavior of Miller's boys was not based upon any problem that they personally would recognize. The problem lay in the fact that their mode of adjustment ran counter to the standards of the larger society.

With Miller's formulation, the dormant distinction between the macrosocial and microsocial conceptions of the delinquent subculture becomes explicit. Moreover, Miller's work shows the degree to which they are incompatible with one another. Each derives from a quite different perspective. In advancing his theory Miller elaborated it from the perspective of the boys themselves and in a larger sense from the perspective of the inhabitants of the lower classes. The macrotheorists, in contrast, do not formulate their theories from the perspective of the gang boys themselves but from that of the larger encompassing social system. This awareness permitted Miller to criticize the functionalists for incorporating middle-class biases into their theories. Douglas made a very similar point in his comments on Cohen's theory:

> In one of the best works on delinquency Albert Cohen has argued that the actions of "delinquent boys" are clearly "non-utilitarian." This statement involves an implicit assumption, possibly unseen by Cohen, that what is "utilitarian" and what is "non-utilitarian" is no different for these boys from what it is to a sociologist; i.e., a sociologist can look at the actions committed by these boys and tell right away from his understanding of such things as a member of the culture that these actions are "non-utilitarian" for the boys themselves. The same assumption is made concerning the criteria of "rationality." "There is no accounting in rational and utilitarian terms for the effort and the danger run in stealing things which are often discarded, destroyed or casually given away." [52]

At another level of analysis it is instructive to contrast the implications of Matza's and Short's work with that of Miller, for Miller may be regarded in some ways as an intermediate figure, standing midway between the position of the subcultural theorists Cohen and Cloward and Ohlin, on the one hand, and that of Matza and Short, on the other. Miller challenged the other macrotheorists with a microtheory; however, he shared with them the assumption that behavior is normatively regulated. He challenged only one of the assumptions that we have imputed to the functionalists while the work of Matza and Short challenged both assumptions. In principle, and in this respect, their work would be just as critical of Miller's formulations as they would be of the work of Cohen and of Cloward and Ohlin. Miller was not concerned with the independent influence of interpersonal relationships; his was still a totally cultural explanation. Matza and Short, in contrast, advanced a fundamentally different conception of the relationship between cultural norms and behavior, one in which the relationship between norm and behavior becomes problematic, one that places its stress upon the situation as a matrix of interpersonal relationships, and one that incorporates the idea of contingency.

One can understand the differences between Matza and Short and the subcultural theorists, including Miller, only by suggesting that their notion of a theory of delinquent behavior implies a different image of man from that implied by the subcultural theorists. For the functionalists the view that the individual's behavior is system determined implies a view of the human being as a neutral agent who mediates and expresses in his behavior influences that originate outside of himself. The most striking contrast in image of man is that offered in the perspective of symbolic interactionists:

> Fundamentally, group action takes the form of a fitting together of individual lines of action. Each individual aligns his action to the action of others by ascertaining what they are doing or what they intend to do—that is, by getting the meaning of their acts. For Mead, this is done by the individual "taking the role" of others—either the role of a specific person or the role of a group (Mead's "generalized other"). In taking such roles the individual seeks to ascertain the intention or direction of the acts of others. He forms and aligns his own action on the basis of such interpretation of the acts of others. This is the fundamental way in which group action takes place in human society.[53]

Ironically, in working their way to this position in which the theory of delinquency would place its central emphasis upon self-other relationships working in specific situations, students were reverting to the position that Shaw had abandoned several decades earlier when he had committed himself to a cultural interpretation of delinquency.

NOTES

1. William F. Whyte, "Social Disorganization in the Slums," *American Sociological Review* 8 (1943): 34-39.

2. Ralph H. Turner, ed., *Robert E. Park: On Social Control and Collective Behavior* (Chicago: University of Chicago Press, 1967), p. xvii.

3. Michael Parenti, Introduction to *The Unadjusted Girl* by William I. Thomas (1923; reprint ed., New York: Harper & Row, 1967), p. xx.

4. Solomon Kobrin, "Chicago Area Project—A Twenty-five-Year Assessment," in Rose Giallombardo, ed., *Juvenile Delinquency: A Book of Readings* (New York: John Wiley & Sons, 1966), p. 475.

5. Edwin H. Sutherland, *Principles of Criminology*, 3d ed. (Philadelphia: J. B. Lippincott Co., 1939). Sutherland's theory was presented in revised form in the fourth edition of the *Principles* (Philadelphia: J. B. Lippincott Co., 1947).

6. Ibid., 3d ed., pp. 4-9; ibid., 4th ed., pp. 5-9.

7. Roscoe C. Hinkle, Jr., and Gisela J. Hinkle, *The Development of Modern Sociology: Its Nature and Growth in the United States* (Garden City, New York: Doubleday & Co., 1954), p. 44.

8. Ibid., pp. 48-49.

9. Edwin H. Sutherland, "A Statement of the Theory," in *The Sutherland Papers*, ed. Albert Cohen, Alfred Lindesmith, and Karl Schuessler (Bloomington: Indiana University Press, 1956), p. 9.

10. Sutherland, *Principles*, 3d ed., p. 7.

11. Albert K. Cohen, *Delinquent Boys: The Culture of the Gang* (Glencoe, Illinois: The Free Press, 1955), p. 42.

12. Lee Rainwater, *Behind Ghetto Walls: Black Families in a Federal Slum* (Chicago: Aldine, 1970), p. 362.

13. Howard W. Jensen, "Editorial Note," in Milton M. Gordon, *Social Class in American Sociology* (New York: McGraw-Hill Book Co., 1950), p. v.

14. W. Lloyd Warner, *Democracy in Jonesville: A Study of Quality and Inequality* (New York: Harper, 1949), p. xiii.

15. Ibid., p. 297.

16. Gunnar Myrdal, *An American Dilemma: The Negro Problem and Modern Democracy* (New York: Harper & Brothers, 1944).

17. Otis Dudley Duncan and Beverly Duncan, *The Negro Population of Chicago* (Chicago: University of Chicago Press, 1957), p. 1.

18. Robert C. Weaver, *The Urban Complex: Human Values in Urban Life* (Garden City, New York: Doubleday, 1964), pp. 243-244.

19. Peter Marris and Martin Rein, *Dilemmas of Social Reform* (New York: Atherton Press, 1967), p. 13.

20. Herbert Blumer, "Race Prejudice as a Sense of Group Position," *Pacific Sociological Review* 1 (1958): 3. Quoted in Lewis M. Killian, "Herbert Blumer's Contributions to Race Relations," in Tamotsu Shibutani, ed., *Human Nature and Collective Behavior: Papers in Honor of Herbert Blumer* (Englewood Cliffs, New Jersey: Prentice-Hall, 1970), p. 184.

21. Oscar Handlin, *The Newcomers: Negroes and Puerto Ricans in a Changing Metropolis* (Garden City, New York: Doubleday, Anchor Books, 1962).

22. James F. Short, Jr., and Fred L. Strodtbeck, *Group Process and Gang Delinquency* (Chicago: University of Chicago Press, 1965), p. 214.

23. Irving Spergel, *Street Gang Work: Theory and Practice* (Reading, Massachusetts: Addison-Wesley, 1966), p. xvi.

24. William F. Whyte, "Social Organization in the Slums," *American Sociological Review* 8 (February 1943): 36-37.

25. Rainwater, *Behind Ghetto Walls*, pp. 363-365.

26. Don Martindale, *The Nature and Types of Sociological Theory* (Boston: Houghton Mifflin, 1960), p. 465.

27. Walter L. Wallace, *Sociological Theory: An Introduction* (Chicago: Aldine, 1969), p. 24.

28. Dennis H. Wrong, "The Oversocialized Conception of Man in Modern Sociology," *American Sociological Review* 26 (April 1961): 187.

29. Ibid., 185.

30. Robert K. Merton, "The Social-Cultural Environment and Anomie," in Helen L. Witmer and Ruth Kotinsky, eds., *New Perspectives for Research on Juvenile Delinquency*, U.S. Department of Health, Education, and Welfare, Children's Bureau (Washington, D.C.: U.S. Government Printing Office, 1956), pp. 25-26.

31. Cohen, *Delinquent Boys*, p. 18.

32. Ibid., p. 194.

33. Ibid., p. 61.

34. David Matza, *Becoming Deviant* (Englewood Cliffs, New Jersey: Prentice-Hall, 1969), p. 67.

35. Short and Strodtbeck, *Group Process and Gang Delinquency*.

36. Cohen, *Delinquent Boys*, p. 194.

37. Alvin W. Gouldner, "Reciprocity and Autonomy in Functional Theory," in N. J. Demerath III and Richard A. Peterson, eds., *System, Change, and Conflict* (New York: The Free Press, 1967), p. 158.

38. David J. Bordua, "A Critique of Sociological Interpretations of Gang Delinquency," *Annals of the American Academy of Political and Social Science* 338 (November 1961): 136.

39. James F. Short, Jr., "Gang Delinquency and Anomie," in Marshall B. Clinard, ed., *Anomie and Deviant Behavior* (New York: The Free Press, 1964), p. 116.

40. Richard A. Cloward and Lloyd E. Ohlin, *Delinquency and Opportunity: A Theory of Delinquent Gangs* (Glencoe, Illinois: The Free Press, 1960).

41. Ibid., pp. 13-14.

42. Ibid., p. 40.

43. Ibid., p. x.

44. Ibid., p. 160.

45. David Matza, *Delinquency and Drift* (New York: John Wiley, 1964).

46. Ibid., p. 49.

47. Ibid., pp. 49-50.

48. Short, Jr., "Gang Delinquency and Anomie," 25.

49. Ibid., 126.

50. Ibid., 124.

51. Walter B. Miller, "Lower Class Culture As a Generating Milieu of Gang Delinquency," *The Journal of Social Issues*, 14, no. 3 (1958): 5-19.

52. Jack D. Douglas, *The Social Meanings of Suicide* (Princeton: Princeton University Press, 1967), pp. 239-240.

53. Herbert Blumer, "Society as Symbolic Interaction," in *Symbolic Interactionism: Perspective and Method* (Englewood Cliffs, New Jersey: Prentice-Hall, 1969), p. 82.

chapter 8

The labeling theory

During the 1960s the tempo of social change in American society accelerated. Movements of social reform—the civil-rights movement, the women's movement, and the gay movement—cumulatively induced a change in the collective self-image of the American people. Their view of their society as a cohesive organic whole, dedicated to the pursuit of common goals, was increasingly replaced by an image of America as a mosaic of diverse groups, each with its own separate goals and its own insistent demands for justice, equality, and freedom. The belief that public life was based upon a far-reaching consensus was belied by the emergence of many competing perspectives. The issues of the cold war increasingly shared the public stage with issues generated by the internal divisions of American society.

Partially in response to the impetus provided by these social changes and partially in response to its own internal development, the discipline of sociology experienced a major reorientation during the 1960s. Since World War II it had been dominated by functionalist theories of society postulating consensus in basic values and norms. Now, many sociologists rejected this postulate and sought to replace it with a pluralistic view of society. Many types of social behavior they had assumed to be uniform in meaning throughout society now seemed to be subject to varying interpretations. Pluralistic relativism tended to replace the single societal perspective presupposed by functionalist theory. The labeling approach was an attempt to formulate a conception of deviance that would be compatible with such a pluralistic view of society.

The Antecedents of Labeling Theory

In many respects labeling represented a revival of the symbolic interactionism associated with the Chicago school and especially with the work of G. H. Mead, C. H. Cooley, and W. I. Thomas. This social psychological view of society, with its emphasis upon the flexibility and pliability of the mutual responses of individuals in social settings, was particularly suited to the study of human conduct during eras when the forms of human association are undergoing change. It was well adapted to inquiry into movements of immigration and urbanization, since during each of these processes individuals tended to reconstruct their institutions and group life. Consequently it was highly appropriate that this perspective should be revived during a new era of social flux and collective uncertainty, even though the focus of change was now no longer immigration and related social processes but the claims of hitherto largely acquiescent, silent, or unorganized groups. Symbolic interactionism emphasized the concept of meaning and its variable nature as individuals sought to coordinate their behavior in more or less novel circumstances.

Paradoxical as it may seem, in the light of its emphasis upon social life as a constant process of adaptation to changing situations, symbolic interactionism was formulated during an era of American society, the early decades of the twentieth century, when the image and values of the small town were still in the ascendant. In such a setting, the consensual base of accepted values was unquestioned. Both Cooley and Mead were profoundly influenced by this image in their conception of society. Both viewed social relationships as primarily personal, and group activity as conforming to the model of the small-town voluntary association. The presupposition of consensus found exemplary expression in Mead's view that individuals participated in society by virtue of their ability to take the role of the "generalized other," that is, their ability to abstract and organize the expectations communicated by their various personal relationships into a single, coherent personification.

Because of their preoccupation with the voluntary aspects of social conduct, Mead and Cooley minimized the role of power as a factor in human society. In thus tending to underestimate the importance of political processes, their work paralleled the apolitical character of sociological thought during the early decades of the twentieth century. Nevertheless, Blumer has argued that symbolic interactionism is a completely general sociological perspective, applicable to all forms of human relationships, including those involving power differences:

> In making the process of interpretation and definition of one another's acts central in human interaction, symbolic interaction is able to cover the full range of the generic forms of human association. It embraces equally well such relationships as cooperation, conflict, domination, exploitation, consensus, disagreement, closely knit identification, and indifferent concern for one another. The participants in each of such relations have the same common task of constructing their acts by interpreting and defining the acts of each other.[1]

Applying symbolic interactionism to political processes was one of the central tasks confronting the labeling theorists of deviance. They faced this problem in a society that had changed dramatically from the days of Mead and Cooley. The small-town image had long since been replaced by that of a pluralistic, highly differentiated society; that of a society in which personal relationships were central was replaced by one in which intergroup relationships had become increasingly important; and that of a society based upon consensus was replaced by one in which political processes had become central.

In a pluralistic society the significance of intergroup relationships as distinguished from personal relationships greatly increases. Group differences are accommodated through political processes, and social processes tend to become increasingly politicized. Inevitably the increasing importance of political processes in the functioning of society induces more and more groups to assume the form of interest groups that enter the political arena in order to attain their objectives.

Issues of social control and deviance become deeply influenced by these tendencies. First, many interest groups attempt to have their rules legislated into law and in this way to endow them with a legitimacy that makes them applicable to all groups in society. Second, the cumulative growth in the number of criminal statutes results in increased governmental control; moreover, in a pluralistic society, such governmental agencies themselves increasingly become interest groups. The ideologies of social control with which they are identified become political issues. This trend toward the multiplication of formal agencies of social control has been intensified by the growth of the welfare state:

> The welfare state is the institutional outcome of the assumption by a society of legal and therefore formal and explicit responsibility for the basic well being of all of its members. Such a stage emerges when a society or its decision-making groups become convinced that the welfare of the individual . . . is too important to be left to custom or to informal arrangements and private understandings and is therefore a concern of government.[2]

If it is necessary for a conception of social control compatible with a pluralistic society to take account of political processes, it is equally necessary for it to take into account the increasingly problematic nature of meaning. In such a society, many social situations become ambiguous in meaning and often fraught with potential conflict. The more complex and differentiated a society, and the more sensitive individuals become to their group identifications, the more problematic become the social encounters among individuals of competing groups. Those who work with deviance must ask the questions: Who says a particular act is deviant? Who has the power to make this concept of deviance stick?

The fundamental problem confronting Lemert and the labeling theorists who succeeded him was to coordinate their insights into social control as an expression of power processes and into deviance as a mode of making problematic situations determinate. The conceptual challenge that they confronted can be indicated by contrasting the problems of formulating a theory of deviant behavior under the varying assumptions of consensus and pluralistic relativism. Under the postulate of consensus, with its implication that basic values and norms are uniformly distributed throughout the society, theoretical interest turns to the distinctive conditions, qualities, and motives of those who violate these norms and challenge these values. The central question becomes that of asking why such individuals differ from those who conform to the societal norms and values. Under the influence of positivism, for example, this mode of inquiry provided the dominant model for the study of crime and delinquency for well over a century. In contrast, under the assumption of pluralistic relativism, the central issue becomes that of asking what kinds of social situations mobilize the application of social control. A pluralistic society is characterized by a wide gamut of behavior. Under what circumstances does certain behavior become selected out, adjudged, and treated as deviant? The central focus of theory becomes the process of such judgment and its consequences. As Lemert indicated, each of these models of theory construction may be viewed as appropriate to different social and historical circumstances:

> In rapidly changing societies and in relatively unstructured situations emphasis is properly placed on the societal reaction in deviance study. In societies and situations with stable, patterned values and norms having sacred connotations it may be more profitable to place the emphasis on attributes of persons and their actions. Still it has to be heeded continually that deviance outcomes flow from interaction between the two sets of factors, to which their identifiable attributes contribute at all times. Interaction clarifies the changing weight of the two.[3]

Lemert was the pioneer in formulating a theory of deviant behavior compatible with pluralistic relativism. He recognized that such a presupposition required a reconceptualization of both social control and the image of human nature.

Lemert's Labeling Theory

SOCIAL CONTROL AND THE CHANGING ROLE OF THE JUVENILE COURT

Any study of juvenile delinqueny, as Lemert approached it, had to try to answer two questions: What are the implications of a pluralistic society for modes of relationship between youth and society, and what issues of social control are posed by such patterns of relatedness? If there has been increasing differentiation between the youth and adult segments of our society, there should also be an increasing number of ambiguous and conflict situations involving the two generations. Moreover, nowhere should this trend be more manifest than in the family and school settings where the interdependence between the generations is so intimate, enduring, and inescapable. Given such circumstances, we would expect formal agencies of social control *to be increasingly resorted to* by those adults who were searching for modes of resolving their antagonistic relationships with youth.

This is what appears to have occurred. Indeed, this development was the starting point of Lemert's analysis of juvenile delinquency: "One of the most striking developments in the picture of child and youth problems has been the great increase in contacts between youth, law enforcement bodies, and the juvenile court."[4] The data bear out this statement: Between 1957 and 1973 the rate of cases of delinquents disposed of by juvenile courts per 1,000 child population increased from 19.8 in 1957 to 34.2 in 1973, an increase in the rate during this sixteen years of more than two-thirds.[5]

Lemert sought to formulate a conception of social control appropriate to a pluralistic, self-consciously changing society. As already discussed, in such a society specific groups are constantly organizing and seeking to attain hegemony for their rules among the adherents of other groups, frequently by means of legislation. Lemert believed that such a society, in which groups contended with each other in the effort to realize their values, implied a conception of social control, which he designated as "active" in contrast to an alternative view of social control as reactive or "passive." He sought to distinguish between the two:

> The distinction . . . makes passive control an aspect of conformity to traditional norms; active social control, on the other hand, is a process for the implementation of goals and values. The former has to do with the maintenance of social order, the latter with emergent social integrations. More precisely stated, active social control is a continuous process by which values are consciously examined, decisions made as to those values which should be dominant, and collective action taken to that end. While it has individual aspects it is more typically a function of group interaction.[6]

In an earlier study of the grand jury, Lemert had provided a concrete illustration of what he meant by "passive" social control:

The identification of the grand jury with the courts tended to make its control activities passive and post-critical, intervening in the governing process only after conflict or crimes arose, then moving in the direction of adjusting the controversy and ending its function. As such, its rationale and internal organization were oriented to static conditions disturbed irregularly by odd personal deviants.[7]

An important example of social control as active has been the ever-increasing influence of the "rehabilitative ideal" in the functioning of agencies of social control. This ideal sanctions extensive intervention into a person's life in order to alter such intimate aspects of his existence as his personality, his values, his group affiliations, and his identity. The legitmacy upon which the exercise of such authority is based is not only legal but is presumably also derived from the theories and findings of the psychological and social sciences and the professional competence of practitioners who apply these theories and findings.

The rehabilitative ideal is itself a complex of ideas which, perhaps, defies an exact definition. The essential points, however, can be identified. It is assumed, first, that human behavior is the product of antecedent causes. These causes can be identified as part of the physical universe, and it is the obligation of the scientist to discover and to describe them with all possible exactitude. Knowledge of the antecedents of human behavior makes possible an approach to the scientific control of human behavior. Finally, and of primary significance for the purposes at hand, it is assumed that measures employed to treat the convicted offender should serve a therapeutic function; that such measures should be designed to effect changes in the behavior of the convicted person in the interests of his own happiness, health, and satisfactions and in the interest of social defense.[8]

There is some evidence, indirect yet persuasive, indicating that the rehabilitative ideal, as applied to the social control of youth, has grown considerably in importance during the present century. As an example we can observe the growing limits upon the discretion police exercise in their disposition of juvenile cases. In particular we can contrast police practices with juveniles in Chicago of the 1920s, recorded by Burgess and Bogue, with the corresponding police practices of the 1960s, noted by Lemert and other students.

> In Chicago of the 1920's, only about 10 per cent of the children handled by the police were being brought into juvenile court. The cases brought to court were restricted primarily to more serious offenders over twelve years of age. The less serious cases were disposed of by the police—usually by calling in the child's parents. . . . It is apparent that the number of cases of delinquent children brought to court in a given year represents only a fraction of the total number of cases of serious delinquents known to the police.[9]

This pattern contrasts with that Lemert noted in the late 1960s and early 1970s: "Approximately one-half of police arrests of juveniles result in their referrals to juvenile courts."[10]

Wheeler, Cottrell, and Romasco attribute this decline in the discretion police exercise in juvenile cases to the association between the degree of their professionalization and their commitment to the rehabilitative ideal:

> The current trends toward professionalization in the field of delinquency prevention and control services may lead toward a broader category of persons being defined as "in need of service" than in the past. For there is at least a modicum of evidence that the more sophisticated personnel become, the greater is their tendency to see symptoms of problem behavior, and therefore the greater the tendency to engage in some form of intervention. It is the very feeling of confidence in the sophisticated techniques of modern intervention methods that may serve as justification for placing children in special therapeutic settings, in residential treatment centers, and in institutions thought to be beneficial for them. Thus a study of police relations with juveniles suggests that the more professional a police system, the larger is the percentage of the juvenile population formally charged with delinquency.[11]

Lemert is convinced that the whole theory of juvenile delinquency must be altered to take account of such trends; for the term "juvenile delinquency" has come increasingly to refer to a mode of interpreting and resolving highly ambiguous conflict-ridden situations in family, school, and local community, rather than to acts that theoretically could be subsumed under the categories of the criminal law. What is known as juvenile delinquency becomes increasingly a social artifact of the functioning of governmental control agencies. As Lemert illustrates in his discussion of the term "incorrigibility," the application of such verbal tags to the behavior of specific youth is frequently a result of the tendency of official control agents to intervene on the side of adults in the latter's conflicts with youth:

> Incorrigibility when put into its social context is a term which many times connotes little more than conflict between a teen-age youth and parents, in which unreasonable demands are made by the latter and in which a probation officer becomes a partisan. Sometimes the application of this term is merely a convenient vehicle for abdicating parental responsibility for a child. Outside the family it may mean that a teacher or vice principal has concluded that a child is a trouble-maker whom he will not tolerate further in the school.[12]

Because such acts come under the jurisdiction of the juvenile court and the youths involved are defined as delinquent as surely as those who commit serious offenses, Lemert argues that theories of delinquency must incorporate such processes of definition: "The task of sociology is not to study the theoretically conceived 'stuff' of delinquency but the process by which a variety of behaviors in contexts are given the unofficial and official meaning that is the basis for assigning special status in society."[13] He maintains that such processes of social control and definition actually tend to reinforce deviant behavior among the young by limiting their social participation and resulting in their self-definition as deviant. His argument is largely theoretical, however, and we shall return to it later in presenting his theory of deviant behavior.

Pluralism and the Image of Human Nature

Lemert insisted that the postulate of a pluralistic society in which numerous interest groups vie in pursuit of their respective ends presupposes individuals who consciously, rationally, and voluntarily form and subordinate themselves to groups in order to attain through collective action that which they could not aspire to attain as individuals. More specifically, in relation to deviant behavior, it presupposes individuals who construct their acts in more or less full awareness that such acts are potentially subject to negative sanctions on the part of control agents. Lemert stated the implications of this view for the understanding of deviant behavior: "We should like to note that new ways of thinking can be opened up by assuming that, in the absence of pressures to conform, people will deviate, or more precisely, express a variety of idiosyncratic impulses in overt behavior."[14]

Under the assumption that individuals consciously guide and control their overt acts through symbolic means, the question of why they conform to certain rules becomes as problematic as why they deviate from them. Theoretical interest is directed to the relationship between social controls and behavior: Under what conditions are social controls effective? Under what conditions are they ineffective? Reciprocally, how do individuals respond to rules and to the control agents who enforce them? Under what conditions will they take the risk of sanctions? What impact does the application of sanctions have upon the subsequent social and psychological functioning of individuals?

Lemert's view of human nature may be clarified by contrasting it with both the Freudian view and the "oversocialized" view associated with functionalist theories. Orthodox Freudians believe human beings are born with criminal tendencies; the latter require proper socialization in order to be brought under the individual's personal control. Lemert, in contrast, asserts that individuals may develop idiosyncratic orientations that are not necessarily congruent with the controls of groups to which they belong, and that if they can evade such controls they may act in accordance with their personal values or interests. A pluralistic society is highly conducive to such moral independence on the part of the individual. Individuals are not "oversocialized"; that is, their behavior is not solely to be interpreted as an expression of their internalization of the values and norms of their groups or of their struggle for status in such groups. This does not imply that their behavior is any the less oriented to others and therefore any less social than that posited by the oversocialized conception; it does imply that there is a component of unpredictability inherent in the course of human conduct, deriving from the potential capacity of individuals to define situations in a very personal manner.

Lemert's image of human nature had important methodological implications for the study of deviance. It gave relevance to the social psychological aspects of the behavior of both control agents and deviants. What are the covert symbolic processes of interpretation through which control agents decide to employ sanctions in particular situations? Reciprocally, what are the covert symbolic processes of interpretation through which individuals arrive at the decision to conform or deviate from particular rules when they are aware of the possible sanctions?

It was on the basis of his conception of human nature that Lemert attacked the epidemiological implications of Merton's structural theory. This theory assumes that deviant behavior is a product of structural strain. Since such strain is constituted by a disjunction between common success goals and the normative means to such goals, and since such normative means are least accessible to the lower social classes, it follows that deviant behavior should occur most frequently among the lowest social classes of the society. Lemert strongly disagreed with this conclusion on both empirical grounds and on the ground that it would be inconsistent with his conception of the image of human nature. Reviewing how unreliable, ambiguous, or inconclusive available empirical data are on the epidemiology of such types of deviant behavior as crime, alcoholism, suicide, and drug addiction, he commented, "A general purview of extant research leaves serious doubts that deviant behavior is proportionately more common at lower than at other class levels of our society."[15] From Lemert's perspective the whole meaning of the concept of the epidemiology of deviant behavior becomes problematic. It becomes dependent on the mode of functioning and relative effectiveness of the agencies of social control, their modes of keeping records, and the values and goals of individuals in different parts of society. But whatever the nature of the influence attributable to these various factors, there is no theoretical reason to expect norm violation to occur more frequently among the lower classes.

Lemert's Theory of Deviant Behavior

Lemert proposed a theory of behavior based upon the view of deviation as a consequence of the extent and form of social control. This view "rests upon the assumption that social control must be taken as an independent variable rather than as a constant, or merely reciprocal, societal reaction to deviation. Thus conceived, social control becomes a "cause" rather than an effect of the magnitude and variable forms of deviation."[16]

A theory based upon such premises would necessitate the integration of power and definitional processes. Moreover, since power was envisioned as an aspect of the social organization of society, and definitional processes as social psychological, Lemert's conception of a theory of deviant behavior required a synthesis between social organization and social psychology. He sought to incorporate both within a single conceptual framework by treating power as an organizational constraint that limited the scope of the definitional process. Furthermore, power was viewed as being merely one among a number of both social and nonsocial constraints:

> Human interaction always occurs within limits: biological, psychological, ecological, technological, and organizational.[17]

> Our position here is that there are limits to the variable meanings which interaction can give to geographic, biological, and socio-cultural facts. For example, while there is undoubtedly a great range of attitudinal reactions or "meanings" to such things as blindness, feeble-mindedness, or selling sexual favors, there is also a common core of meaning or an average impact of sociocultural facts upon a person or persons differentiated from others in these ways. Blind persons are incapable of reacting to the visual-esthetic aspects of our culture; there are no feeble-minded mathematicians; and most prostitutes dissociate sentiment and emotion from the occupational sex act.[18]

Lemert's attempt to formulate the idea of power as an organizational constraint upon the scope of definitional processes is clearly evident in several of the postulates of his theory. From an organizational point of view the process of becoming deviant could be construed as a coerced change in status or role; from a social psychological point of view as a transformation in the individual's identity.

· · ·

4. Sociopathic behavior is deviation which is *effectively* disapproved.

5. The deviant person is one whose role, status, function, and self-definition are importantly shaped by how much deviation he engages in, by the degree of its social visibility, by the *particular* exposure he has to the societal reaction, and by the nature and strength of the societal reaction.

6. There are patterns of restriction and freedom in the social participation of deviants which are related directly to their status, role, and self-definitions. The biological strictures upon social participation of deviants are directly significant in comparatively few cases.

7. Deviants are individuated with respect to their vulnerability to the societal reaction because: (a) the person is a dynamic agent, (b) there is a structuring to each personality which acts as a set of limits within which the societal reaction operates.[19]

Power themes and definitional themes predominate in each of these postulates. "Deviation which is *effectively* disapproved" is a product of power processes, which contribute to the shaping of "the role, status, function and self-definition" of deviant persons. It is the constraints attributable to the exercise of power that effect "patterns of restriction" in "the social participation of deviants." In contrast, the definitional theme enters into the conceptualization of the variation in the manner in which different individuals may define their exposure to measures of social control. "Deviants are individuated with respect to their vulnerability to the societal reaction because: (a) the person is a dynamic agent." The definitional process is also implicit in "patterns of . . . freedom in the social participation of deviants."

The task that Lemert confronted of developing concepts that would integrate power and definitional themes within a single conceptual framework adequate for the analysis of deviant behavior may be clarified by noting Goldhamer's and Shils' definition of power:

A person may be said to have *power* to the extent that he influences the behavior of others in accordance with his own intentions. Three major forms of power may be distinguished in terms of the type of influence brought to bear upon the subordinated individual. The power-holder exercises *force* when he influences behavior by a physical manipulation of the subordinated individual (assault, confinement, etc.); *domination* when he influences behavior by making explicit to others what he wants them to do (command, request, etc.); and *manipulation* when he influences the behavior of others without making explicit the behavior which he thereby wants them to perform. [20]

For present purposes it will be assumed that a social control theory of deviant behavior such as Lemert proposed would be primarily concerned with the exercise of two forms of power: force and domination. Such recognition has two implications. First, it suggests that an analytical distinction between power and definitional processes is indispensable since the relationship between them is likely to be highly variable and problematic. To the extent that power is exercised through force, social control tends to become unilateral, and the definitional processes of the deviant person are irrelevant. Conversely, to the extent that power is exercised through domination, social control tends to become a reciprocal process between superordinate and subordinate individuals. Second, a social control theory would assume that the blend of force and domination constitutive of social control will tend to vary with different types of deviant behavior, and among individuals defined as belonging to the same deviant category. Simmel made it clear that the application of power does not destroy the freedom of the subordinated individual:

> Within a relationship of subordination, the exclusion of all spontaneity whatever is actually rarer than is suggested by such widely used popular expressions as "coercion," "having no choice," "absolute necessity," etc. Even in the most oppressive and cruel cases of subordination, there is still a considerable measure of personal freedom. . . . More precise analysis shows that the super-subordination relationship destroys the subordinate's freedom only in the case of direct physical violation. [21]

Lemert named and applied his basic concepts in his hypothetical depiction of the process of becoming deviant:

> Most frequently there is a progressive reciprocal relationship between the deviation of the individual and the societal reaction, with a compounding of the societal reaction out of the minute accretions in the deviant behavior, until a point is reached

where ingrouping and outgrouping between society and the deviant is manifest. At this point a stigmatizing of the deviant occurs in the form of name calling, labeling, or stereotyping.

The sequence of interaction leading to secondary deviation is roughly as follows: (1) primary deviation; (2) social penalties; (3) further primary deviation; (4) stronger penalties and rejections; (5) further deviation, perhaps with hostilities and resentment beginning to focus upon those doing the penalizing; (6) crisis reached in the tolerance quotient, expressed in formal action by the community stigmatizing of the deviant; (7) strengthening of the deviant conduct as a reaction to the stigmatizing and penalties; (8) ultimate acceptance of deviant social status and efforts at adjustment on the basis of the associated role.

As an illustration of this sequence the behavior of an errant schoolboy can be cited. For one reason or another, let us say excessive energy, the school-boy engages in a classroom prank. He is penalized for it by the teacher. Later, due to clumsiness, he creates another disturbance and again he is reprimanded. Then, as sometimes happens, the boy is blamed for something he did not do. When the teacher uses the tag "bad boy" or "mischief maker" or other invidious terms, hostility and resentment are excited in the boy, and he may feel that he is blocked in playing the role expected of him. Thereafter, there may be a strong temptation to assume his role in the class as defined by the teacher, particularly when he discovers that there are rewards as well as penalties deriving from such a role. There is, of course, no implication here that such boys go on to become delinquents or criminals, for the mischief-maker role may later become integrated with or retrospectively rationalized as part of a role more acceptable to school authorities. [22]

Lemert's three fundamental concepts—societal reaction, primary deviance, and secondary deviance—are all illustrated in the preceding passage. The range of the teacher's responses to the boy, such as reprimands, penalties, and stigmatization, exemplify the societal reaction: "The societal reaction is a very general term summarizing both the expressive reactions of others (moral indignation) toward deviation and action directed to its control." [23] As this definition indicates, the concept of societal reaction is designed to encompass both social organizational and social psychological perspectives, both the application of power to the alleged deviant and the definition of the latter's behavior. As an organizational response it refers to the capacity of control agents to impose such constraints and limitations upon the behavior of the deviant as are reflected in terms like "isolate," "treat," "correct," or "punish."[24]

The two other concepts of Lemert's framework, primary and secondary deviation, can be defined in relation to the societal reaction. Primary deviation is norm violation that escapes exposure to societal reaction, for example, a classroom prank that escaped detection or response by the teacher. Secondary deviation, in contrast, refers to the consequences for norm violators of being exposed to societal reaction. Acts of primary deviation are interpreted by the actor as being consistent with his existing self-definitions, and by others to whom his acts may be known as congruent with his existing social roles. Consequently primary deviation is not accompanied by change either in the actor's place in the group or in his perspective toward himself. Secondary deviation, in contrast, deals with the consequences for the norm violator of exposure to societal reaction. If this occurs he is subject to the expression of moral disapprobation (for example, being tagged a "bad boy") and the application of actual constraints upon his behavior as applied by control agents. He must now confront the image of himself as a stigmatized person together with possible restrictions on the scope of his social participation. The concept of secondary deviation assumes that the actor may respond to such a situation by engaging in further norm violative behavior. Secondary deviance exhibits both an organizational component, a change in the actor's status, and a definitional component (a change in his conception of himself).

Judging from Lemert's illustration and his use of his concepts, the premise that social control "causes" deviance appears to be a shorthand statement for a complex process of interaction. At a certain juncture in a developing social situation a crisis occurs, which is marked by a transformation in the response of the superordinate person. For example, in Lemert's classroom illustration, up to the point of crisis, the teacher utilized penalties in order to induce the errant boy to conform to the rules established for the class. The crisis occurs when this effort is abandoned, and the boy is reidentified as "bad" and consigned to a morally inferior position in the class. It is at this point that the interaction between the two begins to manifest irony. The boy's motives for disrupting the class now change in reaction to the teacher's imputation of stigma. Nevertheless, his disturbing behavior, though differently motivated, merely serves to confirm the latter's previous definition of him as a "bad boy." It is to be noted, too, that as the conflict between teacher and student becomes more and more explicit, the constraints upon both increase, and the alternative definitions of the situation available to both become more and more restricted. Finally, stigmatization does not occur as the ascription of a formal role but as the application of a stereotype—"bad boy," or "mischief maker." This observation suggests that organizations such as the school do not have formal institutionalized roles for those who deviate, and they resort to stereotypes.

The Major Labeling Theorists

Lemert's conception of social control as a determinant of deviant behavior attained prominence in the 1960s and was reformulated by Becker, Kitsuse, and others as the "labeling" perspective. Some of its features were reinforced by the work of Short, Miller, and Matza in gang delinquency. During the post-World War II era, the sociological approach to the problem of delinquent gangs had been dominated by the subcultural theories of Cohen and of Cloward and Ohlin. As discussed in the previous chapter, Short had sought to test these theories empirically, Matza had subjected their assumptions to critical analysis, and Miller had confronted them with an alternative subcultural statement based upon microsociological rather than macrosociological assumptions. All three had tended to converge in their views that gang delinquency could not be interpreted solely as a subcultural response on the part of gang members to their disadvantaged position in the social structures of the larger society. It was also (and perhaps even primarily) to be viewed as a mode of resolving problematic situations that arose in the group and personal experience of gang boys. Short and Matza, in particular, argued for the necessity of reintroducing social psychological factors into theoretical formulations of gang delinquency.

It was Lemert who had first envisioned the possibility of integrating social psychological and social organizational perspectives into a social control theory of deviant behavior. This effort was continued in the work of Becker and Kitsuse, who like Lemert before them, shared the conviction that the pluralistic nature of society called for a new conception of deviant behavior. Becker made this point as follows:

> A society has many groups, each with its own set of rules, and people belong to many groups simultaneously. A person may break the rules of one group by the very act of abiding by the rules of another group. Is he, then, deviant? Proponents of this definition may object that while ambiguity may arise with respect to the rules peculiar to one or another group in society, there are some rules that are very generally agreed to by everyone, in which case the difficulty does not arise. This, of course, is a question of fact, to be settled by empirical research. I doubt there are many such areas of consensus and think it wiser to use a definition that allows us to deal with both ambiguous and unambiguous situations. [25]

Becker also revealed his continuity with Lemert's work in his image of human nature. Like Lemert he assumed that the individual had a potential for behavior that was not solely determined by his internalization of societal norms and values. Instead, he postulated a human being characterized by impulses toward rule violation, whose behavior was guided by the nature of his relationship to social controls:

> There is no reason to assume that only those who finally commit a deviant act actually have the impulse to do so. It is much more likely that most people experience deviant impulses frequently. At least in fantasy, people are much more deviant than they appear. Instead of asking why deviants want to do things that are disapproved of, we might better ask why conventional people do not follow through on the deviant impulses. [26]

Kitsuse had limited himself to the formulation of a theory of the societal reaction. Becker, like Lemert, sought to pave the way for a comprehensive social control theory of deviance. In addition to giving general currency to the concept of labeling, he also developed the concept of career as a mode of analyzing the deviant's experience in society from a temporal vantage point:

> *Social groups create deviance by making the rules whose infraction constitutes deviance*, and by applying those rules to particular people and labeling them as outsiders. From this point of view, deviance is *not* a quality of the act the person commits, but rather a consequence of the application by others of rules and sanctions to an "offender." The deviant is one to whom that label has successfully been applied; deviant behavior is behavior that people so label. [27]

From this statement it might appear that Becker was interested in labeling only insofar as it generated a social object, the deviant. The latter was the one to whom the rules were applied, being thereby converted into an "outsider" upon whom sanctions were imposed. He was, however, equally interested in the process of interaction, which eventuated in the imposition of the label. From such a perspective, that of symbolic interactionism, it was important to study the process itself as distinct from its products. So viewed labeling was the end result of a sequence of communicative actions, during the course of which, a distinctive type of meaning—deviance—became ascribed to particular individuals. Labeling thus became the resolution of a problematic situation. Such a resolution was not attained through the enforcement of preexisting norms but through a sequence of transactions during which rules applicable to the specific social setting were identified and applied in order to define the situation. In this sense rules were social objects that were forged within the give and take between the alleged offender and others. Labeling was a highly contingent outcome:

> Deviance is not a simple quality, present in some kinds of behavior and absent in others. Rather, it is the product of a process which involves responses of other people to the behavior. The same behavior may be an infraction of the rules at one time and not at another; may be an infraction when committed by one person, but not when committed by another; some rules are broken with impunity, others are not. In short, whether a given

act is deviant or not depends in part on the nature of the act (that is, whether or not it violates some rule) and in part on what other people do about it.[28]

The most striking formulation of the process leading to labeling as problematic and contingent was made by Kitsuse in his concept of *retrospective interpretation*. The latter emerged from his analysis of the responses obtained from his questionnaire study of homosexuality:

> When an individual's sexual "normality" is called into question, by whatever form of evidence, the imputation of homosexuality is documented by *retrospective interpretations* of the deviant's behavior, a process by which the subject re-interprets the individual's past behavior in the light of the new information concerning his sexual deviance.[29]

Retrospective interpretation refers to the possibility that certain aspects of the behavior of individuals may pass unnoticed or be viewed as normal at one period of time and then, retrospectively at some subsequent period, become criteria for the imputation of deviance.

Becker recognized that the process postulated by symbolic interactionism did not cease with the application of the deviant label, since the latter itself became subject to reinterpretation during subsequent social interaction:

> I will be less concerned with the personal and social characteristics of deviants than with the process by which they come to be thought of as outsiders and their reactions to that judgment.[30]

> The person who is thus labeled an outsider may have a different view of the matter. He may not accept the rule by which he is being judged and may not regard those who judge him as either competent or legitimately entitled to do so. Hence, a second meaning of the term emerges: the rule-breaker may feel his judges are *outsiders*.[31]

Despite this evidence of Becker's commitment to the symbolic interactionist perspective, he abandoned it in the middle of his analysis of the process through which individuals became deviant and re-placed it with a social organizational perspective. When this shift occurred labeling was no longer an aspect of a larger interactive process that both preceded and followed it but a unilateral mechanism through which individuals were assigned to a social status:

> The application of power forces the individual into a new status. Being caught and branded as deviant has important consequences for one's further social participation and self-image. The most important consequence is a drastic change in the individual's public identity. Committing the improper act and being publicly caught at it place him in a new status. He has been revealed as a different kind of person from the kind he was supposed to be. He is labeled a "fairy," "dope fiend," "nut" or "lunatic" and treated accordingly.[32]

What occurred here was a sudden shift in conceptual framework. The sequence of events that leads to the imposition of the label of deviant is analyzed from the perspective of social interaction; however, once the label is imposed the analytical framework shifts to that of social structure. This shift is signaled by the introduction and continued usage of the concept of status. Before he is labeled the alleged deviant is participating in a process of interaction; once he has been labeled he becomes the occupant of a status within a social structure. The notion of status precludes the notion of interaction as a formative process.

Blumer has sought to make this distinction clear. He has argued that symbolic interactionism and the structural approach are two quite different perspectives upon human conduct even though both may be based upon the empirical study of human conduct:

> The study of the social organization of human groups shows always an arrangement of social positions, whether they be conceived in terms of a division of labor or in terms of hierarchy of status. It is to be noted, further, that each one of these positions is socially defined by expectations as to how the occupant is to act and be socially valued in relation to other positions. . . .
>
> Here I merely wish to point out that the conceptions of culture, social structure and role playing have not been derived

from the study of human association as an on-going process. Rather, they have been formed through the study of certain products of human association.[33]

This shift in conceptual framework coincided with the introduction of the concept of power into the analysis. Such a development suggests that Becker found this concept more amenable to sociological treatment within a social organizational than within a symbolic interactionist perspective. The outcome of his theoretical strategy, however, was the production of an analytical scheme in which the potentialities of symbolic interactionism as applicable to deviant phenomena became truncated.

The contention that Becker shifts from a *process* orientation to a *structural* orientation after the imposition of the deviant label is supported by his conception of the deviant career. The imagery implied by the concept of career is that of movement from status to status, presumably within some encompassing social structure:

> A useful conception in developing sequential models of various kinds of deviant behavior is that of *career*. Originally developed in studies of occupations, the concept refers to the sequence of movements from one position to another in an occupational system made by any individual who works in that system. Furthermore, it includes the notion of "career contingency," those factors on which mobility from one position to another depends. Career contingencies include both objective facts of social structure and changes in the perspectives, motivations, and desires of the individual.[34]

Lamert has commented upon the notion of deviant career as follows:

> The deviant career concept also has been linked with or partly derived from an occupational model, examples of which are found in the descriptions of criminal behavior systems, such as thieving, and the marginal deviance of dance musicians. The occupational parallel, of course, can be demonstrated in the professionalization of some types of thieves, prostitutes, political radicals, vagrants, bohemians (beatniks), beggars, and to some extent the physically handicapped. In contrast to these,

however, there is little indication of an occupational orientation among alcoholics, mentally disordered persons, stutterers, homosexuals and systematic check forgers.

A career denotes a course to be run, but the delineation of fixed sequences or stages through which persons move from less to more serious deviance is difficult or impossible to reconcile with an interactional theory. . . .

A more defensible conception of deviant career is that of recurrent or typical contingencies and problems awaiting someone who continue [sic] in a course of action, with the added notion that there may be theoretically "best" choices set into a situation by prevailing technology and social structure. There is some predictive value of a limited or residual nature in concepts like "turning points" or "points of no return," which have been brought into the sociological analysis of careers. These allow it to be said that persons having undergone certain changes will not or cannot retrace their steps; deviant actions act as social foreclosures which qualitatively change meanings and shift the scope of alternatives within which new choices can be made. Even here a caveat is necessary, for alcoholics, drug addicts, criminals, and other deviants do sometimes make comebacks in the face of stigma, and an early history of deviance may in some instances lead to success in the conventional world.[35]

I suggest that the inconsistencies that have been found in Becker's conceptualization of deviance may be attributed to the lack of resolution within his work of logical difficulties resulting from his attempt to synthesize symbolic interationist and social organizational perspectives. Perhaps the greatest difficulty has resulted from the ambiguous role of norms in his schemes. The social structural approach he used tends to presuppose consensus over norms. This assumption of consensus is particularly evident in his discussion of becoming a marijuana user, in which the central issue confronting the novice is that of learning to master preexisting norms that define the various facets, implications, and consequences of marijuana usage. The assumption of preexisting norms is also presupposed by the notion of subculture as applied to the way of life of jazz musicians. Indeed, this consensual perspective is evident in many parts of *Outsiders*. The folowing passage is an example:

When deviant behavior occurs in a society—behavior which flouts its basic values and norms—one element in its coming into being is a breakdown in social controls which ordinarily operate to maintain the valued forms of behavior. In complex societies, the process can be quite complicated since breakdowns in social control are often the consequence of becoming a participant in a group whose own culture and social controls operate at cross-purposes to those of the larger society. Important factors in the genesis of deviant behavior, then, may be sought in the processes by which people are emancipated from the controls of society and become responsive to those of a smaller group. [36]

Since the ascription of deviance occurs during labeling, the notion of deviant career necessarily refers to the deviant's post-labeling experience; however, it is to be noted that Becker provides a paucity of empirical illustrations of deviant careers subsequent to labeling. He applied the career notion to the stages of becoming a marijuana user prior to or in abstraction from the labeling experience. He also applied it to the experience of jazz musicians; in this instance the concepts of career contingencies were applied in their original occupational context rather than analogically in a deviance context. In short, Becker made few empirical connections between his central concepts—labeling and deviant career.

The preceding analysis of Becker's conceptual framework may assist in clarifying an anomaly of the labeling perspective. According to Schur,

An ambivalence in the labeling view of the individual deviator as social actor has already been noted. On one hand, the actor is viewed as largely at the mercy of the reaction processes; what they are determines what he is to become. At the same time, the approach incorporates from symbolic interactionism a view of the actor as significantly shaping his own projects and lines of action. [37]

It is suggested that this ambivalence in the image of the deviant arises from the manner in which the political processes involved in the ascription of deviance are believed to function. Prior to labeling the potential deviant is viewed at least in part as master of his own fate; after labeling his fate is totally determined by others. In forcing the individual into a deviant status, the application of power results in a metamorphosis in his nature. Status as a structural conception presupposes an individual whose action is determined by his position in a system of positions; in its emphasis upon the pressures exerted by the expectations of others, it provides little scope for the individual's determination of his own behavior. It is to be noted that there is a second anomaly in the labeling perspective as viewed from symbolic interactionism. The political processes that produce deviance apparently impose constraints only upon the self-determination of the behavior of those labeled, not upon that of those who do the labeling. Consequently it is possible for Becker to discuss entrepreneurship among rule makers and rule enforcers but to ignore the possibility of entrepreneurship among deviants. Blumer—in fact any classical symbolic interactionist—would deny that such an asymmetrical resolution of power differences is inherent in symbolic interactionism.

Evaluation and Critique

According to Becker the goal of labeling theory was not to explain discrete deviant acts, but to study the processes through which individuals came to engage in deviant behavior as a consistent ongoing pattern of activity expressive of their identity:

> We are not so much interested in the person who commits a deviant act once as in the person who sustains a pattern of deviance over a long period of time, who makes of deviance a way of life, who organizes his identity around a pattern of deviant behavior. It is not the casual experimenters with homosexuality . . . . that we want to find out about, but the man who follows a pattern of homosexual activity throughout his adult life. . . .
> One of the most crucial steps in the process of building a stable pattern of deviant behavior is likely to be the experience of being caught and publicly labeled as a deviant.[38]

How much has labeling theory clarified the processes through which individuals become committed to deviant behavior and the role of public labeling in these processes? One can grant the power of agencies of social control to "isolate," "treat," "correct," or "punish," but what effects do such experiences exert upon the subsequent behavior of deviants? What are the consequences of stigmatization, the arousal of a sense of injustice, the exposure to status degradation ceremonies, or incarceration for the individuals subjected to such sanctions? Under what conditions is the application of sanctions to specific individuals likely to confirm them in deviant behavior? The labeling perspective tends to be most applicable to situations in which the application of power to the sanctioned individual virtually restricts the latter to one alternative: continued deviance. In short, it presupposes very extensive differentials in power between labeler and labelee. However, the assertion that definitions of the situation can be totally imposed upon individuals is incompatible with the assumptions of symbolic interactionism, which presuppose that interaction in the end is almost always one-to-one. There is always the possibility of some autonomy and consequently of some unpredictability in response. Indeed, the power situation itself may be transformed through interaction, as Park, for example, suggested in his discussion of slavery in the South:

> The regime of slavery, constantly threatened from without, was at the same time steadily undermined and weakened from within; weakened by the claims of the slave, on the one hand, and the conscience of the master, on the other.
>
> ... We know how friendships sometimes corrupt politics. In a somewhat similar way the intimate association of master and slave may be said steadily to have corrupted the institution of slavery, and in so doing hastened it on its course to its predestined extinction. [39]

Conceptions of the relationship between social organization and definitional processes that do not misrepresent or truncate the definitional process are required. At the same time, the role of power processes must also be recognized.

I would like to suggest one process through which the application of social control transforms the self-definition of the individual into that of a deviant. The argument maintains that the individual comes to conceive of himself as a deviant as a result of the joint functioning of power and consensual processes. Such a change occurs when the labeling of the individual by official agencies of social control is validated by his subsequent experiences in his personal associations in the control agency and community. Where such validation in personal interaction does not occur, the official label is not incorporated into the self of the sanctioned individual. For labeling to be effective in transforming the identity of the individual into that of a deviant, a two-phased process is required. The first is that of official labeling. The second is one in which this label influences the social typing of the individual in his informal associations. As evidence for this argument I would like to present three considerations:

1. Lemert illustrated the devastating efficacy of the moral premises that could be mobilized through informal means; his example was Victorian England, which, without the application of formal sanctions, had shown virtual unanimity in its ostracism of unchaste women:

> An assertion, by no means new, is that for stigmatization to establish a total deviant identity it must be disseminated throughout society. Lecky spoke strongly on this point, contending that the solid front of public opinion against the "slightest frailty" among women in mid-nineteenth century England did much to add to the ranks of habitual prostitutes. To his view the "terrible censure" of opinion and the deep degradation of unchaste women caused the status of the prostitute to be irrevocable, and likewise contributed heavily to the associated crime of infanticide. [40]

2. In discussing the conditions under which individuals might voluntarily accept morally degrading identities, Lemert noted that such transformations were facilitated by unanticipated developments in the personal interaction between control agents and deviants in institutional settings:

> The accretion of special meanings which attach to ameliorative services, and their subversion to ends other than those intended, often explains why deviant statuses may be more amenable than they are or than can be officially represented. Organized social control of deviance, as with social control in general, at most has a marginal influence on the interactional processes which gave it existential meaning. Collective efforts to organize systems of rewards and punishments to repress deviance and promote reformation along expected lines are always subject to vicissitudes

of interpretation, diversion, and cooptation of agents of authority at their points of intervention in social interaction. [41]

3. Labeling itself is not solely a formal process. Whenever the labeling theorists depict the process of labeling they typically resort to
stereotypes as distinct from formal role designations. Thus, in
Lemert's hypothetical classroom illustrations, when the interaction
comes to a point of crisis, the teacher labels the student a "bad boy" or
"mischief maker." Similarly, Becker illustrates the process of labeling by the use of such terms as "fairy," "dope fiend," "nut," or "luna-
tic." It is not the formal functioning of control agencies alone that
produces stigmatized individuals but the informal processes that are
mobilized.

Methodologically, a view of labeling that would approach it as a
two-phased process would be concerned with the interaction between
stereotyping at the formal or organizational level and social typing at
the interpersonal level. For this distinction between stereotyping and
social typing I am indebted to Klapp:

> The social type, as here conceived, may be contrasted with the
> stereotype. A stereotype is often, if not generally, viewed as an
> inaccurate, rigid popular concept playing an important part in
> prejudice. It is not rational and interferes with insight. The im-
> plicit aim of many of those who study stereotypes seems to be to
> analyze them so as to get rid of them. The conception of the so-
> cial type presented here is in marked contrast with this view.
> Social types, according to the present argument, are as realistic
> as most concepts used in everyday life may be expected to be;
> they are needed for effective participation in modern secondary
> society, and are characteristically applied within the system to
> promote insightful relations rather than to hold people at a dis-
> tance or portray outside groups in an inaccurate way. [42]

Klapp's distinction opens the way for analyzing the highly ambivalent attitudes toward the deviant that are characteristic of our
society. The stereotyping of the deviant at the formal organizational
level denotes the centrifugal forces through which society seeks to
transform him into an outcast and place him beyond the social pale.
Social typing denotes a centripetal process, operative in certain
informal settings, by means of which the deviant finds acceptance and

a personal niche, albeit a precarious one. Such a conception of the labeling process as dualistic in nature is consistent with symbolic interactionism. It goes beyond the formal imposition of the label in order to examine how the label gets interpreted in the social worlds in which the deviant lives. It is a conception that also contributes analytic clarity to the idea of labeling. The acceptance or rejection of the deviant label involves a change in the self-oriented sentiments, in the "looking glass self," in the traditional phrase of Cooley. Accepting or rejecting the label is a matter of sentiment as well as of power, and the processes that each imply are analytically distinguishable.

Such a two-phased approach, with its emphasis upon both formal and informal processes of interaction, is especially applicable to the issues of juvenile delinquency, for the latter reflects the problems of adolescents in extremis. Moreover, adolescence in our society is a time when the individual's ties to both formal organizations, such as the school, and to informal associations, such as the peer group, are highly significant, more replete with tensions, and yet more interdependent than in earlier or later life stages. It is during this period therefore that a study of the reciprocal impact of the processes of stereotyping and social typing becomes particularly appropriate.

Practical Implications of Labeling

In its practical implications for dealing with the problems of juvenile delinquency, labeling represents both an end and a beginning. It represents an end to the hopes, mostly fostered during the first half of the twentieth century, that the findings of science in general, and of the application of the rehabilitative ideal in particular could have a significant impact upon the problem of juvenile delinquency. The rehabilitative ideal assumed that the problem of delinquency could be delegated to the technical skills of the experts. It was a faith that proved to be misplaced because it omitted a central but all-important fact: delinquency is inseparable from political processes. Labeling theory fundamentally represents a crisis in the legitimacy of authority, a crisis that is quite inconsistent with the acceptance of legitimate authority in any form, even under the guise of dispassionate, professionally trained experts, for it attributes delinquency precisely to professionals and experts.

It is this observation that provides one link between the era in which the labeling perspective has been ascendant with the era of subcultural theories of gang delinquency. Cloward and Ohlin and Matza recognized that gang delinquents were not bound by the legitimacy of the authority of the existing laws. There was no basis for assuming that they should be amenable to treatment offered by the court. Francis Allen had early warned about this limitation of the court:

> Is it possible that the traditional view of the court as exclusively or largely a therapeutic or rehabilitative agency has obstructed identification of areas of legitimate community interest that the court may properly be expected to serve? . . .
> It is an unfortunate fact that the juvenile court of every large urban community is confronted by significant numbers of adolescents whose behavior cannot be ignored because it imperils the basic security of the community, and who, as a class, elude the reformative capabilities of the court. [43]

Such inadequacies were never frankly admitted, perhaps because the court was in an institutional rut from which it could not escape, perhaps because of political reasons in which court and public colluded in the belief that a job was being done when it was not. In effect, under such circumstances, paradoxically but inevitably, the rehabilitative ideal became a euphemism for a misuse of power—and a misuse of the most blatant kind since it was exercised by experts under cover of the authority provided by their professional standing and prestige.

Another phrase that has served as a euphemism to mask the inefficacy of the court has been the doctrine of parens patriae. According to this doctrine the state acts in the role of parent, and the court becomes a surrogate for the family. This analogy between the court and family has been nullified, if indeed it ever was applicable, by the growing bureaucratization of the court.

Labeling inevitably has moral implications for the problem of juvenile delinquency, implications that are clarified by contrasting it with the positivist theories of delinquency that preceded it. As long as delinquency could be attributed to class, poverty, broken homes, and other social ills, the problem it posed could always be blamed upon impersonal factors that absolved the conforming members of society from all involvement in the difficulties and suffering of their less fortunate youthful contemporaries. Into this unruly crowd of competing yet somehow consoling theories of delinquency, labeling throws a pitiless beam of light: accountability. Since its focus of attention is upon agencies of social control, of which the juvenile court is a prime example, and since such agencies are the society's own deliberate creations, labeling implies a need for honesty on society's part about itself even, if need be, honesty about its ambivalence toward such problems as juvenile delinquency. If unanticipated consequences have developed that serve to defeat the declared aims of such institutions as the juvenile court, these can be uncovered and their technical and political ramifications publicly discussed; goals can be reformulated and means aligned to them in a more straightforward and rational manner. More generally, social control processes and their consequences for youth and society become a crucially important problem for theory, research, and practice. One of the most relevant contributions of labeling has been to introduce an image of the human individual, borrowed from symbolic interactionism, as capable of guiding and controlling his own behavior. Such an image provides a sound basis for accountability, applicable to delinquents, control agents, and all members of society alike.

If one practical implication of labeling and delinquent subculture theories has been to raise the questions of the accountability of official institutions, another has been to promote the exploration of community-based corrections. This last need, however, is already beginning to show some internal limitations leading to the realization that community-based corrections will not be able to substitute for formal official institutions without potentially disastrous results. Hence, while official institutions must be made more accountable, a renewed analysis of delinquent behavior is in order to locate the proper role of community-based corrections.

NOTES

1. Herbert Blumer, "Sociological Implications of the Thought of George Herbert Mead," in his *Symbolic Interactionism* (Englewood Cliffs, New Jersey: Prentice-Hall, 1969), p. 67.

2. Harry K. Girvetz, "Welfare State," *International Encyclopedia of the Social Sciences* (New York: Macmillan, 1968), 16: 512.

3. Edwin M. Lemert, "Social Problems and the Sociology of Deviance," *Human*

Deviance, Social Problems, and Social Control, 2d ed. (Englewood Cliffs, New Jersey: Prentice-Hall, 1972), p. 21.

4. Edwin M. Lemert, *Instead of Court*, National Institute of Mental Health, Center for Studies of Crime and Delinquency (Washington, D.C.: U.S. Government Printing Office, 1971), p. 1.

5. *Juvenile Court Statistics, 1973*, Office of Youth Development, U.S. Department of Health, Education, and Welfare (n.d.), p. 10.

6. Lemert, "Social Structure, Social Control, and Deviation," in *Human Deviance, Social Problems, and Social Control*, pp. 53-54.

7. Edwin M. Lemert, "The Grand Jury as an Agency of Social Control," *American Sociological Review* 10 (December 1945): 757.

8. Francis A. Allen, "Legal Values and the Rehabilitative Ideal," *The Borderland of Criminal Justice* (Chicago: University of Chicago Press, 1964), p. 26.

9. Ernest W. Burgess and Donald J. Bogue, "The Delinquency Research of Clifford R. Shaw and Henry D. McKay and Associates," in Burgess and Bogue, eds., *Urban Sociology* (Chicago: University of Chicago, Phoenix Books, 1967), p. 294.

10. Lemert, *Instead of Court*, p. 1.

11. Stanton Wheeler, Leonard S. Cottrell, Jr., and Anne Romasco, "Juvenile Delinquency: Its Prevention and Control," *Juvenile Delinquency and Youth Crime*, The President's Commission on Law Enforcement and Administration of Justice (Washington, D.C.: U.S. Government Printing Office, 1967), p. 419.

12. Lemert, *Instead of Court*, p. 10.

13. Lemert, "Social Structure, Social Control, and Deviation," p. 59.

14. Ibid., p. 49.

15. Ibid., p. 40.

16. Ibid., p. 49.

17. Lemert, "Social Problems and the Sociology of Deviance," p. 22.

18. Edwin M. Lemert, *Social Pathology* (New York: McGraw-Hill, 1951), p. 12.

19. Ibid., p. 23.

20. Herbert Goldhamer and Edward A. Shils, "Types of Power and Status," *American Journal of Sociology* 45 (September 1939): 171-172.

21. Kurt H. Wolff, ed., *The Sociology of Georg Simmel* (Glencoe, Illinois: The Free Press, 1950), p. 182.

22. Lemert, *Social Pathology*, pp. 76-77.

23. Edwin M. Lemert, "The Concept of Secondary Deviation," in *Human Deviance, Social Problems, and Social Control*, p. 64.

24. Edwin M. Schur, *Labeling Deviant Behavior* (New York: Harper & Bros., 1971), p. 24.

25. Howard S. Becker, *Outsiders* (New York: The Free Press, 1963), p. 8.

26. Ibid., p. 26.

27. Ibid., pp. 8-9.

28. Ibid., p. 14.

29. John J. Kitsuse, "Societal Reaction to Deviant Behavior: Problems of Theory and Method," *Social Problems* 9 (Winter 1962): 253.

30. Becker, *Outsiders*, p. 10.

31. Ibid., pp. 1-2.

32. Ibid., pp. 31-32.

33. Blumer, *Symbolic Interactionism*, pp. 106-107.

34. Becker, *Outsiders*, p. 24.

35. Lemert, "The Concept of Secondary Deviation," p. 79.

36. Becker, *Outsiders*, pp. 59-60.

37. Schur, *Labeling Deviant Behavior*, p. 19.

38. Becker, *Outsiders*, pp. 30-31.

39. Robert E. Park, "The Etiquette of Race Relations in the South," in *Race and Culture*, ed. Everett C. Hughes, Charles S. Johnson, Jitsuichi Masuoka, Robert Redfield, and Louis Wirth (Glencoe, Illinois: The Free Press, 1950), p. 179.

40. Lemert, "The Concept of Secondary Deviation," p. 65.

41. Ibid., p. 65.

42. Orrin E. Klapp, "Social Types: Process and Structure," *American Sociological Review* 23 (December 1938): 675.

43. Francis A. Allen, "The Juvenile Court and the Limits of Juvenile Justice," *The Borderland of Criminal Justice* (Chicago: University of Chicago Press, 1964), pp. 50-52.

selected bibliography

Addams, Jane. *The Spirit of Youth and the City Streets.* 1909. Reprint. Urbana, Illinois: University of Illinois Press, 1972.

Aichhorn, August. *Wayward Youth.* New York: Viking Press, 1963.

Alexander, Franz, and Healy, William. *Roots of Crime.* New York: Alfred A. Knopf, 1935.

Alinsky, Saul D. *Reveille for Radicals.* Chicago: University of Chicago Press, 1946.

Allen, Francis A. *The Borderland of Criminal Justice.* Chicago: University of Chicago Press, 1964.

Arnold, Robert. "Mobilization for Youth: Patchwork or Solution." *Dissent* 11 (Summer 1964): 347-354.

Bakan, David. "Adolescence in America: From Idea to Social Fact." *Daedalus* 100 (Fall 1971): 979-995.

Becker, Howard S. *Outsiders.* New York: The Free Press, 1963.

Berg, Ivar. "Economic Factors in Delinquency." In *Task Force Report—Juvenile Delinquency and Youth Crime*, President's Commission on Law Enforcement and the Administration of Justice, pp. 305-316. Washington, D.C.: U.S. Government Printing Office, 1967.

Berman, Louis. "Crime and the Endocrine Glands." *American Journal of Psychiatry* 12 (September 1932): 215-238.

Bloch, Herbert A., and Niederhoffer, Arthur. *The Gang: A Study of Adolescent Behavior.* New York: Philosophical Library, 1958.

Blumer, Herbert. "Sociological Implications of the Thought of George Herbert Mead." *American Journal of Sociology* 71 (March 1966): 535-544.

Bordua, David J. "Delinquent Subcultures: Sociological Interpretations of Gang Delinquency." *Annals of the American Academy of Political and Social Science* 338 (November 1961): 119-136.

―――. "Recent Trends: Deviant Behavior and Social Control." *Annals of the American Academy of Political and Social Sciences* 369 (January 1967): 149-163.

Bowlby, John. *Forty-four Juvenile Thieves: Their Characters and Home Life.* London: Bailliere, Tindall and Cox, 1946.

Breckenridge, Sophonisba P., and Abbott, Edith. *The Delinquent Child and the Home.* New York: Russell Sage Foundation, 1912.

Brown, Claude. *Manchild in the Promised Land.* New York: Macmillan, 1965.

Burgess, Ernest W. "The Study of the Delinquent as a Person." *American Journal of Sociology* 28 (May 1923): 657-679.

Burgess, Ernest W., and Bogue, Donald J. "The Delinquent Research of Clifford R. Shaw and Henry D. McKay and Associates." In *Urban Sociology*, edited by Ernest

W. Burgess and Donald J. Bogue, pp. 293-317. Chicago: University of Chicago Press, Phoenix Books, 1967.

Burt, Cyril. *The Young Delinquent*. London: University of London Press, 1925.

Cabot, Philippe Sidney de Q. *Juvenile Delinquency: A Critical Annotated Bibliography*. Westport, Connecticut: Greenwood Press, 1971.

Chein, Isidor et al. *The Road to H: Narcotics, Delinquency, and Social Policy*. New York: Basic Books, 1964.

Chilton, Roland J. "Continuity in Delinquency Area Research: A Comparison of Studies for Baltimore, Detroit, and Indianapolis." *American Sociological Review* 29 (February 1964): 71-83.

Cicourel, Aaron V. *The Social Organization of Juvenile Justice*. New York: John Wiley & Sons, 1968.

Clark, Kenneth B. *Dark Ghetto*. New York: Harper & Row, 1965.

Clarke, Michael. "On the Concept of 'Sub-culture.'" *British Journal of Sociology* 25 (December 1974): 428-441.

Cloward, Richard A., and Ohlin, Lloyd E. *Delinquency and Opportunity: A Theory of Delinquent Gangs*. New York: The Free Press, 1960.

Cohen, Albert K. *Delinquent Boys: The Culture of the Gang*. New York: The Free Press, 1955.

————. "The Sociology of the Deviant Act: Anomie Theory and Beyond." *American Sociological Review* 30 (February 1965): 5-14.

Cohen, Albert K.; Lindesmith, Alfred; and Schuessler, Karl. eds. *The Sutherland Papers*. Bloomington: Indiana University Press, 1956.

Cohen, Albert K., and Short, James F., Jr. "Juvenile Delinquency." In *Contemporary Social Problems*, edited by Robert K. Merton and Robert A. Nisbet. 2d ed. New York: Harcourt, Brace & World, 1966, pp. 84-135.

Coleman, James C. *The Adolescent Society*. New York: The Free Press, 1953.

Connor, Walter D. *Deviance in Soviet Society: Crime, Delinquency, and Alcoholism*. New York: Columbia University Press, 1972.

Cressey, Donald R. "Changing Criminals: The Application of the Theory of Differential Association." *The American Journal of Sociology* 61 (September 1955): 116-120.

————. "Epidemiology and Individual Conduct: A Case from Criminology." *The Pacific Sociological Review* 3 (Fall 1960): 47-58.

Demos, John, and Demos, Virginia. "Adolescence in Historical Perspective." *Journal of Marriage and the Family* 31 (November 1969): 632-638.

Dollard, John. *Criteria for the Life History*. New Haven: Yale University Press, 1935.

Eissler, Kurt R., ed. *Searchlights on Delinquency*. New York: International Universities Press, 1949.

Elliott, Delbert S., and Voss, Harwin L. *Delinquency and Dropout*. Lexington, Massachusetts: Lexington Books, 1974.

Emerson, Robert M. *Judging Delinquents: Context and Process in Juvenile Court*. Chicago: Aldine Press, 1969.

Empey, Lamar T. and Jerome Rabow. "The Provo Experiment in Delinquency Rehabilitation." *American Sociological Review* 26 (October 1961): 679-695.

————. "Delinquency Theory and Recent Research." *Journal of Research in Crime and Delinquency* 4 (January 1967): 28-42.

Empey, Lamar T., and Lubeck, Steven G. *The Silverlake Experiment*. Chicago: Aldine, 1971.

England, Ralph W., Jr. "A Theory of Middle Class Juvenile Delinquency." *Journal of Criminal Law, Criminology and Police Science* 50 (April 1960): 535-540.

Faris, Robert E. L. *Chicago Sociology, 1920-1932*. Chicago: University of Chicago Press, 1970.

Ferdinand, Theodore N. *Typologies of Delinquency: A Critical Analysis*. New York: Random House, 1966.

Fink, Arthur E. *Causes of Crime: Biological Theories in the United States, 1800-1914*. Philadelphia: University of Pennsylvania Press, 1938.

Frazier, E. Franklin. *The Negro Family in Chicago*. Chicago: University of Chicago Press, 1931.

Friedlander, Kate. *The Psycho-analytical Approach to Juvenile Delinquency: Theory, Case Studies, Treatment*. New York: International Universities Press, 1947.

Furman, Sylvan S., ed. *Reaching the Unreached*. New York: New York City Youth Board, 1952.

Glaser, Daniel, and Rice, Kent. "Crime, Age, and Employment." *American Sociological Review* 24 (October 1959): 679-686.

Glueck, Sheldon, and Glueck, Eleanor. *One Thousand Juvenile Delinquents*. Cambridge: Harvard University Press, 1934.

——. *Unraveling Juvenile Delinquency*. Cambridge: Harvard University Press, 1950.

Goddard, Henry H. "Levels of Intelligence and the Prediction of Delinquency." *Journal of Juvenile Research* 13 (October 1929): 262-265.

Gold, Martin. *Status Forces in Delinquent Boys*. Ann Arbor: Institute for Social Research, 1963.

Goldman, Nathan. *The Differential Selection of Juvenile Offenders for Court Appearance*. New York: National Council on Crime and Delinquency, 1963.

Goodman, Paul. *Growing Up Absurd*. New York: Random House, 1960.

Gouldner, Alvin W. "The Sociologist as Partisan: Sociology and the Welfare State." *The American Sociologist* 3 (May 1968): 103-116.

Haines, Thomas H. "Defect in Germ Plasm as a Cause of Delinquency." *Journal of Delinquency* 1 (July 1916): 154-155.

Hakeem, Michael. "A Critique of the Psychiatric Approach to the Prevention of Juvenile Delinquency." *Social Problems* 5 (Winter 1957-1958): 194-205.

Hartung, Frank E. *Crime, Law and Society*. Detroit: Wayne State University Press, 1966.

Hathaway, Starke R., and Monachesi, Elio D., eds. *Analyzing and Predicting Juvenile Delinquency with the MMPI*. Minneapolis: University of Minnesota Press, 1953.

Hawes, Joseph M. *Children in Urban Society: Juvenile Delinquency in Nineteenth-century America*. New York: Oxford University Press, 1971.

Healy, William. *The Individual Delinquent*. Boston: Little, Brown, 1915.

Healy, William, and Bronner, Augusta F. *Delinquents and Criminals: Their Making and Unmaking*. New York: Macmillan, 1926.

——. *New Light on Delinquency and Its Treatment*. New Haven: Yale University Press, 1936.

Hinkle, Roscoe C., Jr., and Hinkle, Gisela J. *The Development of Modern Sociology: Its Nature and Growth in the United States.* Garden City, New York: Doubleday, 1954.

Hirschi, Travis. *Causes of Delinquency.* Berkeley and Los Angeles: University of California Press, 1969.

Hirschi, Travis, and Selvin, Hanan C. *Delinquency Research: An Appraisal of Analytic Methods.* New York: The Free Press, 1967.

Hollingshead, August de Belmont. *Elmtown's Youth: The Impact of Social Classes on Adolescents.* New York: Wiley, 1949.

Jenkins, Richard L. *Breaking Patterns of Defeat.* Philadelphia: J. B. Lippincott, 1954.

Jonassen, Christen F. "A Reevaluation and Critique of the Logic and Some Methods of Shaw and McKay." *American Sociological Review* 14 (October 1949): 608-618.

Keller, Oliver J., Jr., and Alper, Benedict S. *Halfway Houses: Community-Centered Correction and Treatment.* Lexington, Massachusetts: Heath Lexington Books, 1970.

Kett, Joseph F. "Adolescence and Youth in Nineteenth-century America." *Journal of Interdisciplinary History* 2 (Autum 1971): 283-298.

Kitsuse, John I. "Societal Reaction to Deviant Behavior." *Social Problems* 9 (Winter 1962): 247-256.

Kitsuse, John, and Cicourel, Aaron. "A Note on the Uses of Official Statistics." *Social Problems* 11 (Fall 1963): 131-139.

Kitsuse, John I., and Dietrick, David C. *"Delinquent Boys:* A Critique." *American Sociological Review* 24 (April 1959): 208-215.

Klein, Malcolm W. *Street Gangs and Street Workers.* Englewood Cliffs, New Jersey: Prentice-Hall, 1971.

————, ed. *Juvenile Gangs in Context: Theory, Research, and Action.* Englewood Cliffs, New Jersey: Prentice-Hall, 1967.

Kobrin, Solomon. "The Chicago Area Project—A Twenty-five-year Assessment." *The Annals of the American Academy of Political and Social Science* 322 (March 1959): 20-29.

————. "The Conflict of Values in Delinquency Areas." *American Sociological Review* 16 (October 1951): 657-658.

Kvaraceus, William C., and Miller, Walter B. *Delinquent Behavior: Culture and the Individual.* Washington, D.C.: National Education Association, 1959.

Lander, Bernard. *Towards an Understanding of Juvenile Delinquency.* New York: Columbia University, 1954.

Lemert, Edwin M. *Social Pathology.* New York: McGraw-Hill, 1951.

————. *Human Deviance, Social Problems, and Social Control.* 2d ed. Englewood Cliffs: Prentice-Hall, 1972.

————. "The Juvenile Court—Quest and Realities." In *Task Force Report—Juvenile Delinquency and Youth Crime,* edited by The President's Commission on Law Enforcement and Administration of Justice. Washington, D.C.: U.S. Government Printing Office, 1967.

————. *Instead of Court.* National Institute of Mental Health, Center for Studies of Crime and Delinquency. Washington, D.C.: U.S. Government Printing Office, 1971.

Lerman, Paul, ed. *Delinquency and Social Policy*. New York: Frederick A. Praeger, 1970.

Linder, Robert M. *Rebel Without a Cause*. New York: Grune and Stratton, 1944.

Lohman, Joseph D. "The Participant Observer in Community Studies." *American Sociological Review* 2 (December 1937): 890-898.

Lou, Herbert H. *Juvenile Courts in the United States*. Chapel Hill: University of North Carolina Press, 1927.

Lubove, Roy. *The Professional Altruist: The Emergence of Social Work as Career, 1880-1930*. Cambridge: Harvard University Press, 1965.

McCord, William, and McCord, Joan. *Origins of Crime*. New York: Columbia University Press, 1959.

McCorkle, Lloyd; Elias, Albert; and Bixby, F. Lovell. *The Highfield Story*. New York: Holt, 1958.

McKay, Henry D. "Report on the Criminal Careers of Male Delinquents in Chicago" and "A Note on Trends in Rates of Delinquency in Certain Areas in Chicago." In *Task Force Report—Juvenile Delinquency and Youth Crime*, edited by The President's Commission on Law Enforcement and Administration of Justice, pp. 107-118. Washington, D.C.: U.S. Government Printing Office, 1967.

Marris, Peter, and Rein, Martin. *Dilemmas of Social Reform: Poverty and Community Action in the United States*. New York: Atherton Press, 1967.

Martin, John M., and Fitzpatrick, Joseph P. *Delinquent Behavior: A Redefinition of the Problem*. New York: Random House, 1964.

Matza, David. *Delinquency and Drift*. New York: John Wiley, 1964.

Matza, David, and Sykes, Gresham M. "Juvenile Delinquency and Subterranean Values." *American Sociological Review* 26 (October 1962): 712-719.

Mennel, Robert M. *Thorns and Thistles: Juvenile Delinquents in the United States, 1825-1940*. Hanover, New Hampshire: University Press of New England, Hanover, 1973.

Merton, Robert K. *Social Theory and Social Structure*. Rev. ed. Glencoe, Illinois: The Free Press, 1957.

Miller, Walter B. "Lower Class Culture as a Generating Milieu of Gang Delinquency." *The Journal of Social Issues* 14 (1958): 5-19.

———. "Inter-Institutional Conflict as a Major Impediment to Delinquency Prevention." *Human Organization* 17 (Fall 1958): 20-23.

———. "The Impact of a 'Total Community' Community Delinquency Control Project." *Social Problems* 10 (Fall 1962): 181-191.

Monahan, Thomas P. "Family Status and the Delinquent Child: A Reappraisal and Some New Findings." *Social Forces* 35 (March 1957): 251-258.

Morris, Terence. *The Criminal Area*. London: Routledge and Kegan Paul, 1957.

Murphy, Fred J.; Shirley, Mary M.; and Witmer, Helen L. "The Incidence of Hidden Delinquency." *The American Journal of Orthopsychiatry* 16 (October 1946): 686-696.

Nye, F. Ivan. *Family Relationships and Delinquent Behavior*. New York: Wiley, 1958.

Ohlin, Lloyd E. "Indigenous Social Movements." In *Social Welfare Institutions; A Sociological Reader*, edited by Mayer N. Zald, pp. 180-185. New York: John Wiley, 1965.

Park, Robert E. "Community Organization and Juvenile Delinquency." In *The City*, edited by Robert E. Park, Ernest W. Burgess, and Roderick D. McKenzie, pp. 99-112. Chicago: University of Chicago Press, 1925.

Parsons, Talcott. "Certain Primary Sources and Patterns of Aggression in the Social Structures of the Western World." *Psychiatry* 10 (May 1947): 167-181.

Pickett, Robert S. *House of Refuge: Origins of Juvenile Reform in New York State, 1815-1857*. Syracuse: Syracuse University Press, 1969.

Platt, Anthony. *The Child Savers*. Chicago: University of Chicago Press, 1969.

Polk, Kenneth, and Schafer, Walter E. *Schools and Delinquency*. Englewood Cliffs, New Jersey: Prentice-Hall, 1972.

Polsky, Howard W. *Cottage Six: The Social System of Delinquent Boys in Residential Treatment*. New York: Russell Sage Foundation, 1962.

Porterfield, Austin L. *Youth in Trouble*. Fort Worth, Texas: Leo Potishman Foundation, 1946.

Powers, Edwin, and Witmer, Helen L. *An Experiment in the Prevention of Delinquency: The Cambridge-Somerville Youth Study*. New York: Columbia University Press, 1951.

Puffer, Joseph A. *The Boy and His Gang*. Boston: Houghton Mifflin, 1912.

Quay, Herbert C., ed. *Juvenile Delinquency; Research and Theory*. Princeton: Van Nostrand, 1965.

Rainwater, Lee. *Behind Ghetto Walls: Black Families in a Federal Slum*. Chicago: Aldine, 1970.

Reckless, Walter C. "A Non-Causal Explanation: Containment Theory," *Excerpta Criminologica*, 2 (March-April, 1962), 131-134.

Reckless, Walter; Dinitz, Simon; and Murray, Ellen. "Self-Concept as an Insulator Against Delinquency." *American Sociological Review* 21 (December 1956): 744-746.

Reiss, Albert J., Jr. "Delinquency as the Failure of Personal and Social Controls." *American Sociological Review* 16 (April 1951): 196-207.

Rice, Stuart A. "Hypotheses and Verifications in Clifford R. Shaw's Studies of Juvenile Delinquency." In *Methods in Social Science: A Case Book*, edited by Stuart A. Rice, pp. 549-565. Chicago: University of Chicago Press, 1931.

Robins, Lee N. *Deviant Children Grown Up*. Baltimore: Williams and Wilkins, 1966.

Robinson, W. S. "Ecological Correlations and the Behavior of Individuals." *American Sociological Review* 15 (June 1950): 351-357.

Robison, Sophia M. *Can Delinquency Be Measured?* New York: Columbia University Press, 1936.

Rosenheim, Margaret K., ed. *Justice for the Child*. New York: Free Press of Glencoe, 1962.

Rothman, David J. *The Discovery of the Asylum: Social Order and Disorder in the New Republic*. Boston: Little, Brown, 1971.

Savitz, Leonard. "Delinquency and Migration." In *The Sociology of Crime and Delinquency*, edited by Marvin E. Wolfgang, Leonard Savitz, and Norman Johnston, pp. 473-480. 2d ed. New York: John Wiley, 1970.

Schur, Edwin M. *Labeling Deviant Behavior: Its Sociological Implications*. New York: Harper & Row, 1971.

Schwitzgebel, Ralph K. *Streetcorner Research: An Experimental Approach to the Juvenile Delinquent*. Cambridge: Harvard University Press, 1964.

———. *Development and Legal Regulation of Coercive Behavior Modification Techniques with Offenders*. National Institute of Mental Health, Center for Studies of Crime and Delinquency. Washington, D.C.: U.S. Government Printing Office, 1971.

Sellin, Thorsten. *Culture Conflict and Crime*. New York: Social Science Research Council, 1938.

———. *The Criminality of Youth*. Philadelphia: The American Law Institute, 1940.

Sellin, Thorsten, and Wolfgang, Marvin E. *The Measurement of Delinquency*. New York: John Wiley, 1964.

Selling, Lowell S., and Stein, Seymour P. "Vocabulary and Argot of Delinquent Boys." *American Journal of Sociology* 39 (March 1934): 674-677.

Shanas, Ethel. *Recreation and Delinquency*. Chicago: Chicago Recreation Commission, 1942.

Shaw, Clifford R. *The Jack-Roller*. Chicago: University of Chicago Press, 1930.

———. "Case Study Method." *Papers and Proceedings of the Twenty-first Annual Meeting, American Sociological Society*. Chicago: University of Chicago Press, 1926. 21: 149-157.

———. "Correlation of Rate of Juvenile Delinquency with Certain Indices of Community Organization and Disorganization." *Papers and Proceedings of the American Sociological Society*. Chicago: University of Chicago Press, 1927. 22: 174-179.

Shaw, Clifford R., et al. *Delinquency Areas*. Chicago: University of Chicago Press, 1929.

Shaw, Clifford R., and Moore, Maurice E. *The Natural History of a Delinquent Career*. Chicago: University of Chicago Press, 1931.

Shaw, Clifford R., and McKay, Henry D. *Social Factors in Juvenile Delinquency*. Report on the Causes of Crime, vol. 2, Report of the National Commission on Law Observance and Law Enforcement. Washington, D.C.: U.S. Government Printing Office, 1931.

———. *Juvenile Delinquency and Urban Areas*. Chicago: University of Chicago Press, 1942.

Sheldon, William D.; Hartl, Emil M.; and McDermott, Eugene. *Varieties of Delinquent Youth*. New York: Harper & Row, 1949.

Sherif, Muzafer, and Sherif, C. W. "Group Processes and Collective Interaction in Delinquent Activities." *Journal of Research in Crime and Delinquency* 4 (January 1967): 43-62.

———. *Reference Groups: Exploration into Conformity and Deviation of Adolescents*. New York: Harper & Row, 1964.

Short, James F., Jr. "Gang Delinquency and Anomie." In *Anomie and Deviant Behavior*, edited by Marshall B. Clinard, pp. 98-127. New York: The Free Press, 1964.

Short, James F., Jr., and Nye, F. Ivan. "Reported Behavior as a Criterion of Deviant Behavior." *Social Problems* 5 (Winter 1957-1958): 207-213.

Short, James F., Jr., and Strodtbeck, Fred L. *Group Process and Gang Delinquency*. Chicago: University of Chicago Press, 1965.

Spergel, Irving. *Racketville, Slumtown, Haulburg: An Exploratory Study of Delin-*

quent Subcultures. Chicago: University of Chicago Press, 1964.

———. "Community-based Delinquency-Prevention Programs: An Overview." *The Social Service Review* 47 (March 1973): 16-31.

Stinchcombe, Arthur L. *Rebellion in a High School.* Chicago: Quadrangle, 1964.

Street, David; Vinter, Robert D.; and Perrow, Charles. *Organization for Treatment: A Comparative Study of Institutions for Delinquents.* New York: The Free Press, 1966.

Sutherland, Edwin H. "Mental Deficiency and Crime." In *Social Attitudes,* edited by K. Young, pp. 357-375. New York: H. Holt, 1931.

Sykes, Gresham M., and Matza, David. "Techniques of Neutralization: A Theory of Delinquency." *American Journal of Sociology* 22 (December 1957): 664-670.

Tannenbaum, Frank. *Crime and the Community.* Boston: Ginn, 1938.

Tappan, Paul W. "Treatment Without Trial." *Social Forces* 24 (March 1946): 306-311.

Thomas, Piri. *Down These Mean Streets.* New York: Alfred A. Knopf, 1967.

Thomas, William I. *The Unadjusted Girl.* Boston: Little, Brown, 1931.

Thomas, William I., and Thomas, Dorothy S. *The Child in America.* New York: Alfred A. Knopf, 1928.

Thrasher, Frederic M. *The Gang: A Study of 1,313 Gangs in Chicago.* Chicago: University of Chicago Press, 1927.

Tobias, John J. *Crime and Industrial Society in the Nineteenth Century.* London: Batsford, 1967.

Toby, Jackson. "An Evaluation of Early Identification and Intensive Treatment Programs for Predelinquents." *Social Problems* 13 (Fall 1965): 160-175.

Tulchin, Simon H. *Intelligence and Crime: A Study of Penitentiary and Reformatory Offenders.* Chicago: University of Chicago Press, 1939.

Van Waters, Miriam. *Youth in Conflict.* New York: Republic Publishing Co., 1925.

Vold, George B. *Theoretical Criminology.* New York: Oxford University Press, 1958.

Warren, Marguerite Q. "The Case for Differential Treatment of Delinquents." *The Annals of the American Academy of Political and Social Science* 381 (January 1969): 47-59.

Werthman, Carl. "The Function of Social Definitions in the Development of Delinquent Careers." *Task Force Report—Juvenile Delinquency and Youth Crime.* President's Commission on Law Enforcement and the Administration of Justice, pp. 155-170. Washington, D.C.: U.S. Government Printing Office, 1967.

Wheeler, Stanton, ed. *Controlling Delinquents.* New York: John Wiley, 1968.

Whyte, William F. *Street Corner Society.* Chicago: University of Chicago Press, 1943.

———. "The Social Role of the Settlement House." *Applied Anthropology* 1 (October-December 1941): 14-19.

———. "Social Organization in the Slums." *American Sociological Review* 8 (February 1943): 34-39.

Wirth, Louis. "Culture Conflict and Misconduct." *Social Forces* 9 (June 1931): 484-492.

Witmer, Helen L., and Kotinsky, Ruth, eds. *New Perspectives for Research on Juvenile Delinquency.* U.S. Department of Health, Education, and Welfare, Children's Bureau. Washington, D.C.: U.S. Government Printing Office, 1956.

Witmer, Helen L., and Tufts, Edith. *The Effectiveness of Delinquency Prevention Programs*. U.S. Department of Health, Education, and Welfare, Children's Bureau. Washington, D.C.: U.S. Government Printing Office, 1954.

Wolfgang, Marvin E.; Figlio, Robert M.; and Sellin, Thorsten. *Delinquency in a Birth Cohort*. Chicago: University of Chicago Press, 1972.

Wolfgang, Marvin E., and Ferracuti, Franco. *The Subculture of Violence*. London: Tavistock Publications, 1967.

Wootton, Barbara. *Social Science and Social Pathology*. New York: Macmillan, 1959.

Yablonsky, Lewis. "The Delinquent Gang as a Near-Group." *Social Problems* 7 (Fall 1959): 108-117.

index

about the author

Harold Finestone is professor of sociology at the University of Minnesota. Specializing in the study of deviant behavior, he was a research sociologist with the Illinois Institute for Juvenile Research for eleven years. His articles have appeared in such journals as *Social Problems, Law and Contemporary Problems*, and the *American Journal of Sociology*.